AN INTRODUCTION TO
FOLK-LORE

AN INTRODUCTION TO
FOLK-LORE

BY

MARIAN ROALFE COX

NEW AND ENLARGED EDITION

LONDON
DAVID NUTT, 57–59 LONG ACRE
1904

Now Reissued by
Singing Tree Press
1249 Washington Blvd., Detroit, Michigan 1968

Copy 1

TO MY FRIEND

EDWARD CLODD,

WHO SUGGESTED ITS THEME, THIS BOOK
IS GRATEFULLY DEDICATED.

PREFACE TO THE SECOND EDITION

THE reception accorded to this little book affords
me the opportunity, in re-issuing it, of giving some
effect to the various criticisms upon it. These appear to resolve themselves into the suggestion that
the list of selected authorities should be somewhat
increased. Accordingly, as the main object of the
book is to afford persons interested in the subject
some key to the general literature of Folk-lore, that
list has now received material additions. I have to
thank Mr. Nutt, the President of the Folk-lore Society,
for valuable suggestions as to its compilation.

The kindly critic in *The Nation* suggests that such
list should be embodied in an appendix explaining
the general methods of Folk-lore investigation ; but,
not to repeat work already admirably done, it suffices
to call attention to Miss Burne's exhaustive paper in
Folk-lore, vol. i. pp. 313–330.

As stated in the Preface to the First Edition, the

general and rapid survey of Folk-lore attempted in the following pages is taken from the anthropological standpoint. The old interpretation of Folk-tales, and of the large groups of myths with which they have alliance, was mainly based upon the etymologies and meanings of the proper names in both. That method not only failed through the uncertainty and conflicting character of its results, but it also excluded its materials—all drawn from literary sources—from comparison with the raw, but more valuable, materials supplied by savage tales and customs.

On the enlarged bases of the anthropological method, Folk-lore is expanded, from the mere telling of stories and recording of old wives' fables, into an inclusive interpretation of early man's way of looking at the world. To this attention is drawn in the Introductory Chapter.

As it would be impossible to give references in foot-notes without very materially increasing the bulk of the present volume, I have decided, for the convenience of the reader, again to omit them. The fact that this little " Introduction " is written, not for the expert or scientist, but for the uninitiated, reconciles me to the necessity for this omission.

The examples have been carefully selected, and I desire gratefully to acknowledge indebtedness to all authorities from whom information has been drawn.

M. R. C.

CONTENTS

INTRODUCTORY

CHAPTER I

THE SEPARABLE SOUL

The beginnings of Folk-lore—How the belief in a second self, or
soul, may have originated—The soul's means of ingress and
egress—Poets' imagery and popular legends in illustration of

xi

CONTENTS

CHAPTER II

ANIMAL ANCESTORS

The savage mind naturally credulous ; treats all nature alike as personal and animated—Observation of changes of form in the order of nature engenders belief in the transformation of men into animals—Especially sorcerers have this power—Witch stories in illustration—Or a man's double may enter the body of an animal ; or animals may be possessed by the doubles of dead persons—Certain animals thus regarded as transformed ancestors—Resulting confused theories of descent from and kinship with animals—Men named after animals—Regard for animal namesake—Totemism—Its universal traces —A digression anent the family tie—Influence of totemic beliefs on savage conduct—Relics of totemism amongst civilised races

CONTENTS

CHAPTER III

ANIMISM—GHOSTS AND GODS

xiii

CONTENTS

CHAPTER IV

THE OTHER-WORLD

CHAPTER V

MAGIC

CONTENTS

CHAPTER VI

MYTHS, FOLK-TALES, ETC.

xv

AN

INTRODUCTION TO FOLK-LORE

INTRODUCTORY

" Homo sum, humani nil a me alienum puto."
—TERENCE.

Antiquity of the human race—Primitive savagery of man—General resemblance in the mental character of all savages—Definition of Folk-lore—Its value as a science—The power of tradition—Traces of savage belief seen in some habitual expressions and irrational practices of the civilised—Examples—Superstitious observances—Butter bewitched—Cows bespelled—Counter-charms—Luck and ill-luck—Sir Thomas Browne on right and left omens—Salt-spilling—Various safeguards—Charms—Virtue of things stolen—Napoleon's talisman—Sympathetic cures—Disease transference—Principles of leechcraft: folk-medicine—Stone-axes and arrow-heads as amulets—Amber—Written charms—The lucky horse-shoe: potency of iron against spells—Why the peacock's feather is unlucky—Rice-throwing and kindred practices—The "toom" cradle—May marriages—Relics of sun and moon worship—The moon in weather-lore—Lucky and unlucky days—Lucky numbers—Telling the bees—Various modes of divination—Catoptromancy, augury, dreams, palmistry, &c.—The divining-rod—Use of plants in divination—Some festival and ceremonial customs—Local customs—Duty of the folk-lorist—Nursery tales and children's games as contributions to the history of man's life.

AFTER applying the resources of his noble intellect to determine the distance and composition of the stars above him, and the formation of the earth

I   A beneath him, man has at length arrived at the discovery that " the proper study of mankind is man " ; and in the whole universe there is no more interesting subject.

Within the present century, flints bearing marks of artificial chipping were found in certain strata of the earth, the age of which is known to geologists. The discovery proved to be of inestimable moment, establishing beyond question the fact of the great antiquity of the human race. The men who used these flints as weapons and implements lived upon the earth during that geological age known as the Tertiary Epoch, and were the contemporaries of the mammoth, the mastodon, the cave-bear, the megatherium, the wingless birds, and other huge and extinct creatures. Not alone in Europe, which has been the principal field of research, have these traces of the early races of men been found, after their burial of countless ages in beds of river drift, but also in India and Japan, Assyria and Palestine, Egypt, Algeria, and other parts of Africa, throughout the whole of America, in Australia and in Polynesia ; while every year adds to the number of finds in fresh countries.

The evidence thus gathered is conclusive as to the primitive savagery of man, a condition which has its survivals in the black fellows of Australia, the Bushmen of South Africa, the Veddahs of the interior of Ceylon, the Nagas and other hill tribes of the Indian Peninsula, and in the Andamanese Islanders, all of whom would, but for the introduction of metals by white people, be in the Stone age of culture.

It is reasonable to assume a resemblance between man of the old Stone age and existing savage races, for the observations of travellers have proved that, whether on this side of the world or the other, man at the same level of culture has everywhere made shift with the same rough implements, chipped in much the same way, until his history was revolutionised by the discovery of metal.

But with that remote time, of which we have no traditions or written records, when man's thought, as far as any relics prove, was only exercised for supplying the wants of his body, we have nothing whatever to do. Folk-lore—in other words, the records of man's beliefs and customs—begins only with the traces or records of his thought. The term *Folk-lore* was first suggested by the late Mr. Thoms, in 1846, to designate " that department of the study of antiquities and archæology which embraces everything relating to ancient observances and customs, to the notions, beliefs, traditions, superstitions, and prejudices of the common people." It is with these that this little book is concerned. " In our lower classes are still to be found sedimentary deposits of the traditions of remotely distant epochs." It is the task of the folk-lorist to construct the philosophy of primitive man from these still surviving relics. The modern savage helps to supply the key to primitive modes of thought ; for, just as man at the same level of culture makes use everywhere of the same tools and weapons, so he everywhere explains his surroundings in much the same way. The following pages will illustrate the substantial uniformity in the working of the human mind under the same physical conditions everywhere. The most irrational and rudimentary mythologies are substantially identical with those of the Greeks, Scandinavians, and Hindus, however much these may be overlaid and adorned by successive generations of culture. Even the religious rituals and ceremonial traditions of the most civilised peoples contain survivals which link them in close relationship with the beliefs and customs of present-day savages.

If, therefore, we would inquire

" How our own minds were made,
What springs of thought they use,"

it is clear that we must concern ourselves not only with the ancestors of the many different races, sometimes conquerors, sometimes conquered, whose commingled blood flows in the veins of our English nation; but we must acknowledge some ultimate relationship with the first cave men, as well as with the many forgotten peoples who buried their dead in those huge funeral mounds, or built the vast stone dolmens to preserve their bones.

And it is necessary to bear this in mind. We who have emerged from our original lowly estate, and by slow steps have raised ourselves to the level of civilised man, still retain quite sufficient vestiges of the old barbarous condition, and of the stages that succeeded it. And unless we admit this fact in explanation of many a superstitious and wholly irrational act which civilised persons are wont to perform,

> " One point must still be greatly dark,
> The moving Why they do it."

Man clings to tradition. In the Hebrides at this day he will occupy bee-hive habitations, constructed of rough, undressed stones, on precisely the model of those erected by the population of Great Britain ages before the Romans set foot there. Similar dome-shaped huts are found in France, in the desert of Beersheba, in Cornwall and in the Pyrenees, and are very generally associated with megalithic monuments. Wherever they are found, they are either the remains of a primitive people, or they have been erected in later ages, because the traditions of that race have been continued.

5

The most consciously rational mind is ever unconsciously swayed by impulses and habitudes the origins of which are unsuspected. We are constantly proving by unconscious actions " how use doth breed a habit in a man." We are, in truth, the very slaves of custom ; our minds are biased— prepossessed, as it were, by the minds of our forefathers and foremothers.

" To tunes we did not call, our being must keep chime."

Much of the lore of our ancestors is turned into foolishness, the clearest judgment, as Pindar says, being that of the after days. Yet many expressions which they originated we still use from force of habit, though they carry no longer their literal meaning ; which meaning, like many of our irrational actions, can be explained only in connection with the beliefs and practices of a far fore-time.

Nowadays a man raises his hat as a simple mark of courtesy, but the act was originally one of homage ; just as the curtsey was the bowing of the knee in worship. The wearing of a hat, or covering to the head, was a symbol of authority and power. Afterwards the possession of freedom was signified by covering the head ; the slave was bareheaded till he obtained the Cap of Liberty.

We talk of *self-possession ;* we say, " I wonder what possessed him," without intending to admit

that a fiend may take charge of one's wits. We say, " God bless you ! " or " Good luck to you ! " when a person sneezes, with no intention of helping to cast out a devil, or acknowledging a spiritual presence. It is simply a very old habit, and a widespread one ; for it has been detected in Florida, in Zululand, in West Africa, in ancient Rome, in Homeric Greece, and in many countries besides. The exclamation so often attendant on a sneeze originated in the belief that a spirit could take possession of a man ; then, as with some, the act of sneezing served to " cast him out with monstrous potency"; or, as with others—for example, the Zulus —it was a sign that the ancestral spirit was a beneficent visitant. So when Telemachus, in the 17th Odyssey, sneezed loudly, Penelope thought it a lucky sign.

When the housemaid, to induce the fire to burn, lays the poker across the bars and pointing up the chimney, she is ignorant of the original motive of the act—namely, to make the form of the cross, and thus frustrate the thwarting purpose of the spirits inhabiting the chimney, who are as mischievous as those other sprites " that bootless make the breathless housewife churn." In our own country districts, when there is difficulty in the butter-making, the spell is believed to be the work of a witch, and the remedy is to plunge a

7

red-hot poker into the contents of the churn. The supposed potency of iron against evil spells will be presently explained. Another popular means of preserving dairy operations from the interference of witches is to bind a branch of the rowan or mountain-ash round the churn on May Eve.

On a May morning, while the dew is on the grass, witches are most active in devising their uncanny deeds. Their favourite amusements are stealing children and bewitching cattle. An old woman was once found mixing what looked like butter, and muttering strange words over it, on a May morning. This was a charm, and the mixture was to be stuck on the cow-house door. When an old woman cuts the tops of watercresses with a pair of scissors at a spring, and mutters strange words and the names of certain persons, she is assuredly working a spell against their cows. Probably a lump of butter, and other things for working charms, will be found about her. It is well for the farmer to sprinkle his cattle with water blessed on Easter Sunday. This, if anything, is believed to preserve them from evil influence.

The nursemaid who puts the child's shift on inside out, and dares not risk ill-luck by correcting her mistake, is in a like frame of mind to the great Augustus himself, who would have been grievously disquieted had he inadvertently squeezed a right-hand foot into a left-hand shoe. A fretful child is said to have got out of bed wrong foot foremost. In Sussex one is recommended for luck to put on the right stocking before the left ; but in Shropshire just the contrary practice is enjoined. Marcellus, in the fourth century of the Christian era, said that a person should put on his left shoe first if he would escape a pain in the stomach. Pliny tells us that a wasp or beetle caught in the left hand was used medicinally. You must enter a house right foot foremost in Madagascar. Dr. Johnson was so particular about this in our own country, that if he happened to plant his left foot on the threshold of a house, he would turn back and re-enter right foot foremost. In Scotland you must plait a cord with your left hand to keep out witches. Saxo Grammaticus, who wrote his history of the North in the twelfth century A.D., tells us that the men of Rügen used to take omens by a certain sacred white horse. After a solemn prayer the horse was led in harness out of the porch by the priest. Three rows of spears with points downwards had been set out, and if the horse crossed the rows with the right foot before the left, it was taken as a lucky omen of warfare ; if he put the left first, so much as once, the plan of attack was dropped.

But, as Sir Thomas Browne, writing in 1646,

says, "What admission we owe unto many conceptions concerning right and left requireth circumspection. That is, how far ought we to rely upon . . . the *left* eye of an hedgehog fried in oil to procure sleep, or the *right* foot of a frog in deer's skin for the gout, or that to dream of the loss of *right* or *left* tooth presageth the death of male or female kindred, according to the doctrine of Artemidorus." Yet there are those among us who have not even attained to the guarded scepticism of Sir Thomas Browne.

Though it is always unlucky to spill salt, it is thought that calamity may be averted if some of the salt be thrown over the left shoulder, a precautionary measure which is practised all over Europe. It may be hoped that the Chinese are not without resource in the event of the upsetting of the oil-jar, a *contretemps* considered quite as unlucky with them as the spilling of salt with us. Safeguards of all sorts are remembered and resorted to on occasion. For instance, if two persons wash their hands in the same basin, the sign of the cross should be made in the water. We avoid passing under a ladder, though spitting between the rungs will avert mischance. Some carry a cramp-bone to ward off pain—the older the bone the greater its virtue; another tries, as a cure for rheumatism, a new potato, dishonestly come by, worn in the heel of the right boot ; instead of this the Walloons carry three horse-chestnuts in the pocket ; they are equally efficacious, and they will also relieve giddiness. The Wiltshire labourer wears, in a bag round his neck, the forelegs and one of the hindlegs of a mole to secure immunity from toothache. Louis Napoleon in his will exhorts his son to keep as a talisman the seal that he used to wear on his watch-guard. It is said that when the Empress Eugenie was escaping from Paris in September 1870, she took special precautions for the safety of the casket containing this talisman. It is a large sapphire, and perhaps the secret of its virtue as a talisman was due to the fact that, as in the case of the potato, it was stolen ! Napoleon I. had cribbed it from the crown in the coffin of Charlemagne ! Numerous cures are supposed to be effected by means of amulets and jewel talismans ; for example, red beads worn round the neck will prevent nosebleeding ; the amethyst, as its name implies (from Greek ἀμέθυστος, without drunkenness), is a remedy for the intoxicated. The principle of leechcraft or folk-medicine herein involved is nearly allied, as will presently be seen, to the savage's method of cure by sympathetic magic. Dryden, in his " Tempest," makes Ariel say, with reference to the wound which Hippolito received from Ferdinand : " Anoint the sword which pierced him with this weapon-salve, and wrap it close from air, till I have time to visit him again." To salve the weapon and not the wound, to take the hair of the dog that bit one, to stick a pin into a wart and throw the pin away, so that the finder of the pin will have the wart, or to rub it with meat or snails, then burying the meat or impaling the snail so as to cause its death—such practices as these are amongst the relics of barbarism found in our own country, and after all these things do the folk-lorists seek. Martin Luther, who was very superstitious, believed that three toads, spitted on a stick, extracted poison from wounds. The practice of disease-transference is very ancient, and is met with everywhere, with local variation. In Devonshire and in Scotland alike, when a child has hooping-cough, a hair of its head is put between slices of bread and butter and given to a dog. The dog will probably cough, but the child will go free. Transference of disease to inanimate objects is also not uncommon. When sacred wells, such as those in the Isle of Man and elsewhere, were visited for the cure of diseases, it was usual for the patients to drink the water, and to moisten with it a fragment of their clothing, which they would then leave hanging to a bush or tree near the well. It was thought that when the rag had rotted away, the disease would depart ; but if any one were rash enough to take away this rag, he would be certain to catch the disease that had been communicated to it. The pins, coins, buttons, and other objects found in wells, and generally considered to be offerings, may formerly have been vehicles of the diseases which patients have thought thus to throw off. Another cure for hooping-cough is to pass the child under a donkey. To crawl under a bramble which has formed a second root in the ground is said to cure rheumatism, boils, and other complaints; and it is a very common custom to pass ailing children through cleft trees. The virtues of a gold wedding-ring for styes are celebrated throughout Christendom. Rings of various descriptions are efficacious as amulets, and the mere touch of the ring finger is believed to have healing power. The carnelian heart, another of the many lifeless things to which virtue is ascribed, is a degraded imitation of a very old charm or " fetich," the heart-shape being accidentally reached by a process of evolution. From very early times the stone-axes, and arrow-heads, which are somewhat heart-shaped, once used by primitive peoples, were regarded as lucky possessions, because they gave one a certain hold over the ghosts of the people who originally formed them, and who might be summoned by rubbing or anointing them, just as the genius of the lamp was commanded to appear in the " Arabian Nights " story. Modern Europeans regard the stone arrow-heads as fairy-darts, and for this reason value them as amulets. Amber was once used as a charm to protect the wearer from evil influences, and, as may be inferred from the custom of burying a bead in graves, to help the dead man in his journey to the other world. Necklaces of amber have been frequently found in British tumuli.

Written charms are worn as amulets in various parts of the world. It is on the same principle that Chinese physicians direct their patients to swallow the written prescription when the drug recommended is not handy. The written command " Febra fuge," used in a particular way, would cure the ague. " That blessed word Mesopotamia " has no doubt proved as efficacious as the mystic Abracadabra and the rest of its class which magicians use to conjure by. A Scotch mother will leave an open Bible beside her child to keep the fairies away. The Chinese scares away the evil spirits by placing his classics under his pillow. In ancient Assyria written texts were bound round a sick man's brains, and the Jews believed that the phylacteries would avert all evil and drive away demons. In Saxo we read how some dreadful spells graven on wood and put under a dead man's tongue forced him to utter a strain terrible to hear.

Many persons pick up old horse-shoes and hang them up for luck, shunning the more decorative peacock's feather whose neighbourhood is baleful. But then a horse-shoe effectually hinders the power of witches: they cannot step over cold iron. We have seen before (p. 8) how the use of this metal was resorted to in order to frustrate their malevolence. Now, the practices of modern witches have descended from prehistoric times, a curious proof of this fact being seen in their use of old flint implements and arrow-heads as weapons against persons whom they desired to injure. It was the entrance of the iron age that prepared the way for man's emancipation, still only partially effected, from the tyranny of witchcraft; for his intellect, ever expanding with his means of wider experience, submitted no longer to the old cramping thraldom. A knowledge of the use of iron has everywhere enabled man to dispossess the rude stone man, and drive him further afield, or to make him a vassal. It is easy to see, therefore, whence comes the witch's dread of iron, and its power to overcome magic influences. In European folk-lore it destroys the power of fairies and elves. Barrows and stone circles are under the special protection of fairies; stone-implements, celts, arrow-heads, &c., when found by peasants, are called fairy-darts or elf-stones: Irish peasants wear them set in silver round their necks to protect them against elf-shots. The very name of iron is a charm against the

Oriental jinn. In fine, the iron horse-shoe nailed to stable doors keeps away the witches, just as the shades were held at bay when Ulysses brandished his falchion. We forget, it would seem, that the virtue is principally in the material of the horse-shoe, when we wear for luck jewelled imitations of it in gold. But the form may possibly have something to do with it. All heathendom, our own ancestors in common with several Slavic and Finnish nations, with Persians and Indians, saw something sacred and divine in the horse, whose neigh is an omen of luck. It was a favourite animal for sacrifice; its flesh was eaten. Omens were taken from it (see p. 9); and all sorts of magic has been practised by cutting off horses' heads and sticking them up. The devil is sometimes horse-footed, so is a kobold. Oddly enough, a horse's hoof hung up in a house has the same preservative virtue in China as the horse-shoe amongst ourselves. Belief in the potency of iron to counteract evil may be further exemplified in the Roman practice of driving nails into the walls of cottages as an antidote against the plague. L. Mantius (A.U.C. 390) was named dictator to drive the nail. On the other hand, to touch the king of Korea with a weapon or instrument of metal is the highest treason. So entirely is the law observed by king and people that ninety-four years ago Tiengtsong-tai-dang allowed an abscess to end his life rather than that his body should be touched with a knife.

The following story is told to explain why peacocks' feathers bring ill-luck. When God created the peacock, the seven Deadly Sins gazed with envy at the splendid plumage of the bird, and complained of the injustice of the Creator. " You are quite right ; I have been unjust," said the Creator, " for I have already bestowed too much on you ; the Deadly Sins ought to be black as Night, who covers them with her veil." And taking the yellow eye of Envy, the red eye of Murder, the green eye of Jealousy, and so on with the rest, he placed them all on the feathers of the peacock and gave the bird its liberty. Away went the bird, and the Sins, thus despoiled, followed close on his track, trying in vain to recover their lost eyes. This is the reason why, when a man decks himself with a peacock's feather, the sins incarnate dog his steps, and assail him each in its turn.

Why do we throw rice over a bridal pair ? Some will say it is " for luck," rice being used as an emblem of plenty, of fruitfulness. The barbarous practice has doubtless a barbaric origin ; possibly we have forgotten to perform the rite with due discrimina· tion, inasmuch as the bride is not exempted from the bruising shower. They order this matter better in Celebes, where it is believed that the bridegroom's soul is especially liable to take flight at marriage, and rice is therefore scattered over him with the object of inducing it to stay. With the Wadders, one of the early races of South India, of the class Dravidian, it is part of the very long and elaborate marriage ceremony for the bride and bridegroom to pour rice over each other, while the elders pour some over both. This rice is retained for the feast to follow. The next day the bridal pair swear eternal fidelity to each other by pouring milk over each other's head. " The wandering gipsies of Transylvania are said to throw old shoes and boots on a newly married pair when they enter their tent, expressly to enhance the fertility of the union." At a Turkish wedding the bridegroom " has to run for his life to the harem under a shower of old shoes ; " for, according to the Turks, an old slipper thrown after a man is an infallible charm against the evil eye. Wheat was cast on the bride's head in some parts of England, as is done in Sicily. This was also a Hebrew custom. In Russia, when the priest has tied the nuptial knot at the altar, his clerk throws a handful of hops on the head of the bride. Our North Country goodwives throw a plateful of short-cakes over her as she goes to her future home; and the Chinese perform the same ceremony with rice, the emblem of abundance. Natives of the Sulu Islands, north-east of Borneo, always put a few grains of rice in a packet of gold, or of precious stones, believing that the rice will cause the gold or stones to increase.

Neither in China nor in our North Countree must one commit " a crime so inhuman " as the rocking of a " toom " or empty cradle.

> " Oh, rock not the cradle when the baby's not in,
> For this by old women is counted a sin."

This belief holds its ground also in Scotland, in Holland, and in Sweden.

" If you marry in Lent you will live to repent," says the old North Country rhyme. Ovid knew that the month of May was unlucky for marriages; and the first column of *The Times* leads one to suppose that the idea has survived through eighteen centuries. The Romans objected on religious grounds to marriages in May, because the funeral rites of the Lemuralia were performed in that month. The Roman Calendar actually forbade marriages on certain days—*e.g.*, February 11th, June 2nd, November 2nd, December 1st.

What we call "luck" may often be associated with a matter of ritual. Superstitious fear of the consequences of any infraction of established rule serves to ensure the preservation of many savage rites and observances, till they come to be followed as a matter of habit, and quite independently of

19

reason. For instance, we are careful at table to pass the bottle from right to left, for it must travel the way of the sun. The habit of moving sun-wise, from east to west, has survived as a vestige of sun-worship, which is also reflected in the devotions of the Irish peasant, who crawls three times round the healing spring, imitating the circuit of the sun. The crank of a churn must be turned, or eggs beaten and mixtures stirred, always in the same direction, usually "with the sun." Evil spells are wrought "withershins," a word thought to be analogous to the German "wider Schein," or contrary to the appearance of the sun; and ill-luck consistently attends all actions performed withershins. Similarly, the various superstitions concerning the moon, the curtseys and the prayers to the new moon, the money-turning charms, the cures, &c., may all be connected with moon-worship. Many educated people persist in associating changes of weather with the different phases of the moon, and would be loth to see, in their faith in this fanciful weather-lore, a survival from the doctrines of the astrologist, which are largely based on symbolism, such as that which connects the sun with gold, the moon with silver, and the moon's waxing and waning with growing and declining nature. The symbolic magic of the Middle Ages, the confusion of ideal analogy with real connection, can in its turn be traced back to its deep root in the imagination of the savage, whose belief that like affects like will be presently illustrated.

Like Virgil, we incline to the belief that all days are not equally lucky. " Eschew the fifth day," he says, in his elaborate almanac of lucky and unlucky days ; " it is the birthday of the ghastly Orcus and of the Furies." But the seventeenth day, he assures us, is lucky ; while the ninth is good for the runaway, adverse to the thief. Choosing of days prevailed among the Jews, Greeks, and probably all heathen. Hesiod distinguishes between mother - days and stepmother-days ; he goes over all the good days of Zeus, and all the bad. Though our names for the days of the week were imported from abroad, yet native superstitions may have been mixed up with them from very early times. The ill character of the Friday amongst Christian peoples was gained through its association with the day of the Crucifixion. Even the nails should not be cut on a Friday, and no work can be expected to prosper if begun on that day. A lodging-house keeper in Macclesfield caught her servant-girl cutting her finger-nails one Friday, and, snatching the scissors from her, shouted : " Is that what I had you from the workhouse for, to cut your nails on a Friday, and bring bad luck to this house ? " On the other hand, it is one of the superstitions of the Rio

Grande that if you cut your finger-nails every Friday, you will not have toothache.

The belief in " luck in odd numbers " is frequently expressed and acted upon. Shakespeare makes Falstaff say : " This is the third time ; I hope good luck lies in odd numbers. . . . They say there is divinity in odd numbers, either in nativity, chance, or death." [1]

So thought Virgil, who wrote (Ecl. viii. 75), *" Numero deus inpare gaudet ; "* accordingly three threads of three hues were used in the thrice repeated charm to draw Daphnis home. Three, or some multiple of three, is the most popular of mystic numbers in Britain. It enters largely into all prescriptions of leechcraft ; thus, three times is the child passed under the donkey on nine consecutive mornings for the cure of hooping-cough. Nine knots on a string hung round a Lancashire child's neck are to cure the same complaint. Pliny mentions the virtues of nine knots being known to the Magi ; knots are frequently used in enchantments. Nine times should the stye be rubbed with the cat's tail. " Thrice the brindled cat hath mew'd," says the witch in " Macbeth."

Seven is not popular in England, in spite of its

---

[1] The people of Rügen, however, according to Saxo, held the reverse opinion. " Their women," he says, " would sit by the hearth and draw random lines in the ashes without counting. If these, when counted, were even, they were thought to bode success ; if odd, ill-fortune."

mystical associations in Scripture; and but few examples of it are met with in folk-medicine, and these chiefly with reference to the personal powers of a seventh son. But seven was a number sacred to the Semites, a belief in its magic virtues having descended to them from their Accadian predecessors. The Deluge lasted seven days, and after it the first act of the Chaldean Noah was to build an altar and to set vessels by sevens. The Sabbath of rest fell on each seventh day of the week; the planets and three groups of stars were each seven in number; " the god of the number seven " received peculiar honour. Seven occurs in Assyrian talismans; it is used in exorcisms. " Seven by seven had the magic knots to be tied by the witch, seven times had the body of the sick man to be anointed with the purifying oil."

It would be impossible in brief space to catalogue the various superstitions that are met with even in this last decade of the nineteenth century, when burglars invariably carry a small piece of coal " for luck " in their deeds of darkness; love philtres are not wholly out of fashion; and there are certain who believe that carrying the bones of a toad from which the flesh has been eaten by ants will compel the affections of the opposite sex.

When the bees swarm, and our country folk straightway beat an old kettle or pot, or anything that makes a metallic din, they are using the same means which Virgil recommended to induce the bees to go back to the hive. " Raise tinkling sounds," he said, " and rattle the cymbals." Bees are proverbially busy and intelligent, and it would appear that they particularly resent a slight of any kind. Virgil says that some have thought them possessed of a share of the Divine mind. We know that they supplied the sacred mead, and so came into direct contact with the gods ; perhaps it was expected of them as messengers of the gods to herald the arrival of a new-comer to the land of spirits. However this may be, if there is a death in the house the bees must be told of it, or they will fly away. A member of the writer's family on one occasion neglected this little act of courtesy, and lost a hive ! Their supposed sensitiveness upon this point is recognised nearly all over Europe. It is also a Hindu custom to tell the bees of the death of their owner. The following lines from a Greek epigram enjoin the same practice :—

" Naiads and chill cattle-pastures, tell to the bees, when they come on their spring-tide way, that old Leucippus perished on a winter's night, setting snares for scampering hares, and no longer is the tending of the hives dear to him."

The granny who prophesies the weather by observing the course of the bubbles in her tea-cup, or who foresees the advent of a stranger, tall or short, in the floating tea-leaf, is "using divination" no less than the Babylonian king of whom we read in Ezekiel xxi. 21 (though his method was certainly more elaborate) : " He stood at the parting of the way, at the head of the two ways ; he made his arrows bright, he consulted with images, he looked in the liver." Examining the entrails of animals is a common method of divination ; so is casting different objects into water and observing the ripples that they make. Lobengula, the late Matabele king, gazed into a dark pool before starting on the warpath. The Wahuma, another African race, a pastoral people, who do not cultivate the soil, but live on the flesh and milk of their cattle, keep fowls for purposes of divination only. They would on no account eat them ; they use them solely in obtaining auguries by their entrails, just as the Romans did in the days of the foundation of their empire, some 2600 years ago. Saxo Grammaticus tells us that the magicians of the North were skilled in the same art.

Pausanias explains by what method sick persons read their fate in a certain spring in front of the temple of Ceres, at Patras. From of old the Egyptians have seen visions in a drop of ink ; the Maoris similarly use a drop of blood. Equally portable as an apparatus is the crystal ball which serves the modern spiritualist ; so are the beryl and the magic mirror. The art of catoptromancy, or divination by means of a mirror, has been practised by necromancers and clairvoyants of all ages. The Romans called such persons *specularii ;* perhaps even nowadays every speculator is more or less a visionary. Varro, the contemporary of Cicero, says that the art originated in Persia. Pythagoras (550 B.C.) consulted a highly polished steel mirror at the full of the moon. In a " Book of all Forbidden Arts," written in 1455 by the Duke of Bavaria's physician, a similar use of a " beautiful bright polished sword " is mentioned. It has been conjectured that the Urim and Thummim, worn in the breastplate of the high priest of Israel, were objects used in a similar way. At any rate, he consulted them, and they gave oracular responses. The words signify " lights and perfections." King Saul tried to foresee the issue of the battle with the Philistines by means of Urim ; then as a *pis aller* he consulted the witch of Endor.

The flight of birds is another means of augury, a word which is in part derived from Latin *avis*, a bird. The Romans called the bird-seer *auspex*. We still talk of favourable auspices. The art of taking omens from birds and animals is familiar to savages, and extends upwards to the civilised. In classic writings there are many allusions to the divining powers of the seer, the feeder of the

oracular birds. English people have their curious
superstitions about birds, quite on a par with those
of the Maori, the Tatar, the Dayak, and the Kalmuc.
In North India the crow is a bird of evil omen ; so
are kites and vultures. If a man answers the owl,
he is sure to die. When a wagtail first appears
every one bows to it. The Greeks bowed to the
kite. Aristophanes, in his play of " The Birds," in
which he burlesques the national mythology, makes
Peisthetairus say that when the kite was ruler and
king over the Greeks he first taught the people to
prostrate themselves before kites. The Scholiast
explains that the kites' appearing betokened the
coming of spring, wherefore the Greeks bowed the
knee to them.

These are among " the many modes of the divining
art " which, in the tragedy of Æschylus, Prometheus
claims to have taught to men : to discriminate
among dreams as to which are destined to be a
true vision ; obscure vocal omens ; the flight of
birds of crooked talons, both the auspicious and
the ill-omened ; the smoothness of the entrails, and
their hue ; the various happy formations of the gall
and liver, and the limbs enveloped in fat. All these
" modes " are practised by savages, and survivals
of some may be detected amongst the civilised.
Nine-tenths of Europeans firmly believe still that
dreams are prophetic, just as in ancient times

dreams were interpreted and their warnings followed. Examples of dream-divination, so common in the classics, might be compared with those which English mediæval poems afford, and with the familiar details and interpretations of Joseph's dreams (Gen. xxxvii., xl., xli.). In a Northern lay the poet makes Atli say: "I dreamed that thou, Gudrun, thrust me through with a poisoned sword." And Gudrun answered: "To dream of iron means fire, to dream of a woman's anger means sickness and sorrow," &c. In another lay, Gudrun, vexed with unhappy dreams, goes to Brunhild to have them interpreted. She had dreamt about a fair hawk with wings of golden hue, and about a great hart with hide of gold. Animals and birds in dreams were read as persons then as now; and the symbolical interpretation of dreams is not unknown either to the lower races.

Others divine by means of sieve and shears, or of a shoulder-blade, or a key and Bible. Chiromancy, or palmistry, which once flourished in ancient Greece and Italy (as it still does in India, where to say "It is written on the palms of my hands" is the usual way of expressing a sense of inevitable fate), has its modern votaries not merely among gipsy fortune-tellers; while the divining-rod, inevitably recalling the rod of Moses, is still in use for finding springs. When one of the Bacchæ struck the rock with her thyrsus, a dewy stream of water flowed. According to the Scholiast on Euripides, Neptune struck his trident in the ground at Triæna, in Argolis, and immediately water sprung up. Allat, the queen of the Assyrian Hades, had a divining-rod ; and the Greek Hermes carried a magic staff or rod, by means of which he could raise the dead. The priest in the temple of Demeter, in Arcadia, smote the earth with rods, calling on the people under the earth ; and when the Zulus practise divination they strike the ground and invoke the spirits. The magic rod is brought into use in popular tales for opening treasure-rocks, the idea being no European monopoly. The Zulus, the Hottentots, the Kaffirs, the Malagasians have all very similar stories about rocks that open like the cavern in the " Forty Thieves."

Children sport with divination when they strip the pinnate leaves from a stem, with lightsome heart linking their future with " tinker, tailor, soldier, sailor, gentleman, apothecary, ploughboy, or thief." More momentous to dreamy maidenhood is the question which a flower shall decide. One by one Margarete pulls the petals from the aster, murmuring—

" He loves me, loves me not . . ."

The lovelorn goatherd, in the beautiful idyll of

Theocritus, gently chiding his wayward Amaryllis, sings how the poppy petal clung not, but withered on his smooth fore-arm, when he asked, " Loves she, loves she not ? " Nor did the soothsayer's divination with the sieve prove more auspicious. But his right eyelid throbs ; haply this is a good sign, and she will relent and come to him. Two thousand years and more have not sufficed to stifle faith in these " strange arts " and portents.

It is unnecessary to multiply instances of the countless irrational practices which are based upon the traditional lore of the folk, and are the outcome of customs and beliefs of great antiquity. They are not peculiar to any one race or country, being found in regions very wide apart. This fact, however, does not prove that all mankind have inherited their beliefs from a common source. There is no reason why the savage intellect should differ in its work-ings in different parts of the globe. Like causes everywhere produce like effects. Just as at the same level of culture man all over the world makes shift with the same rude tools—the accidental chip of flint, which teaches him the use of a cutting or scraping instrument ; the heavier stone, which he uses as a hammer wherewith to crush or break (the Scandinavian word *hamarr* means both rock and hammer) ; the pebble as a missile ; these being the natural prototypes of all implements of stone, which by slow degrees man comes to shape and improve for himself—so the savage intellect, grappling everywhere with the same problems, supplying everywhere the same crude solutions, has laid enduring foundation for many elaborate structures of beliefs and ritual observances.

In old Aryan myth the spring-tide sun was typified by a red or golden egg, which in after-times was made by the early Christians the emblem of the Resurrection. Hence the Easter egg, and the many curious customs connected with it throughout Europe. In the household accounts of King Edward I. stands the following item against Easter Day : " Four hundred and a half of eggs, eighteenpence." The Pope gave an Easter egg in a silver case to Henry VIII. Quite recently Cheshire children begged (as is still the custom in the Midlands and in Scotland) for pace or pasch eggs (so called from the Hebrew word Pascha, meaning the Passover), which are usually boiled hard in water stained with different dyes, red, blue, or violet, and otherwise ornamented. These eggs are sometimes hung up in the cottages till another year. In Yorkshire the coloured eggs are hidden out of doors in little nests, and the children hunt for them. In Swabia a hare is set on the nest, and the children find the hare's eggs. But you must first catch your hare. In past years, in our own country, if lads could do this, and bring it to the parson of the parish of Coleshill, in Warwickshire, before 10 A.M. on Easter Monday, he was bound to give them " a calf's head, a hundred eggs, and a groat in money." In many parts of Germany eggs are made into cakes in the form of a hare. In England long ago the clergyman and choristers actually played at ball with Easter eggs as part of the service in church. Afterwards they retired for refreshments, including a gammon of bacon and a tansy pudding. Amongst other nations, the Parsees used to distribute eggs, coloured bright red, at their spring festival.

All festival and ceremonial customs, such as those observed at harvest, at birth, at death, or at marriage ; all local customs, such as the Dunmow Flitch, the Lady Godiva procession at Coventry ; the use of the curfew bell, of ducking stools, of scold bridles—all such like curiosities come under the notice of the folk-lorist. The original meaning of many of them is forgotten, customs being observed often as mere matters of habit. We have seen that the folk—that is, the uneducated classes— retain many of the beliefs and ways of savages. It is the aim of the student of folk-lore to collect and compare the surviving superstitions and stories of old races, to treasure the " idle tale and fading legend of the past ; " for all scraps of folk-lore are of value as capable of throwing light backwards upon the history of human civilisation. Certain usages and myths which seem unintelligible when found among civilised races, are the relics of a stage of thought which is dying out in Europe, but which still exists amongst savages. The European may find among the Greenlanders or Maoris many a trait for reconstructing the picture of his own primitive ancestors.

Much information is to be derived from a comparative study of nursery tales and children's games, as contributing to the history of man's life. Indian hill tribes have many of the same games as European children, including peg-tops, and several games with a ball; they have also a kind of cat's cradle. The Egyptians played at draughts as long ago as B.C. 1500, and probably long before that. Children everywhere play at imitating their elders; this is noticeably the case amongst savages. For instance, amongst tribes whose custom it is to capture their wives by force from neighbouring tribes, children play at the game of wife-catching, just as English children play at catching a " sweetheart." As Mr. Tylor says, " It is quite a usual thing in the world for a game to outlive the serious practice of which it is an imitation ; " and he instances the bow and arrow, and sling and stone, still deadly weapons amongst a few savage tribes, but surviving cnly as toys or sports amongst the civilised.

The Chinese, the oldest and most populous nation of the globe, are still in the condition that Europe was in during the Middle Ages; for, whereas our ignorant and semi-barbarous usages were but a step towards a higher civilisation, they have stereotyped their low level of civilisation, and strive for nothing better. Many of the ceremonies of the Chinese wedding are survivals of the time when a bride was carried off by force; and among some of the tribes of Western China it is customary for the bride to perch herself on the high branch of a large tree, while her elderly female relatives station themselves on the lower limbs, armed with switches, and through this protecting force the bridegroom has to make his way, being merrily attacked by the dowagers as he scrambles up to his bride. In the Spartan marriage ceremony also the pretence was kept up of carrying the bride off by force, although the bride's guardians had sanctioned the union. The same custom is found among the Circassians and in South America. On the large islands of the Fiji group, a woman is often seized upon by apparent or actual force in order to be made a wife. If she does not approve the proceeding, she runs off when she reaches the man's house; but if she is satisfied, she stays. In these cases, says Mr. Tylor, the abduction is a mere pretence; but it is kept up seemingly as a relic of a ruder time when, as among the modern Australians, it was done by no means as a matter of form, but in grim earnest.

The following pages will exhibit the essential identities and analogies between European and savage customs and superstitions, as well as the affinities between our own village and homestead customs and those of other lands. It is only in traversing " the eternal landscape of the past " that the student of folk-lore will find the source of all myth and of all superstition, the origin of the countless ancient notions which still survive, though sometimes in strangely altered form.

CHAPTER I

THE SEPARABLE SOUL

" Who can see the green earth any more
As she was by the sources of Time?
Who imagines her fields as they lay
In the sunshine, unworn by the plough?
Who thinks as they thought,
The tribes who then roamed on her breast,
Her vigorous, primitive sons?"—MATTHEW ARNOLD.

TRAVELLING backwards towards the morning of
Time in our search for the origins of folk-lore, we

36

must halt at that stage in the evolution of the
mental life of man when an intelligent curiosity
concerning himself and his surroundings took the
place of mere animal inquisitiveness ; when *homo
sapiens* thus further manifested his ever-widening
divergence from his prime brethren, the " apes with
foreheads villainous low." Man at his lowest was
naked, toolless, fireless ; his endowments had to be
acquired step by step. Ingenuity of the rudest
character necessarily requires a past of many generations of slow mental progress ; and the lowest
savage who has inherited weapons, or the ability to
devise them, cannot be called " primitive." The
most barbarous and childish of myths, therefore,
were evolved amongst races who had reached a
considerable degree of intellectual activity, though
they were far from having attained to clear rational
thought—" they who," as Prometheus describes them
in the play of Æschylus, " at first seeing, saw in
vain ; hearing, they heard not. But, like to the
forms of dreams, for a long time they used to huddle
together all things at random, and naught knew
they about brick-built and sunward houses, nor
carpentry ; but they dwelt in the excavated earth
like tiny emmets in the sunless depths of caverns.
And they had no sure sign either of winter, or of
flowery spring, or of fruitful summer : but they used
to do everything without judgment."

The brain of the ape-like ancestors of man in Tertiary times was inferior in weight and in structural complexity to that of the ape which Mr. Romanes has succeeded in teaching to count five. Indeed, this intelligent animal treads closely on the heels of some of the living races of men, who are much puzzled to count after five, because they have no spare hand with which to grasp the fingers which they use as units or *digits*, as we still say (from Latin, *digitus*, a finger) ; whose vocabulary is so limited that they largely depend upon signs and gestures, and therefore cannot make themselves wholly understood in the dark ; and who are quite incapable of abstract ideas. In short, in measuring the mental capacity of the rudest savage, we must put him on a plane much more nearly adjacent to that of the anthropoid ape than to the immeasurably higher plane of civilised man.

But there comes a time when the savage, having satisfied the daily wants of his body, finds leisure to concern himself about the causes of things, his explanations taking the form of what we call myth and legend. For most myths may be interpreted as man's early attempts to solve the riddle of the Universe. He was no Œdipus at guessing, nevertheless he was a philosopher in his way—a very limited way.

Ignoring for awhile that we ourselves have either sipped, or largely drunk, of the Pierian Spring, that we have ever tasted of the Tree of Knowledge, whose garnered fruit long ages were required to cultivate, let us put ourselves in the place of our savage progenitors, and, thus bereft of our shrewder wits, endeavour to " think as they thought." " Knowledge is ofttimes nearer when we stoop than when we soar : " a cruder understanding can better realise the attitude of our primitive philosopher, who perceives nothing irrational in the notion of beasts that talk, and of plants as well as lifeless things with souls.

To the mental faculty, in a low state of its development, the events which take place in dreams are indistinguishable from actual occurrences. " Dreams are true while they last, and do we not live in dreams ? " An attempted explanation of dream-acts results in the belief that they are the performances of the spirit when away from the body, just as real acts are performed when the spirit is present in the body. To make this clear, and to show also how, in all probability (following the theory generally set forth in these pages), the notion of a spirit is primarily conceived, let us suppose that the savage hunter, fatigued and famished after an adventurous day with his flint—his sole weapon—gorges himself on the flesh of the animal he has slain, and falls asleep, to go through once more in his dream some thrilling incidents of the chase, with variations.

He secures his prey; it is wrested from him by his fellow, whom he slays. He wakes, boasts of his adventure, and tells his comrade of his bloody deed. For he cannot explain, like Eugene Aram, " My little lad, remember, this is nothing but a dream." The savage, as we have said, cannot distinguish between dream life and real life. Suppose that the little lad insists that the sleeper never left the spot, while his recent vivid experience makes the latter trust to his own memory. How is he to reconcile such contradictory facts ? The simple course is to believe that he has a *second self*, which has been away and come back : while weariness was snoring on the flint, the second self, the soul, the ghost (armed with the ghost of the flint), was abroad. A similar event would take place everywhere and often, with the same resulting impression. Whenever a man has watched his comrade sleeping, and afterwards listened to his account of what he supposes he did, while in reality his body never left the spot, there has seemed only this one explanation possible—namely, that the sleeper's spirit quitted the body, and went forth on its adventures. A dream may be either the experience of the soul when absent from the body of the sleeper, or it may be a visit from the soul of the person or object dreamed of, as phantoms visit and converse with the professional seer. The modern spiritualist believes that while a person is in an insensible state his apparition visits distant parts, and communicates with the living ; and a medium has the power of summoning also the spirits of the dead. Even if the savage suspects some distinction between dream experience and real experience, his language does not enable him to express it. He cannot say, " I dreamt that I saw," instead of " I saw " ; therefore dreams must needs be related as realities, and this strengthens belief in them as such.

Belief in the *other self* thus established, the savage has no trouble to account for the presence in his dreams of parents, comrades, or enemies known to be dead or at a distance; it is a proof that their souls still exist. For he naturally thinks that the persons that his spirit meets in dreams, the horse, the dog, the waving trees, are spirits also, and all inanimate things used in dreams are ghosts of the material things. Many persons have a superstitious objection to waking a sleeper suddenly ; savages are forbidden to do so, lest the soul just then might be wandering, and not have time to return to the body, and then the sleeper would be a dead man.

The common belief is that the soul issues by way of the mouth. Homer frequently speaks of the soul passing " the fence of the teeth " ; and other examples from the Greek may be cited. In Herondas, iii. 3, " Thrash this boy until his miserable soul is at his very lips." (This recalls the common expression about having one's heart in one's mouth.) From Plato, Frag. 1, " Kissing Agathon, I had my soul upon my lips ; for it rose, poor wretch, as though to cross over." From the *Anthology*, v. 14, " Sweet is Europa's kiss, even if it touch but the lips. But it is not so her kiss touches : the pressure of her lips draws up the soul from the toes and finger-tips." " Soul meets soul on lovers' lips," says our own Shelley ; " And our spirits rushed together at the touching of the lips," is a line in " Locksley Hall." The same idea is expressed in Schiller's " Amalia " : " *Seele rann in Seele.*" But enough of poets' fancies.

A well-known story may be cited to illustrate the belief that the mouth is the door by which the spirit enters and leaves the body. Two shepherds sat one summer's day in the open air together. Whilst one of them slept, his comrade saw a bee come forth from his mouth, and watched it as it crept along a blade of grass which hung over a tiny trickle of water, and then flew off amongst the flowers. After an hour the bee returned by precisely the same course, and re-entered the mouth of the sleeper. Thereupon the man awoke, and related how in a dream he had crossed a magnificent bridge over a large river, and had visited Paradise. In a parallel legend, King Gunthram, spent with toil, had gone to sleep on the lap of a faithful follower, who sees a little beast like a snake run out of his lord's mouth towards a streamlet, which, however, it cannot cross. The servant lays his sword across the water, and the creature runs over it, and up into a mountain on the other side. Presently it returns by the same way, and re-enters the mouth of the sleeper, who thereupon wakes, and relates how in a dream he had crossed an iron bridge and gone into a mountain filled with gold.

Matthew Paris, the greatest Latin historian of the thirteenth century, has something to say about the soul leaving the body during sleep, passing out of the mouth, generally in the form of a mouse. One out of a hundred myths to this effect must serve as illustration of the prevalent belief. " In Thuringia, at Saalfeld, a servant girl fell asleep whilst her companions were shelling nuts. They observed a little red mouse creep from her mouth and run out of the window. One of the fellows present shook the sleeper, but could not wake her, so he moved her to another place. Presently the mouse ran back to the former place and dashed about, seeking the girl ; not finding her, it vanished ; at the same moment the girl died." Many will doubtless recall the case of the homeless soul of Hermotimus, according to the familiar classical story. On one fateful occasion, when his prophetic soul had flitted, accord-

ing to wont, to distant regions, his wife inconsider-
ately burnt his lifeless body, and so the poor soul,
on its return, found no dwelling to animate with its
presence. Similarly, when men are in a trance, or
asleep, the soul runs out of them in the shape of a
snake or a weasel.

The insensibility of death is like the unconscious-
ness of sleep or swoon, and the savage intellect
accounts for it as the prolonged, yet possibly only
temporary, absence of the other self. In many cases
of burials, it is certain, from the position given to the
corpse, that the idea of sleep was connected with
death. The Norsemen were buried seated in a
chair or in a boat; but the builders of the megalithic
or " great stone " monuments, the huge dolmens, or
family tombs, were interred lying on their sides,
with their hands folded as though in sleep. In
early days, the barrow, or burial-place, was modelled
after the house. In the case of Wicking princes,
their warships seemed the most appropriate place
to bury them in. After vain attempts to call back
the errant spirit, the savage leaves food in the grave
with the corpse, and weapons ready for use, in case
the spirit should return to reanimate it. The Tupis
buried the dead person " in a sitting posture with
food before it ; for there were some who believed
that the spirit went to sport among the mountains,
and returned there to eat and to take rest." Gar-

ments are hung on trees near the place of interment, for the dead man to put on if he chooses to come out. In the Icelandic saga, the death-shoes are bound tightly on the feet of the dead man, that he may walk safely in the ways of Hela ; then the great cairn is heaped over the body.

In connection with this Hell-shoe, it may be interesting to refer to a Yorkshire superstition which Sir Walter Scott quotes :—" They are of beliefe, that once in their lives it is good to give a pair of new shoes to a poor man, forasmuch as after this life they are to pass barefoote through a great launde full of thornes and furzen, except by the meryte of the almes aforesaid they have redeemed the forfeyte ; for at the edge of the launde an oulde man shall meet them with the same shoes that were given by the partie when he was lyving, and after he hath shodde them, dismisseth them to go through thick and thin, without scratch or scalle." This land of thorns is the terrible whinny-moore which the ghostly traveller must pass in his journey to the other world. Hear the comfortable words of the Lyke-Wake Dirge :—

> " If ever thou gave either hosen or shoon,
>   Every night and alle ;
> Sit thee down and put them on,
>   And Christe receive thy saule.

But if hosen nor shoon thou never gave neean,
Every night and alle ;
The whinnes shall prick thee to the bare beean,
And Christe receive thy saule."

In an Irish folk-tale, the ghost of a woman who had died in America appears to a friend at her former home in Ireland, by whom she sends a message to her mother. " Tell her," said the ghost, " to buy a pair of shoes and stockings and give them to some poor person in my name, for God's sake. I am walking back and forth perishing with the cold." This request was fulfilled, and so the ghost was laid. The Hindus say that if you give water or shoes to a Brahman, you will find water to refresh you, and shoes to wear, on your journey to the next world. But there is priestcraft in this respect of persons as the recipients of charity. In some of the shops in China specially cheap shoes and boots are exposed for sale, it being customary to put them on the feet of the corpse before burial. The soles of the more expensive shoes (*i.e.* those not made of paper, as is the general case), however, are made, not of leather, but of felt. If you ask the reason, you are told that the head of one of the ministering spirits in Hades resembles that of a cow, and that consequently he is very angry with any one who passes under his jurisdiction wearing leather-soled shoes.

46

Almost every people in Europe has at some time observed, as many do still, the custom of keeping candles burning round the coffin after the body has been laid out ; and coffins of those lying in state are surrounded by wax tapers. The original motive for the practice may have been the same as that actuating the Chinese at this day—namely, to light the spirit of the dead upon his way. Jews place a light at the head of their dead ; and in Northumberland, and in the Isle of Man, a candle used to be set upon the corpse.

An interesting account was given in New York papers, towards the close of 1889, of a Chinese funeral which had recently taken place in that city. The deceased, Li Ju Doo, had been a general in the Taeping insurrection, was a Freemason, and had flourishing business establishments at Boston and Philadelphia, as well as New York. Nine days intervened between the death and the funeral. The body was embalmed and laid in a coffin at an under-taker's. On a table at the foot of the coffin were arranged the articles of food with which the Celestials provide their dead for their long journey—a roasted lamb, heaps of sugar confectionery, and some porcelain saucers filled with rice. On another table was a roasted sucking-pig, some packets of tea, flasks of wine, and small heaps of lemons, oranges, and biscuits. There were also chop-sticks, tea-cups, and small baskets of flowers. The corpse was clad in the robes of a mandarin of the Ming Dynasty, the pig-tail wound round the head ; on the breast lay paper money. Some gold pieces were in the left hand, and some money—gold, silver, and paper—was thrown into the coffin, that the deceased might be able to distribute gifts on his journey, and bribe the evil spirits that might otherwise hinder his passage. On the way to the grave, a person sitting behind the hearse flung down paper money from time to time to buy off the obstruction of the spirits. When the grave was filled in—after various cere-monies that there is not space to detail—on the top roasted fowls and cooked rice were placed, and two flasks of wine were poured on it as a libation.

Jewels and large sums of money are often put in graves, for the same motive as that which prompted pious conformity to the Chinese ritual as related above. Saxo Grammaticus, in his account of the Swedish war, relates how the victorious Ring had search made among the carcases for the body of Harald, that the corpse of the Danish king might not wrongfully lack its due rights. In order to make propitiation to the shade of Harald, he har-nessed to the chariot of the king the horse on which he rode, and decked it with a golden saddle. Then he prayed that Harald would ride on this, and outstrip those who shared his death in their journey to Tartarus. Then, raising a pyre, he bade the Danes fling on it the golden chariot of their king. And while the flames were burning he earnestly charged the mourning nobles that they should freely give arms, gold, and every precious thing to feed the pyre in honour of so great a king. Afterwards, the king's ashes, together with the horse and armour, received a royal funeral. The civilised Greeks gave the dead man a honey-cake as a sop for Cerberus, and an obolus for the payment of Charon, the ferry man ; the old Prussians furnished him with money for refreshments on his weary journey ; and the German peasants at the present day bury a corpse with money in its hand or mouth. A North Indian story about a grave-robber shows that silver coins were buried in the mouth of the dead for travelling expenses.

The late Crown Prince of Siam is (Feb. 1895) lying, or rather sitting, in state in a silver urn, in accordance with Siamese custom, with his knees drawn up to his chin, and his hands clasped before his knees. The body is preserved in spirit till the day of its cremation. A silver ribbon connects the silver urn with its gold pedestal, around which prayers and services are held, this ribbon being touched by the priests to convey the prayer to the royal remains. The late Crown Prince's toilet sets, betel boxes, cigarettes, dinner-services, all made of

49   D

gold, surround the urn, together with offerings and food for the departed spirit. The royal symbolic five-fold umbrellas, too, are not forgotten. The custom of burying a man's portable property with him is familiar to all who have studied the funeral ceremonies of uncultured races. The motive is intelligible enough. For if even lifeless objects, such as the hatchet, bow and arrows, food and drink of the dead man, possess other-selves, these, too, can pass with him into the world of ghosts. The dead savage will have to hunt and to fight, and must therefore be armed ; the spirits of the buried weapons and implements accompany his spirit. In the same way, domestic appliances are buried with women, and toys are laid beside dead children. Evidence of the wide prevalence of these funeral rites is afforded by the many interesting survivals in which they may be traced ; many a custom apparently meaningless having its deep significance to the student of folk-wont.

Even in the age of the mammoth, men practised funeral rites, believed in a future, possessed fetiches, perhaps even idols. The discoveries of the last half-century in the caverns of France and Belgium, substantiated by the evidence from Peru, Borneo, and Patagonia, prove this fact beyond a doubt. The Eskimo lays a dog's head on his child's grave, to serve as a guide to the land of souls. Live stock are slaughtered, the favourite horse and dog are killed, that the deceased may miss nothing in the spirit world ; wives, slaves, and friends are sacrificed, that he may not lack companionship and service. Even as late as the seventeenth century Japanese servants would solemnly pledge their bodies to their lord, and when he died would put themselves to death by the " hara kari," or ripping up. As such practices passed into survivals, clay images took the place of the faithful servants in the funeral cere-monies, as paper houses are burnt for the dead Chinaman to live in, and mock money is placed in his tomb. At this day, in the Caucasus, the dead man's widow and his saddle-horse are led thrice round his grave ; and the widow must not re-marry, nor the horse ever be ridden again. In our own country, a survival of the custom of sacrificing the warrior's horse at his tomb may be seen in that pathetic incident of a soldier's funeral, his charger, saddled and bridled, following in the procession. A Hindu widow will often voluntarily perform the rite of suttee, that she may be with her husband in the other world, just as Brunhild threw herself on the pile by Siegfried, and Trojan captives and Messenian widows joined their dead lords. In Saxo Grammaticus we read that when Asmund's body was buried in solemn state at Upsala and attended with royal obsequies, " his wife Gunnhild, loth to outlive him, cut off her own life with the sword, choosing rather to follow her lord in death than to forsake him by living." Saxo also describes how the faithful Signe encompassed her own death whilst her husband was being led to execution. But Hermutrude broke her promise to her husband Amleth not to forsake him in death. Indeed, widow sacrifice was once prevalent among Scandinavians, Gauls, Slavs, and other European Aryans. It is a Fiji custom to strangle all the wives of the deceased at his funeral.

In the German folk-tale of "The Three Snake Leaves," the king's beautiful daughter vows to accept no husband who will not promise to be buried alive with her if she dies first. Such a compact also is made between mere friends. Saxo tells us that Asmund, son of King Alf, and Aswid, son of King Biorn, swore by every vow, in order to ratify the friendship which they observed to one another, that whichever of them lived longest should be buried with him who died.

The practice of sending messages to the world beyond the grave has even been met with amongst savages. It is done in this way : a chief summons a slave, delivers to him a message, and then cuts off his head. A Chinese expedient for communicating with ghosts of the dead may be described in this connection. In various parts of China there is a belief that the souls of very atrocious criminals who have either been executed or who have died in prison, are sent back from Hades by Yenlo, the judge there, to undergo a further term of imprisonment, one death not being enough to expiate their crimes. When the second term of imprisonment is judged to have expired, the district magistrate beseeches the tutelary deity of the city to accompany him to the prison in order to acquaint the ghost with his release. The order is supposed to reach the imprisoned by burning it, a ceremony which is solemnly carried out in the jail. On August 19, 1888, the district magistrate of the city of Soochow had placards posted up inviting subscriptions of imitation money for the ghosts then in the city jail. This was all duly burnt, and thus converted into currency, which would be useful to the ghosts on the long journey before them.

Enough has been said to show with what care the departed spirit is provided with every necessary. Even at the present day the Lithuanians bury or burn with the dead the claws of a lynx or bear, because they share the widely prevalent belief that the soul in its wanderings has to climb a steep mountain (just as we speak of ascent into heaven), and would never reach the summit without some means to prevent its sliding backward. For this same reason, the nails of a corpse must never be

53

pared. The Russians still carry about with them
parings of an owl's claws and of their own nails.
The ascent of a steep mountain, which is often of
glass, is a task frequently met with in popular tales.
In one from Lower Austria, the hero, who keeps
sliding backward in his attempt to scale a glass
mountain, changes himself into a bear, by means of
a hair given him by a grateful bear, and digs steps
with his paws. The expedient is one that would
naturally occur to the story-teller.

In the course of ages the numerous ceremonies
in connection with death have undergone much
transformation ; nevertheless, the barbaric element
in them is still recognisáble. Nowadays, instead
of offering food to the dead (the scattering of
flowers over the dead, a beautiful classic rite which
still obtains, is a practice scarcely less irrational
perhaps, though it has come to be a mere memorial
of affection), soul-cakes are made and eaten by the
living upon certain fixed occasions, though all idea
as to the connection between cakes and the dead
is lost. In Belgium it is said that for every cake
eaten a soul is delivered from purgatory. " In the
Congo district the custom has been described of
making a channel into the tomb to the head or
mouth of the corpse, whereby to send down month
by month the offerings of food and drink." The
cup-like hollows so frequently met with on the

stone slabs covering the tops of dolmens, were probably intended as receptacles for the food furnished to the dead ; and the basins scooped in the soil of a barrow may have served the same purpose. The fact that these cup-like markings are found on Christian tombs shows how a custom can survive all recollection of the motive for its institution.

In Brittany the touching ceremony is annually observed at the grave of dead kinsfolk of filling the hollow of the tombstone with holy water, or of pouring libations of milk upon it. On that night the supper is left spread in every household, and the fire burning, so that the souls of the dead may come from the graveyard to feed and to warm themselves. For

"Les morts, les pauvres morts, ont de grandes douleurs,"

says the poet Baudelaire ; and certainly in France and in Italy their fête on All Souls' Day is most religiously observed, and shows no symptom of dying out. The Feast of Souls is also observed by Letts and Esthonians, who spread a banquet for their spirit relatives. Torches are placed on the graves, to light the ghosts to the repast. Among the Slavs a yearly feast is held for the dead, and little bits of food are thrown under the table, that the departed souls may come and feed on the smell of it.

A Corsican legend thus accounts for the terrible storm that broke over the house of a poor man on the eve of the Day of the Dead. The noise was terrific, cries and curses echoed round : " Cursed be thou, and cursed thy wife ! Cursed also be thy children ! " The wretched man grew cold with fear. " Did you put the water outside the window ? " asked his wife. " Sangu di Cristu ! " cried he, " I forgot ! " And he rose and put vessels of water on the balcony. But this was not the end of the poor man's alarms and punishments from the resentful dead, whose vigil it was, and who had found no water either to drink or to wash and purify their sins in. But we must leave him alone to his subsequent encounters with the *Squadra d'Arozza*, the Dead Battalion, and return to our savage.

While such elaborate care is bestowed on the other-self, the ghost, the corpse itself is not forgotten. Of course it was above all things necessary to guard it from injury ; therefore trees were planted upon the graves with the idea of concealing them, or masses of earth and stones were piled over the corpse, that no man or beast could get at it. It was in consequence of the belief that the soul would at some period revivify the body that the Egyptians used to embalm their dead, and build the enormous pyramids to enshrine the mummy. The elaborate headstone is the modern counterpart of the rude and uninscribed *menhir*, or long stone which marked the resting-place of the corpse, just as the little turf-covered mound now represents the great tumulus or cairn.

Quite on a par with the primitive notions which we are now examining is that which actuated an aged woman who died in North Cornwall nine years ago, and who preserved all her teeth as she lost them, firmly believing that they must be buried with her against the day of Resurrection, otherwise her resurrection body would not be perfect. She made the clergyman promise that the teeth should be placed in her coffin.

If, on the other hand, the return of the dead, instead of being desired, were dreaded, the conduct of the survivors would be quite different. Measures would be taken to lay the ghost, and the corpse of an enemy would be mutilated, that the ghost might be rendered harmless. Thus murderers take every precaution to lay the ghost of a slain man. " The Greek cut off the extremities of his victims, the tips of the hands and feet, and disposed them neatly beneath the armpits of the slain man. In the same spirit, and for the same purpose, the Australian black cuts off the thumbs of his dead enemy, that the ghost too may be mutilated and prevented from throwing at him with a ghostly spear."

Burial barrows or howes were not infrequently broken open for the sake of the sword or the treasure buried with the dead warrior. When Grettir the

Strong won his famous short sword from the barrow of Karr the Old, he had a struggle with the barrow-dweller, and then cut off his head and laid it by his thigh, to lay the ghost in the approved way. Or, as in the story told by Saxo, when Asmund mastered Aswit, the formidable barrow-ghost, he cut off his head and impaled his guilty carcase, to prevent him doing further harm.

When a person had to be buried at sea, it used to be the custom to sew the body up in a hammock, taking the last stitch through the tip of the nose of the deceased. " Without this precaution the body would not stay down, however weighted with shot, but would shake off the trammels of its sailor shroud, and reappear as a ghost to its former ship-mates." Two cannon-balls are generally sewn up with a body to sink it. Once a negro died at sea, and his fellow-negroes rowed him a long way, meaning to commit him to the deep. After a while they returned to the ship with their burden, because they had discovered that they had only one cannon-ball, and it would be disrespectful to cheat their comrade out of half his due.

" In Russia the Chuwashes fling a red-hot stone after the corpse is carried out, for an obstacle to bar the soul from coming back." Savages will either adopt some means to prevent the soul's return, or they will abandon the dead man's house, that the ghost may reside in it. In civilised times a haunted house is similarly abandoned to its ghostly tenant. In Victor Hugo's house in one of the Channel Islands, there is an arm-chair with a chain drawn across it, that no one may sit in it, because it is still occupied by the ghost of his grandfather !

The incorporeal shade, the ghost, is usually conceived of as the counterpart of the deceased. In the 23rd Iliad there appeared unto Achilles, in his deep sleep, the soul of hapless Patroclus in all things like his living self, in stature and fair eyes and voice ; and the raiment of his body was the same. He prayed to be buried with all speed, that he might pass the gates of Hades. But when Achilles reached forth with his hands, he clasped him not ; for like a vapour the spirit was gone beneath the earth with a faint shriek. Even so when Odysseus would fain have embraced the spirit of his mother dead, she thrice flitted from his hands as a shadow, or as a dream (Odyssey XI.). And it was the same with Æneas when he attempted to throw his arms about the neck of his lost wife Creusa ; thrice the phantom fled from his hands as unsubstantial as the winds, and in all points like a fleeting dream. (The *noli me tangere* attitude is characteristic of ghosts. The New Testament affords an example.) The modern spiritualist believes that he receives a visit from a deceased relative,

" in his habit as he lived," even as his father's ghost appeared unto Hamlet, thus admitting, by implication, that clothes have ghosts. The sculptors and glass-painters of the Middle Ages constantly represented the souls of the dead as tiny bodies. In the British Museum there is a tomb from an ancient cemetery at Xanthus in Lycia. It is ornamented with mysterious winged creatures with human faces, who are carrying tiny shrouded figures, in all probability intended to represent the souls of the dead. The conception of the soul as a small human image is found in Australia, in Borneo, amongst the Hindus and the North American Indians ; it is familiar also in German folk-lore. Dr. Nansen tells us that amongst the Eskimos a man has many souls. The largest dwell in the larynx and in the left side, and are tiny men about the size of a sparrow. Other souls, dwelling in other parts of the body, are the size of a finger-joint. It has been thought that the little image seen in the pupil, called by the Indians of Guiana " the man in our eyes," which disappears from the dim eyeballs of the dying, may explain the conception of smallness in size of the shades of the dead.

Even if the body remains dead, the other-self, double or ghost, still mingles among the living, or departs to the other world, the abode of disembodied spirits, whence it can visit the haunts of men.

These spirits of the departed are supposed to be possessed of more extensive powers than before their separation from the body, and they can interfere in the affairs of the living, wherefore they must be cajoled and propitiated. For they may behave as good spirits or as evil spirits. Santal women who die before child-birth are believed to be *kitchni*, or evil spirits, capable of doing any mischief. It is a prevalent feeling everywhere that the ghosts of those who have suffered a violent or untimely death are especially malignant, so are the wandering ghosts of the unburied, in Australian belief. The notion that the spirits of men left unburied are doomed to walk the night seems to be universal. We can understand why the Hindu, in his desire for vengeance, should slay himself. It is in order that he may become a demon with power to haunt and torment his enemy. The dread of the power of spirits is a first step towards a definite worship of ghosts : it is fear which maintains throughout the world sacred temples, lakes, groves, altars, and images of the divinities. In the play of " Hecuba " by Euripides, the son of Achilles sacrifices Polyxena, the young Trojan princess, on the lofty grave-mound to appease his father's ghost, bidding him drink the pure purple blood of the virgin ; and then he prays him to be propitious, " and all the army joined in the prayer." For the ghost of Achilles had appeared above his tomb, and stayed the army of the Grecians as they were directing homeward their sea-dipt oars, and had told them that they should not leave his tomb unhonoured. And Trojan Helen, in the play of " Orestes," sends her daughter Hermione to offer libations and Helen's own hair at the grave-mound of the murdered Clytemnestra, and to pray her to hold kind intentions towards herself and her child and her husband. Hermione is told to promise all fitting offerings to the manes of Helen's sister. If it were the habit of every savage to propitiate the ghosts of his own dead relatives, because of the power for good or ill that they are supposed to exercise, it would follow that remote ancestral ghosts, having for generations been the objects of veneration, would come to be regarded as deities, and probably as creators.

Herodotus relates that the Nasamones go to the tombs of their ancestors and consult with them. After offering prayers they go to sleep by them, and any dream that appears to them is considered an answer. Of the Basutos in modern Africa we read : " Persons who are pursued in their sleep by the image of a deceased relation, are often known to sacrifice a victim on the tomb of the defunct, in order, as they say, to calm his disquietude." It is very clear from a mass of evidence that the savage believes that spirits outlive their bodies; then the notion of an enduring future life is reached by a gradual process of evolution.

Ancestor-worship is widely prevalent at the present day, and survivals of the primitive practice are easily traceable amongst civilised peoples. " Every Chinese household has somewhere within its doors an ancestral hall, a shrine in which are deposited the tablets of deceased ancestors. It may be a separate building, or it may be a mere shelf." Every clan has its ancestral temple, where the members rally to join in the ceremonies at the spring and autumn festivals. In Korea, as in China, ancestor-worship is the real religion, though Confucianism is the avowed religion of the country. In every Korean house burns a perpetual fire sacred to the dead ancestors of the household ; and to tend that fire, and never to let it go out, is the Korean housewife's first and most important duty. The early races of South India feed the spirits of their ancestors on all occasions of festivity, and worship as well as feed them after every death. Cooked rice and incense are offered to the spirit of the deceased. The " Anses," the ancestors of the royal races, were objects of veneration and worship to the Goths ; indeed, habitual and household worship of ancestors was the main cult of the older religion of the ancient Northmen. Sacrificial feasts were held in honour of the dead, who were called Elves, and were supposed to dwell in their barrows or burial-places, or in great hills near the place where they lived in life. Cormac's Saga supplies an account of one of these feasts. " She [Thordis] said, There is a knoll a little way from here where the Elves dwell ; thou shalt take thither the ox that Cormac slew, and sprinkle the blood of the ox on the outside of the knoll, and give the Elves a banquet of the meat ; and thou shalt be healed." Belief in the Banshee, an ancestral spirit, was, until quite recently, generally current in Scotland and Ireland and in many parts of England ; and the household fairy to whom offerings of food are made is a survival from the times of our Aryan-speaking ancestors, whose hearth cult was connected with the worship of ancestral spirits. Half of our ideas about fairies are derived from the heathen beliefs as to the spirits of the dead.

A body deserted by its other-self may be entered by the other-self, friendly or malicious, of some one else, living or dead. Sneezing, yawning, or convulsions are regarded as such cases of malevolent possession (see p. 7) ; hence exorcism is resorted to for the expulsion of an evil spirit. Out of this belief grew the whole practice of sorcery. Amongst savages, the medicine-men, Shamans, or dealers with familiar spirits, were the only priests. A madman was supposed to be possessed by the *manes* or spirit of some dead man, wherefore the Romans

used the word *mania* (which we borrow from them)
to denote madness, even after they had ceased to
hold the belief which suggested the use.

Cases of swoon and apoplexy, or any loss of
consciousness, would be explained as the result of
a temporary absence of the second self ; and here
language preserves the idea in such expressions as
" coming back to himself." This is why in the
Middle Ages it was difficult for a person accused of
witchcraft to prove an *alibi*, for it was argued that
whilst the body was innocently quiescent, the soul
was abroad working evil.

It used to be a common practice, and it is not
even now an extinct one, to open the window in the
room where a person lay dying, to enable the soul
to take flight ; just as the Hottentots, the Samoyeds,
the Siamese, the Fijians, and the Redskins make a
hole in the hut to allow the passage of the deceased,
but cautiously close it again immediately afterwards
to prevent its return. In some parts of China they
make a hole in the roof for the egress of the dead
man's soul. The Iroquois make a small hole in
every tomb, to allow the soul to go out and come in
at its pleasure ; and it has been conjectured that the
holes frequently found in the pre-historic dolmens
or cromlechs, those rude stone receptacles for the
bones of the dead, have been bored for the purpose
of allowing ingress and egress to the spirit, that, in

the belief of the survivors of the deceased, still tenanted the bones. The same explanation may serve for the presence of bored holes in many funeral urns — such, for example, as have been found in the barrows on Salisbury Plain, containing calcined bones.

The natives of Vati Island believe that the souls of their departed friends and relatives enter certain stones, which they therefore preserve. Some of these stones " had a small piece chipped out on one side, by means of which the indwelling ghost or spirit was supposed to have ingress or egress." One is reminded of the story of the Yorkshire old lady who had two holes cut in the sides of the coffin which was destined one day to contain her remains, so that the devil might find his way out in the event of his happening to get shut in with her.

More curious still is the evidence afforded by the skulls of pre-historic man that have turned up in almost every European country, as well as in Algeria and in North and South America. It appears from the witness of these skulls that the men of the polished stone age were in the habit of cutting holes in each other's heads during life. At least in the majority of the European cases this operation of trepanning, as it is called, was undoubtedly performed during life. The surgeon's only instrument in those neolithic days was a flint scraper or knife, and yet there is evidence that the patient in the majority of cases lived for many years after the operation. Now, what could be the motive for this trepanning ? We have seen how cases of convulsions, epilepsy, or any mental derangement, perhaps even of severe headache, were attributed to the possession of the patient by an evil spirit ; what expedient therefore could appear more rational than to provide an outlet for the demon's escape ? This appears to have been the principle, as well as the practice, of the primitive medicine-man. He first cut a hole in the head of the sufferer and then conjured the spirit forth. The Kabyles of Algeria practise trepanning in cases of epilepsy.

The phenomena of shadows and reflections would further tend to confirm belief in a second-self. The fact that a man's shadow is not always beside him only proves that the second-self can go away. Similarly would the savage reason with regard to the reflection which he sees on looking into water. The Basutos think " that if a man walks on the river-bank, a crocodile may seize his shadow in the water and draw him in." In classic languages, as well as in various barbaric tongues, the word for shadow expresses also the soul or other-self. New England tribes called the soul *chemung*, shadow. In the Tasmanian, Quiche, and Eskimo languages, and in several dialects of Costa Rica, as among the Zulus and the Abipones, one word expresses both soul and shade. We ourselves speak of a " shade " or ghost, and we find a similar employment of the Greek word σκιά, and the Latin *umbra*. With the σκιά and *umbra* may be compared the *khaibit* of the ancient Egyptians, which was supposed to have an entirely independent existence, and to be able to separate itself from the body. It was quite distinct from the *ka* or double, and the *ba* or soul.

" Death," says Lucretius, " leaves all things entire, except vital sense and quickening heat." It is the cessation of breathing which characterises death as differing from sleep ; it is therefore not unreasonable to identify the soul with the breath, which really quits the body at death. Again, the evidence of language proves the universality of this idea ; for the word used to express breath also means soul in Hebrew, Sanscrit, Greek, and Latin, and in several barbaric tongues. Possibly, too, the German *geist* and English ghost have the meaning of breath. Animal and *être* mean the same thing, *breather*. Algonkin Indians buried little children by the wayside, that their souls might enter into mothers passing by, and so be born again. In Florida, when a woman dies in childbirth, her infant is held over her face to receive her parting spirit; similarly, the nearest kinsman of the ancient Roman would inhale his latest breath. Quite recently it was said that a certain Lancashire witch could not die till she had transferred her familiar spirit. Accordingly her associate was fetched, and received the witch's last breath into her mouth, and with it her familiar spirit.

Echoes are thought to be the voices of departed souls; for after vain search for a visible owner of the mocking voice, uncivilised man can frame but one explanation of the phenomenon, and, in so doing, finds support for his belief in a soul that can be separated from the body and become invisible.

From the fanciful explanation of natural pheno-mena poetry has derived much of its immortal charm. Before philosophy comes in to " conquer all mysteries by rule and line," and depeople all echo-haunted spots, " such places," as Lucretius says, " the neighbouring people pretend that Satyrs and Nymphs inhabit; and say that there are Fauns in them by whose noise and sportive play, re-echoing through the night, they universally affirm that the dead silence is broken, and that sounds of chords and sweet plaintive notes are heard." It is interesting to recall in this connection that

" the Anglo-Saxon dictionary preserves the curious word *wood-mare* for an echo (*wudu-maer* = wood nymph), a record of the time when Englishmen believed, as barbarians do still, that the echo is the voice of an answering spirit ; the word *mare*, for spirit or demon, appears also in *nightmare*, the throttling dream demon who was as real to our forefathers as he is to the natives of Australia now."

Conceiving that the soul can quit the body during life, the savage supposes that it may temporarily become embodied in a bird or beast. This is an approach to the doctrine of transmigration, which Pythagoras taught, and of which we read in Plato. Shakespeare makes capital of the notion in " Twelfth Night " (iv. 2) :

Clown. What is the opinion of Pythagoras concerning wild-fowl ?

Malvolio. That the soul of our grandam might haply inhabit a bird.

The popular imagination still pictures the soul as a bird which flies out of the mouth of a dying person. Grimm says that this is why old tombstones often have doves carved on them, and these the Christian faith brings into still closer proximity to spirit. It will be remembered that in the popular tale of " The Juniper-Tree," the little brother, when killed, flies out of the juniper-tree as a bird ; and in a large number

of folk-tales, notably those belonging to the " Cinderella " group, a little bird sits on the tree growing
out of the grave-mound, and comforts the orphan
child. The Bohemians thought that the soul
hovered about as a bird till the body was buried,
when it found rest. Finns and Lithuanians call
the Milky-Way the " path of birds "—that is, of
souls. In Woycicki's collection of Polish folk-tales
is one about a robber who confesses his sins under
an apple-tree. As he does so, apple after apple
flies up into the air, converted into a white dove.
They were the souls of those he had murdered. But
one apple remains : it is the soul of his father,
whose murder he has suppressed. When at length
he confesses it, the last apple changes into a gray
dove and flies after the rest. The temptation to
quote other stories in illustration of this graceful
fancy must be resisted.

In Irish mythic belief the souls of the righteous
appear as doves ; in County Mayo the souls of
virgins take the form of swans. The night-jar
in Nidderdale is looked upon as the soul of an
unbaptized child ; while in Cornwall it is believed
that King Arthur still lives in the form of a raven.

In Greece the soul is pictured as a butterfly,
which is called ψυχή, also the word for soul. In
an Irish parish butterflies are called " the soul
of your grandfather." In the Basque language

71

the name for butterfly means literally " ass's soul." Another popular opinion, based on savage philosophy, and which has already been illustrated (*supra*, pp. 43–4), is that the soul runs out of the sleeper's mouth as a mouse, or a cat, or a weasel, or a snake.

Or the departing soul may break into blossom like a flower, of which conception folk-legends afford numberless pretty illustrations. In a story from Abyssinia, seven palm-trees grow on the spot where the girl buries the bones of her seven brothers ; and in the North Indian story, when the brothers kill and eat their sister, a bamboo springs from her bones, just as in numerous stories of the "Cinderella" type, a magic tree springs from some buried portion of the helpful animal. The Lay of Runzifal makes a blackthorn shoot up out of the bodies of slain heathen, a white flower by the heads of fallen Christians ; and the tradition goes that the red poppies which followed the ploughing of the field of Waterloo after Napoleon's defeat, sprung from the blood of the many gallant men who fell during the battle. So tulips, if we may credit the legend, had their origin in the Armenian town of Erzeroum, where they sprung from the life-blood of despairing Ferdad, who threw himself from the rocks at the false alarm of the death of his beloved Shireen. The reader need hardly be

reminded that the anemone sprung from the blood
of dying Adonis, when the boar he was chasing
turned and rent him. From the mounds of buried
lovers flowering shrubs spring up, whose branches
intertwine. In the ballad of " Fair Margaret and
Sweet William " we read :

> " Out of her brest there sprang a rose,
>   And out of his a briar ;
>   They grew till they grew unto the church top,
>   And there they tyed in a true lovers knot."

We have the same fancy in another ballad :

> " They buried the ane in Mary's kirk,
>   The other in Mary's quire,
>   And out of the ane there grew a birk,
>   And out of the other a briar."

In an ancient Romansch ballad—presenting a simple
episode in Swiss peasant life—a camomile plant
grows from the grave-mound of the girl, and from
the grave-mound of her lover a plant of musk.
And, for the great love they bore one another,
the flowers twined together and embraced. In the
Portuguese ballad of Count Nello, a cypress grows
on one grave, and an orange tree on the other.
Their branches join and kiss. The king who had
forbidden the union of these fond lovers, the Count
and the Infanta, now orders their trees to be cut
down. From the cypress flows noble blood, from
the orange tree blood royal ; from one flies forth

73

a dove, from the other a wood-pigeon. They perch before the king as he sits at table. "Ill-luck upon their fondness," he cries, " ill-luck upon their love ! Neither in life nor in death have I been able to divide them." So, again, the rose and the briar of the English ballad are the cypress and the reed of a Greek folk-song, the thorn and the olive of the Norman *chanson*, the vine and the rose of the " Tristram and Iseult " story.

It is necessary, however, to return from this fascinating excursion into later times to an examination of the primitive philosophy in which all these fanciful notions have their origin. The logic of the untutored savage is simple but consistent. He observes that plants and trees, like animals, show undoubted signs of life, and he reasonably attributes souls to them also. For he can only interpret the actions of nature by putting them on a level with his own actions. A spirit stirs the volcano, causing it to belch forth flame. It is a spirit that rides on the wings of the wind uprooting the forest-trees or swamping the canoe in the whirlpool. A spirit in the trees causes them to grow and put forth leaves, and awful spirit eyes look down on men from the host of the nightly stars. The state of mind to which these nature-spirits belong has lingered in the fancies of the Greeks, creating the Naiads of the flowing rivers

74

and springs ; the Nereids that ride the sea-horses ;
Pan, Sylvanus and the woodland Nymphs, the goat-
like Fauns and Satyrs, and the sisterhood of the
Dryads. " The Lorelei is only a modernised version of a river demon, who drowns the swimmer
in a whirlpool ; the healing water-spirits of the
old sacred wells have only taken saints' names.
The little elves and fairies of the woods are only
dim recollections of the old forest spirits."

It is a very general belief amongst savages that
the souls of the dead animate trees. " The Dieyerie
tribe of South Australia regard as very sacred certain trees, which are supposed to be their fathers
transformed ; hence, they will not cut the trees
down, and protest against the settlers doing so.
Some of the Philippine Islanders believe that the
souls of their forefathers are in certain trees, which
they therefore spare." Many other such instances
of the savage's regard for certain sacred trees might
be adduced. It is probable that all the strange
legends of speaking, sentient trees originated in
the belief that trees and plants were tenanted by
the souls of the dead, thus becoming personified
and endowed with human qualities and faculties.
We may recall in this connection the experience
of Æneas with the plants of dogwood and bristling
myrtles which he found growing on a mound.
When he tore the green stems from the ground

75

to deck an altar for sacrifice, he saw that blood was trickling from the roots. This happened a second time. But when with all his might he strove to pluck a third stalk, a lamentable groan was heard from the depths of the mound, and a voice bade him spare the buried and not tear a wretched being. It was the murdered Polydorus who spoke, from the mound which covered his remains. We see from this story that the plants growing on the mound, or barrow, come to be identified with the body underneath. They embody the soul of the dead person, in the same way as, in primitive belief, the living bird or butterfly becomes the habitat of the soul when it quits the dead body.

"In an Annamite story an old fisherman makes an incision in the trunk of a tree which has drifted ashore; but blood flows from the cut, and it appears that an empress and her three daughters, who had been cast into the sea, are embodied in the tree."

A Slovac legend is likewise connected with the belief in the transmigration of souls. Two musicians travelling together noticed a fine plane tree, which would make so excellent a violin that they resolved to cut it down for that purpose. At the first blow the tree sighed; at the second blow out spurted blood; at the third blow the tree spake and said, " Musicians, do not cut me down; I am of flesh and blood, and no tree. My mother cursed

76

me, a lovely girl, and changed me into a broad-leaved plane tree, even while I drew water, chatting with my friend. Go ye, musicians, and play before my mother." And they did so, playing a dirge. " Rend not my heart with your playing," said the mother.

In a large class of folk-tales, belonging to the " Singing Bone " type, a child is robbed by a brother or sister of an apple, or some other coveted acquisition, and then murdered, and buried or hidden away. A plant grows on the spot, and some time afterwards, when attempt is made to pluck the flower, the voice of the murdered child makes known what has been done, exposing the criminal. Sometimes it is a bone of the victim, or a reed growing on the grave, which, when blown through, reveals the crime.

Trees play prominent parts in folk-tales. The Kaffirs have trees which laugh, and the Zulus tell about speaking trees. These are common in Indian as well as in Norse tales, and are believed in by North American tribes. The green reed spoke to Psyche in the story told by Apuleius, and the speaking oaks saluted wandering Io. Jotham's story in the Book of Judges makes the trees talk to one another. So in the Izdubar legends of Babylonia the trees answer Hea-bani. In a North Indian story a king had a terrible secret, like the

Phrygian king Midas, which only his barber knew. The Indian king had horns, and the barber whispered the secret to a tamarind tree. Of this tree a drum was made, and whenever it was beaten it cried, " There are horns on the king's head ! " In the Greek story it was a reed that " was garrulously given, a babbler in the land." It grew from a hole in the earth into which the barber had whispered, and it murmured, " King Midas has ass's ears." Much the same tale was current in Wales and Ireland about King Mark, whose Welsh name March means horse. He used to have every barber who shaved him killed, lest he should betray the secret as to his ears. Now, on the spot where the bodies of the murdered barbers were buried there grew reeds, from among which a certain of March's bards chose one to make a pipe. This reed would discourse of nothing but March ab Meirchion's equine ears. The enraged March would have killed the musician, but was persuaded to blow the pipe himself, and then discovered that the instrument and not the musician was at fault.

In our own country. it has been said that " when an oake is felling, before it falls it gives a kind of shriekes or groans, that may be heard a mile off, as if it were the genius of the oake lamenting." John Aubrey (1686–87), from whose writings this passage is quoted, adds : " It has not unusually

been observed that to cut oak-wood is unfortunate."
Within fifty years of the present day it was believed that a certain larch tree at Nauders, in the
Tyrol, bled whenever it was cut. In England the
superstitious think that the creaking of furniture is
an omen of death in a house. The Aztecs have the
same belief, which is probably associated primarily
with the wood of which the furniture was made.

A mysterious sympathy is supposed to exist
between men and natural objects. Thus, when
children have been passed through cleft trees (see
supra, p. 13), the child's life is supposed in a manner
to be bound up with that of the particular tree
through which he has been transmitted ; and should
an attempt be unadvisedly made to cut the tree, no
efforts will be spared by the man to secure the continued existence of his foster-brother. So was the
Hamadryad's life bound to her tree ; when it was
wounded she was hurt, she cried aloud when the
axe threatened, and when the trunk fell she died.
In some districts of Belgium it is still the custom to
plant a tree in the garden on the birth of a child.
It is thought that the fate of the tree is intimately
connected with the fate of the child. On this subject of the " Life-token " more will be said in the
chapter on Magic. In the ancient Egyptian story
of " The Two Brothers," which was written down
some 3200 years ago by a Theban scribe named

Ennana, the life of the younger brother is bound up in that of the tree in which he has deposited his heart. This story, like a number of others, affords an illustration of the savage belief in a separable soul. In the reign of Romanus Lacapenus it was desirable that Simeon, Prince of Bulgaria, should die. Now, on the arch Xerolophi, in Constantinople, there stood a column, and an astronomer assured Romanus that if the head of this column were struck off, Simeon, whose fate was bound up with it, would perish. The head was accordingly struck from the pillar, and at the same hour on the same day the Prince died in Bulgaria of a disease of the heart.

We have only to turn to Ovid to find stories of metamorphosis of human beings into trees, just as in Samoa it is told that a man can assume a vege-table form, or stand erect as a handsome straight tree.

Trees occupy a conspicuous place in all the classic, Chinese, Finnish, Hindu, Persian, Arabian, and other religions ; besides, the general worship of both Celts and Teutons had its seat in the forest. Amongst the Greeks, trees and flowers were con-nected with the worship and ritual of Apollo, and we have various myths explaining the association. For instance, the nymph Daphne, being pursued by Apollo, who was enamoured of her, implores the aid of her father Peneus, and is changed into a laurel. " Since thou canst not be my wife, at least thou shalt be my tree," said the god. The olive and the oak were sacred to Artemis at Ephesus; at Delos she had a sacred palm tree. Dionysus also was a tree-god. Sacred groves like that of Dodona, and others of which the ancients speak, have likewise been found among the benighted races of Central Africa, and among the American Indians. Even in more recent days the Persians worshipped flowers; and an author writes of the Victorian Gardens at Bombay that " a true Persian, in flowing robe of blue, and on his head his sheepskin hat, would saunter in and stand and meditate over every flower he saw, and always as half in vision. And when the vision was fulfilled, and the ideal flower he was seeking found, he would spread his mat and sit before it until the setting of the sun, and then pray before it, and fold up his mat again and go home." Traces of plant-worship are to be found even in England. Thus, at certain seasons, Devonshire farmers, on the eve of Twelfth Day, go to their orchards after supper with a pail of cider with roasted apples pressed into it. Out of this each person in the company takes an earthenware cup full of liquor, and, standing under the more fruitful apple trees, addresses them thus :—

> " Health to thee, good apple tree,
> Well to bear pocket-fulls, hat-fulls,
> Peck-fulls, bushel bag-fulls."

This formula having been repeated, the contents of the cup are thrown at the tree. In many countries the white thorn is held sacred, the tradition being very ancient, although the sanctity of the tree was enhanced in mediæval times by the belief that the Crown of Thorns was formed from it. The Irish consider it specially unlucky to cut this tree down. The Poles have the same superstitious fear in connection with hollow willow trees, because the devil is supposed to reside in them. Split trees are used for the cure of diseases (see *supra*, p. 13). At the Holi festival in North India a sacred tree is burned, and the people leap over its ashes to get rid of itch, &c. ; and the villagers try to steal one of the rags tied to this tree in a neighbouring village, for the act is very propitious. The worship of the Nim tree is supposed to propitiate the goddesses of all kinds of epidemics which prevail in summer.

In short, relics of ancient tree cults have been found amongst Aryan- and non-Aryan-speaking tribes, in Europe and in Asia, and are seen in our own country in the offerings (like those of the West African negro and of savage tribes elsewhere) of rags and other small gifts on bushes and trees, and also in the May-pole customs and dances. Memories of holy trees and groves are recorded also in the names of *Holyoake* and *Holy-*

wood. But the subject of Tree-worship is too vast for one to do more than touch the borders of it in this brief survey of the ground which Folk-lore covers.

This chapter, dealing with the universal savage belief in a separable soul which sometimes quits the body, may be concluded with a general reference to the many illustrations of this belief which are met with in the folk-tales of all lands. For example, there is the Indian story of the magician Punchkin, whose soul is in a little green parrot in a small cage below a chattee full of water, the lowest of six chattees piled one above another, in the centre of a circle of palm trees growing in the midst of a thick jungle, in a desolate country, hundreds of thousands of miles away. Upon the life of that parrot depends the magician's life. This is how " Koshchei the Deathless," in the Russian story, hides his soul : " Under an oak is a casket, in the casket is a hare, in the hare is a duck, in the duck an egg, in the egg is my death," says he. A Tatar giant kept his soul in a twelve-headed snake, which he carried in a bag as he rode on horseback. The jinn's soul, in the Arabian story, is in the crop of a sparrow imprisoned in a small box inside seven other boxes, which are enclosed in a marble coffer that is sunk in the ocean surrounding the world. Every one knows the Norse story of " The Giant who had no heart in his body." Seven robbers, in a Siberian tale, hang up their hearts on pegs, and they are stolen by a captive swan-maiden and delivered—as the price of her own liberty—to a Samoyed, who smashes the hearts, thus killing the robbers. Variants of the foregoing theme are very numerous in folk-tales. It occurs in the ancient Egyptian story of the " Two Brothers," one of the oldest fairy-tales on record, the MS. of which is in the British Museum. For a classic example of the same notion we may recall the Greek story of Meleager and the firebrand. When he was seven days old, the Fates declared that the boy would die as soon as the piece of wood then burning on the hearth should be consumed. Upon hearing this Althæa, his mother, extinguished the firebrand, and concealed it in a chest. Years afterwards, to revenge the death of her brothers, she threw the piece of wood into the fire, whereupon Meleager expired.

CHAPTER II

ANIMAL ANCESTORS

The savage mind naturally credulous ; treats all nature alike as personal and animated—Observation of changes of form in the order of nature engenders belief in the transformation of men into animals —Especially sorcerers have this power—Witch stories in illustration—Or a man's double may enter the body of an animal; or animals may be possessed by the doubles of dead persons—Certain animals thus regarded as transformed ancestors—Resulting confused theories of descent from and kinship with animals—Men named after animals—Regard for animal namesake—Totemism— Its universal traces—A digression anent the family tie—Influence of totemic beliefs on savage conduct—Relics of totemism amongst civilised races—The Easter hare—Plants identified with ancestors —Vegetable totems—Animal and plant worship—Results of the personification of animals and plants—Guiding beasts and birds— The hawk and the Mikado—Burying alive under foundations—The bell of Peking—Animal omens—Helpful animals in folk-tales— Animals as *dramatis personæ*—Myths of descent from and marriage with animals—Animal children—Animal worship in Egypt —Animal gods—Shape-shifting gods—Greek and savage myths compared—The swallowing trick—Why the savage legends were retained—Attempted symbolical explanation of myths—The right method of interpretation—The Swan-coat—Melusina—Cupid and Psyche—The Werewolf; to be distinguished from the lycanthrope —A recent case of relapse into barbarism.

THERE is a period during the early stages of man's intellectual development when he is readily able to believe anything that may be suggested by an undisciplined fancy, if it be not contradicted by direct experience. Savage man treats all nature alike as personal and animated; he transfers to every object those qualities which he himself possesses, and expects from every object such actions as he can himself perform. If injured by a fellow-creature, he would retaliate with a blow, and seek vengeance for the injury. In like manner, inanimate objects, in contact with which he may suffer pain, come in for his resentment. Of one of the native races of America we read, "If a savage struck his foot against a stone, he raged over it, and bit it like a dog." This is like the conduct of young children, who, bruised by a fall—

> "Lend life to the dumb stones
> On which to vent their rage,
> And bend their little fists
> And rate the senseless ground."

And we should not be surprised to find in the civilised child the psychological representative of primitive man, when we consider that the period during which the human species has existed in any kind of civilisation, making its own conditions, is but a span compared with its long life of simple barbarism. Civilisation is but a thin veneer, and the primeval barbarism is often very near the surface. By an old English law, repealed only in the reign of Queen Victoria, the beast that killed a man, the wheel that ran over him, or the tree which fell and crushed him, was deodand, or given to God;

that is to say, it was forfeited and sold for the poor. According to Pausanias, the Prytaneis at Athens condemned to capital punishment any lifeless object which had accidentally caused a man's death.

The savage asks himself questions, and is satisfied with the first answer that comes to hand. Wherever tradition fails to furnish this answer, invention is his only resource, though he is not consciously inventing. In a rough-and-ready manner he is reasoning from such data as his surroundings afford, and it is in this way that he comes to evolve those curious myths, which are destined to be crystallised in the course of generations into religious traditions. To the savage mind nothing is improbable, nothing is supernatural. It sees nothing remarkable in those extreme changes that are constantly occurring in the order of nature. They only serve to stimulate the dormant imagination and to direct its working. The savage sees a motionless egg suddenly turn itself into a bird, or a chrysalis into a butterfly, without any external agency. From the white kernel of a hard brown nut come a soft shoot and green leaves. He accepts these facts and many similar ones without surprise, and, with a mind naturally credulous, is not disposed to limit his belief in metamorphosis to just those instances of it that he may chance to witness. Therefore, any suggestion of a particular creature having assumed a different shape is instantly acceptable to him, and without difficulty he conceives that men can take the form of animals. The metamorphoses which actually occur are more marvellous than many that he wrongly supposes to occur. There is greater contrast between a maggot and a fly, a tadpole and a frog, than between a child and a puppy, a man and a bull. All races show us that the transformation of men into animals, and animals into men, is a familiar thought ; and we must bear this in mind, as the key to the interpretation of much that we shall have to consider. A few examples must suffice to illustrate the belief in animal-metamorphosis. The Thlinkeets of North America will kill a bear only in cases of great necessity, because the bear is supposed to be a man that has taken the shape of an animal ; and in Abyssinia, blacksmiths are supposed to be able to turn themselves into hyænas and other animals. It is not every savage who believes that he himself possesses this magical power. More generally it is limited to sorcerers, or medicine-men, who can take the shape of any beast, bird, fish, or insect. But they can also change the forms of others besides themselves. This idea is firmly rooted in the savage mind, and bears fruit in many directions. It crops up still in certain nursery tales, where the witch has power to change the heroine's

88

offspring into a cat or a fox. The belief in magic
and in medicine-men has a universal hold on savage
life, and declares itself everywhere in the institutions
of untutored races, the sorcerer having as much
power and influence as in later times has the priest.
For not only can he practise animal-metamorphosis
on himself and others, but he can visit the abodes
of the dead, can move inanimate objects by incantations, can converse with spirits, and magically cure
or inflict diseases. Marvels of the sort have been
reported from very near home. When that great
explorer, Pytheas of Massilia, who lived in the fourth
century B.C., in the age of Alexander the Great,
made his famous voyage to Britain, he found an
island then known as Axantos, or Uxisana, now
called the Isle of Ushant, where he landed, and came
upon a temple where nine Gaelic priestesses main-
tained a perpetual fire in honour of their god (like
the Vestal virgins). They attended to an oracle,
and they professed to be able to assume at will the
form of any animal, to cure all diseases, and to know
the future's secrets. " *Heu vatum ignaræ mentes,*"
said Virgil, as well he might. Alas ! how ignorant
are the minds of priests.

The witch and the Druid priestesses have certain
powers in common. Each claims to be able to
assume animal form, and to rule wind and wave by
spells and incantations. The " magic broth " which

the witch-doctors brew in Matabeleland is still sometimes sprinkled on the trees and the king's kraal and waggons, and even on the royal person of the king himself in time of war, in order to preserve them from evil influences, and to make the bullets of the enemy miss fire. For the Matabele believe in witchcraft, and fear the spells of their own people ; while they think that the witchcraft of the white people is of a wholly beneficial kind, and a sort of antidote to their own. I quote the following passage from a correspondent to the *Times*, Oct. 14, 1893, during the war in Matabeleland :—" The man who is supposed to bewitch others is believed to go about by night and ' lay medicine ' about the country and in the kraals of his victims. He is also supposed to have dealings with certain wild beasts, such as the leopard and the hyæna. One of the missionaries had poisoned a hyæna, or wolf, as it is called in Matabeleland, which had been troubling his station. He was standing looking at the dead beast when one of the Matabele came up. ' Ah ! ' said he, ' that is an umtagati's wolf.' (Umtagati is Setebele for wizard.) The missionary asked what made him say that. The man pointed to a scratch on the hyæna's ear. ' That is an umtagati's mark,' he said ; ' every night an umtagati used to get on the wolf's back and ride him round the kraals.' "

The Khonds believe that witches can transform

themselves into tigers. Often when a tiger carries off a child or a goat, it is thought to be no real beast, but a witch in an assumed form. But enough has been said to show that the power of metamorphosis is especially ascribed to sorcerers and witches, and that a belief in this power is universal amongst savages. And further, the belief in witchcraft has lingered through many centuries of civilisation. Nowadays the hare is popularly regarded as the associate of witches, who can assume its shape. Probably for this cause the hare is an object of disgust in some parts of Russia, as well as in Western Brittany. The old Welsh laws contain several allusions to its magical character.

In various parts of Scotland there is a tale of a " witch who was shot at in the guise of a hare. In this shape she was wounded, and the same wound was found on her when she resumed her human appearance." Precisely the same tale has been met with among the Red Indians, except that their wizards took the form of birds which were wounded by the magical arrow of an old medicine-man, and the arrows were found in the bodies of the human culprits. In fact, tales of this kind are to be found all over the globe. The Japanese version has a fox. " The prince royal of India had a lovely mistress who had bewitched him, and who fell asleep one day in a bed of chrysanthemums, where her lover shot at and wounded a fox in the forehead. The bleeding temple of the girl discovered the evil animal she really was. For the fox, as in China, is in Japan a wicked animal capable of everything in the way of transformation and suggestion." (The above legend is referred to in all those Japanese drawings which associate the chrysanthemum and the fox.) The fairy-fox plays an important part in every native Chinese collection of supernatural tales, filling somewhat the same *rôle* that the werewolf fills in European folk-lore; only the latter is usually malicious, while the fairy-fox is sometimes beneficent, and, when it takes human shape, assumes the form of a woman—like the charming young fox (disguised, of course, as a woman) that, in numerous tales, gets married to some loving Japanese swain and has a family. Generally some little domestic disagreement induces the charmer to resume her foxhood and scamper off, followed by her cubs, leaving the bewildered husband desolate. A story was recently told in Ontario, in a district peopled with Scotch Highlanders from Glenelg, who carried their ancestral traditions with them to another hemisphere. It is a variant of the foregoing, and testifies also to the belief already referred to (*supra*,

p. 7), that when the butter is long in coming, the devil has a hand in the business.

"Thence, countra wives, wi' toil an' pain,
May plunge an' plunge the kirn in vain ;
For oh ! the yellow treasure's ta'en
By witching skill."

A blue butterfly was seen to flutter over a certain farm, and was the subject of much notice, and, subsequently, of suspicion. For some unexplained reason, the butter "would not come" on that farm from the time that the butterfly had been seen. For three weeks this state of things continued, and the butterfly fluttered. Then a man armed himself with a wet towel and felled the insect single-handed. Shortly afterwards a poor lonely woman was found dead on the ground near her own door. Her life, in short, became extinct simultaneously with the destruction of the blue butterfly. Next day the butter came ! Here was circumstantial evidence sufficient to convict that old woman of witchcraft.

These Highland emigrants tell another tale, about a black dog which was suspected of being the perpetrator of all kinds of ridiculous practical jokes. For this ownerless black dog had long been seen stalking about the neighbourhood where the vexations occurred. Some one attempted its life with a gun, but without producing any visible results.

The practical jokes were maliciously continued. Then a sensible man charged his gun with a silver bit, and fired. The body of the dog was never found, but a small boy came running up to say that his grandfather was dead. He had dragged himself into the house as though hurt, and had quickly expired. It may be mentioned that in folk-tales we not infrequently come across the fancy that creatures that are in league with the devil, but more especially sea-monsters, when invulnerable to everything else, can be shot with a silver bullet. It occurs, for instance, in an Irish version of " Cinderella," and it is a common incident in Icelandic tales. " No monster, however fiendish, can withstand a silver shot." It will be remembered that Sir Walter Scott in his " Old Mortality " refers to the belief that witches can only be shot with silver bullets.

The witch sometimes appears as a cat, as in the German story, when, on the cat's paw being chopped off, it turned into a pretty female hand, and the miller next morning found that his wife had a hand missing. In another story the witch is ridden as a horse, and is taken to the farrier's to be shod. Next morning she lies in bed with horse-shoes on her hands and feet.

In Russia, of all living creatures, magpies are those whose shapes witches like best to take. The

wife of the false Demetrius, according to popular
poetry, escaped from Moscow in the guise of a
magpie. The White Russians have a tradition
that once a whole wedding party were transformed
by some hostile magician—the bridegroom and the
other men into wolves, the bride into a cuckoo,
and the rest of the women into magpies. Ever
since that time the metamorphosed bride has flown
about seeking and lamenting her lost bridegroom,
and moistening the hedges with the " cuckoo's
tears," which we less poetically style the " cuckoo's
spittle."

The universal belief in animal-metamorphosis, of
which we have been giving illustrations, has, however, more than one phasis. Sometimes, instead of
a man changing his form, it is his double that
enters the body of an animal ; or animals may be
possessed by the doubles of dead persons. This
is akin to the theory of metempsychosis which we
have already considered. The Apaches, an existing American race, believe that every rattlesnake
contains the soul of a bad man, or is an emissary
of the Evil Spirit ; and the Californians round San
Diego will not eat the flesh of large game, believing such animals to be inhabited by the souls of
generations of people who have died ages ago. A
nearly allied belief regards certain animals as transformed ancestors, and this habit of mind accounts

for all the confused theories of kinship and descent which we must now examine.

It is necessary to keep ever before us the fact that to the savage mind no distinction is perceptible between animate and inaminate nature. Believing that

> " All things the world which fill
> Of but one stuff are spun,"

the savage would readily accept the theories, which we know he holds, of descent from birds, beasts, plants, stars, sun and moon, wind or rain. The widely prevalent habit of naming men after animals, plants, or other natural objects, contributes, by the inevitable misinterpretation of traditions, to the belief in descent other than human—especially as this belief so conveniently fits in with the idea of metempsychosis. The savage shows great regard for his animal-namesake, or *kobong*, as the Australians call it. He would avoid killing an animal of the species after which he is named, and would on no account eat of it. In short, this animal, held so sacred by the tribe who bear its name, does eventually become identified with the ancestor of the tribe, and is worshipped as such. The word *totemism* is usually applied to cover this belief in the sanctity of certain plants and animals from which men claim descent, every tribe having its totem, or crest, or clan-mark, marking his supposed descent from a beaver, a bear, a crocodile, a fish, a wild pig, or an emu, or a honeysuckle tree or a vegetable, as the case may be. The word *totem* (expressing much the same thing as the Australian word *kobong*) is the corruption of an original word which the Red Indians apply to the plant, animal, or other natural object representing the ancestor and protector of the group of persons who share the name and crest. This institution of totemism has been observed by travellers in North and South America, in Australia, Samoa, India, Arabia, in Northern Asia, and in West and South Africa. Moreover, traces of totemism have been found in the early history of Germans, Greeks, and Latins, as well as in the traditions of the Semitic peoples in Arabia and Palestine. It is a question, too, whether the religion of the British tribes may not in some early stages have been connected with totemism. " The names of several tribes, or the legends of their origin, show that an animal or some other real or imaginary object was chosen as a crest or emblem, and was probably regarded with a superstitious veneration. A powerful tribe or family would feign to be descended from a swan or a water-maiden, or a ' white lady ' who rose from the moonbeams on the lake. The moon herself was claimed as the ancestress of certain families. The legendary heroes are turned into ' Swan-

Knights,' or fly away in the form of wild geese.
. . . We hear of 'Griffins' by the Shannon, of
'Calves' in the country round Belfast : the men
of Ossory were called by a name which signifies
the 'wild red-deer.' There are similar instances
from Scotland, in such names as 'Clan Chattan,'
or the Wild Cats." Giraldus Cambrensis gravely
relates how Ossory men were in his day—seven
hundred years ago—periodically turned into wolves ;
and a later writer gives currency to the popular
belief that the descendants of wolves live in that
part of Meath. Early Welsh poems furnish other
examples, and perhaps we may compare such
patronymics as " Dering." " Harting," " Baring,"
and the like. The Merovingian princes traced their
origin to a sea-monster ; and the pedigrees of the
Anglo-Saxon kings contain names which seem to be
connected with legends of a descent from animals.
The beliefs, whose unmistakable traces thus survive
in civilised countries, were probably in their origin
the counterparts of savage beliefs as we find them
at the present day. The Santals, an Indian hill-
tribe, believe themselves to have sprung from two
eggs laid by a wild goose. Leda's twins were contained in two eggs. But the goose in her story
was a swan.

Not only does totemism as a form of religion
largely influence savage conduct, but savage society

also is founded on this belief in kinship with animals and all manner of natural objects. For instance, a man may not marry a woman whose totem is the same as his own, any more than he would eat of the animal which is his totem. It is *tabu*, a thing forbidden ; for it would be equivalent to eating his own flesh. Also he is obliged to avenge a murder in his own stock. In some cases the totem is tattooed into the flesh ; this lessened the risk of infringing the *tabu*. It may here be parenthetically mentioned—in order to show how very deeply rooted is the obligation of the family tie—that the family and blood revenge, which is a binding duty amongst savages, is one of the strongest links of the family in archaic Teutonic society, where also we see the creation of artificial family ties by sworn brotherhood, resembling the blood-mingling of savages at the present day. When about to make a league, says Saxo, the ancients were wont to besprinkle their footsteps with the blood of one another, so as to ratify their pledge of friendship by reciprocal barter of blood. " Dost thou remember how we two in days of old blended blood together ? " says Loki to Woden in Loka-senna ; and a line in the Short Brunhild's Lay, referring to the sworn brotherhood of Sigurd and Gunnar, shows the way the bond was entered into : " Ye twain did let your blood run together in the footprint."

But to return to the question of animal ancestry.

It is always instructive to note how a particular belief affects existing races. The Kaffir who has killed an elephant protests that he did it unintentionally, and in case the elephant's soul should seek vengeance (for in savage belief, as we have seen, all animals as well as inanimate things have souls, just as men have), he cuts off the trunk and buries it, so that the soul of the elephant will have less power in the spirit-world. Similarly, the Chippewas, thinking they will have to encounter in the other world the spirits of slain animals, apologised to a bear for killing him, asked forgiveness, and pretended that an American was to blame. And the Samoyeds, after shooting a bear, offer excuses to the body, and lay the blame on the Russians. In the Kalewala, the epic poem of the Finns, when the people kill a bear they implore his forgiveness. The Hindu is taught to respect the flocks and herds, and will on no account lift his hand against a cow, for there is no knowing that it is not his own grandmother; and in New Caledonia a child is warned not to kill a lizard, lest it should happen to be his own ancestor. On the west coast of Ireland the same superstitious regard is paid to the seal, which the people cannot be bribed to skin. Some members of the Clan Coneely were said to have been transformed into seals, wherefore these animals go by their names.

For this reason many of the clan have changed their patronymic to Connolly. But to this day no Coneely considers that he can kill a seal without afterwards having bad luck, and in some places the tribesmen would no more eat a slaughtered one than they would a human being. A few years ago (says a writer in 1881) a Connelly shot a seal, and every one expected something awful would happen to him. A photograph has been exhibited before the Folk-lore Society, of an old Scotch woman who proudly claims to be the grand-daughter of a seal, and tells the story of her grandfather's capturing and marrying the seal maid.

There are several Irish legends which appear to be based on the notion that a man may not eat of the animal which is his totem. In the story of the Death of Cúchulain, contained in the Book of Leinster, some witches offer the hero some cooked dog. Cúchulain's name signifies " the Hound of Culand," and the story turns on the idea that " one of the things he must not do was eating his namesake's flesh." In another legend, Conaire the Great, a mythical king of Ireland, is the son of the Bird King, and is therefore forbidden to kill birds of any kind.

We read in Cæsar that in Southern Britain it was considered a crime to eat the hare, the goose, and the domestic fowl ; the prohibition had in all probability some connection with a belief in the sacred character of these animals. The hare, as we have seen (*supra*, pp. 31–32), is associated with Easter observances. Now, the name of this Christian festival is derived from Eostre, an Anglo-Saxon goddess, whose worship was celebrated at this season. The hare may have been sacred to Eostre; at any rate, it " probably played a very important part at the great Spring Festival of the prehistoric inhabitants of this island." The hare may have been worshipped as a tribal totem or god.

The practice of begging pardon of the slain animal is in many parts of the world extended to the case of plants; for they, like animals and human beings, manifest the phenomena of life : they are born, they grow, fade away, and die ; wherefore, as we have seen in an earlier chapter, a soul or spirit is attributed to them also. To this day, when " the wind blows the long grass or waving corn, the German peasants will say that the grass wolf or the corn wolf is abroad," and in some districts they leave a sheaf of rye standing throughout the winter, as a shelter to the " rye wolf." Or the plant-spirit may be human; both because it is believed, as we have seen, that the soul of a dead person may enter a plant, and also because the plant may be the ancestor of a certain tribe. For, as in the parallel case of an animal, a misinterpreted tradition arising from the habit of naming after a plant, raises the belief that the race descended from it. At the same time, it must be borne in mind that quite possibly an animal or plant may be worshipped directly for itself, as something superhuman, and apart from any belief in its being the ancestor or totem of a tribe. A third motive for the worship may be found in the doctrine of fetichism, which will be explained subsequently. Similar reasoning must be extended to the case of other natural objects which, through one of these causes, come to be regarded with fear or veneration. Thus the Wadders, one of the early races of South India, show special regard for certain trees after which their gotrams are called. They will not touch leaf, branch, or fruit, and this fact seems to suggest that totemism once obtained amongst them. Among the Frisians a mysterious virtue attached to water-lilies, and Dutch boys are said to be extremely careful in plucking or handling them, for if a boy fall with the flowers in his possession, he immediately becomes subject to fits. The use of plants in love divination may have originated in a direct appeal to the plant-spirit. Reference may also be made to their use in magic.

Very commonly the capture of a wild beast is followed by a feast in propitiation of its manes. Now, when we have arrived at sacrifices being offered to totemic ancestors, we see by what short steps this particular regard for a certain animal or plant leads to a system of animal-worship, or plant-worship. When an animal is believed to be a relative, it is also looked upon as a guardian, and hence arises the faith, so widely diffused, in omens derived from birds and quadrupeds. The ancestor, in his animal form, is supposed to be solicitous for the welfare of his kindred, and therefore warns them by certain signs and sounds of their danger. All ages and countries have had their superstitions about Guiding beasts. Just as the escort of wolf or raven augured victory, so a tribe on its travels was guided by an animal to its place of settlement, and there founded colonies, and built towns, castles, and churches. Greek and Roman story teems with examples. A raven leads Battus and his emigrants to Cyrene (named after κόραξ, the raven). The Irpini are so called from *irpus*, the wolf that led them. The raven and wolf in northern latitudes were Woden's favourites, who presaged victory and weal. Or the bear may act as a guide, just as the hind (in Procopius) shows the way to Cimmerian hunters. A doe showed the Franks the ford of safety over the Main, and a white hart over the Vienne. In German legend a flying hen indicates the site of a future castle. Remus had seen six, and Romulus twelve vultures fly auspicious at the founding of their city. An official document presented in October 1894, to the Mikado, by Mr. Miyoji Ito, the Secretary-General of the Japanese Imperial Cabinet, a translation of which appeared in the *Times*, January 5, 1895, records the following instances of sacred birds giving auspicious signs. When the Emperor Jimmu was marching his troops against Nagasunehiko, a crow of dazzling brilliance perched upon the point of his bow, and the imperial host gained a complete victory over the redoubtable enemy. In the autumn of 1894, after a great naval engagement at the Yalu, says Mr. Ito, a hawk descended upon the masthead of one of his Majesty's ships, the *Takachiho*. " The commander of the ship ordered one of the marines to ascend the mast and seize the bird. The latter, drooping its head, did not attempt to move, but seemed glad to be caught. A bird obtained in this singular manner was naturally welcomed with enthusiasm as Heaven's messenger." There was a rat hunt on board to provide it with food, there being no meat in the ship, and finally the bird was presented to the Mikado, who named it Takachiho, after the vessel on which it alighted. " Taka " means hawk in Japanese. Now, a king of Kudara (the present Korea) once made a present of a hawk to the Emperor Nintoku. Again, Takachiho is the name of a mountain at whose top the Imperial ancestor

105

Niniginomikoto stayed awhile after his advent to this nether world, wherefore it is regarded as a sacred spot. In consideration of these significant historical associations, it was considered by the Japanese a remarkable coincidence that the bird should have alighted on the mast of a war-vessel bearing the hallowed name of Takachiho, just after a memorable victory in Korean waters, and the circumstance could only be interpreted as a sign of the continued success of the Imperial arms! At least, so thought Mr. Ito. In connection with this belief in animal guidance and protection may be mentioned the inhuman rite of immuring live animals, possibly as substitutes for human victims, in the foundation on which a structure was to be raised, so as to secure immovable stability. Danish traditions tell of a lamb being built in under the altar, that the church might stand unshaken; and of a live horse being buried in every churchyard, before any corpse was laid in it; and this horse becomes the walking dead horse. Both lamb and horse occasionally show themselves in church or churchyard, and the apparition betokens a death. Even under ordinary houses, swine and fowls are buried alive. In 1879 the bones of a boar were found under the foundation of a church in Suffolk. It is said that the reason for burying alive a dog or a boar under the corner-stone of a church was

that its ghost might haunt the churchyard and
drive away witches and warlocks.   Too numerous
to cite are the stories of the walling up of persons,
or the bathing of foundation stones with human
blood, as in our own legend of Vortigern, who
could not finish his tower, till the foundation was
wetted with the blood of a child born of a mother
without a father.   When the new bridge at Halle,
finished 1843, was building, the common people
fancied a child was wanted to be walled into the
foundations.   To make Liebenstein Castle impreg-
nable, there was walled in a child, whom its mother
basely sold ;   and the same story is told in connection with Reichenfels and many other castles.
The tradition is common also in Bosnia and Her-
zegovina, and the custom survives in Africa, in
Polynesia, in Borneo, as well as among the more
cultured nations of Southern Asia.   The motive
of the rite seems to be " either to propitiate the
earth-spirits with a victim, or to convert the soul
of the victim himself into a protecting demon."
In Jerusalem a rough representation of a hand
is marked by the natives on the wall of every
house whilst in building.   The Moors generally,
and especially the Arabs of Kairwan, employ the
marks on their houses as prophylactics, and similar
hand-prints are found in El Baird, near Petra.
We have an illustration of a similar notion in the

Chinese legend of the Bell Tower of Peking. The Emperor Yung-lo, having built the tower, ordered a mandarin named Kuan-yu to cast a bell of the proper size. Two attempts having failed—for in each case the casting was " honeycombed "—the Emperor was furious, and threatened to behead the unfortunate official in the event of a third failure. The mandarin had a beautiful daughter of sixteen years, who, grieving at her father's distress, secretly consulted an astrologer to ascertain the cause of these failures. From him she learned that the casting would never succeed unless the blood of a maiden were mixed with the ingredients. The brave girl kept her counsel, and obtained her father's permission to be present at the next casting. Amid dead silence the melted metal was once more poured out, when with a shriek and a cry, " For my father," Ko-ai plunged headlong into the seething, hissing fluid. In an attempt to seize her, some one grasped one of her shoes, which came off in his hand. The father was taken home a raving maniac ; but when the bell was cooled it was found to be perfect. At every stroke its sonorous boom is ever followed by a low wailing sound like a woman's voice in agony, distinctly saying the word *hsieh* (shoe). So to this day the people, hearing it, say, " There's poor Ko-ai calling for her shoe."

But to return to animal omens. It is a popular idea that a prosperous day's work depends upon a favourable encounter at early morning. It is unlucky for a hare to cross your path ; Indians, Laplanders, Arabs, and South African tribes would agree with our own country folk in thinking so. There are diverse opinions in diverse places as to the nature of the luck in connection with a black cat. But when you go a-fishing in Galway it is most unlucky to see a fox. Often it is not the flight of a wayside fowl, nor the chance encounter of a quadruped, but their appearing, their residing in men's dwellings, that bodes weal or woe. The swallow and the stork are birds of luck, while a weasel or snake on the roof has been thought to betoken ill. In Germany, a spider running towards you early in the morning is unlucky ; but there are luck-spinners, too, in many parts of England and Ireland, where the descent of a spider is a favourable omen, as it is also in Polynesia. The howl of a wolf or jackal in a village, the bark of a dog and twitching of its ears, a cat crossing the road when one is starting on a journey— all these events are untoward in North India. A swarm of bees settling on a house betokens fire or some disaster, as we read over and over again in the classics. To Leopold of Austria they foretold the loss of Sempach fight in 1386. The practice of telling the bees has already been mentioned (see *supra*, p. 24). In Germany, the death of master or mistress is told not only to the bees, but to every beast in the stall ; and every sack of corn must be touched, and everything in the house shaken, that information of the death may be conveyed to them.

Or we have notice of a death when the raven caws, when a cock or hen trails straw, when the mole burrows in a human habitation, when crickets chirp and woodworms tick, and mice nibble at the clothes of a sleeper.

All these superstitions and others like them may be referred in their origin to the personification of animals, to the savage man's habit of regarding animals as his kin. Wolves' teeth were used as amulets by the Irish, who at one time considered the wolves their grandfathers. Animals were even supposed to have a speech of their own ; and it is the specially favoured who understand the language of beasts or birds. Helenus, whom Æneas consulted, understood the stars and the language of birds. The actions of animals are interpreted as weather pro- phecies : a cat washing her face being a sign of rain ; an ox licking its forefoot, under its dew-claw, a sign of storm.

It is interesting to trace the influence of savage beliefs on savage invention of stories. We see why an animal is so often an important character in a popular tale, giving protection, advice, or assistance to the hero or heroine. Every country in the world has its stories of helpful animals, like the ants which sorted the mixed grain for Psyche and for Cinderella, or like the cow which in many versions of the latter story is the girl's mother transformed. Perhaps in the original barbaric conception of the Cinderella story, the cow was actually the child's mother; for to the savage mind there is nothing irrational in the notion of animal parentage; and within the last decade a Gaelic version has been related in which the heroine's mother is actually a sheep. Usually, however, the savage element in folk-tales becomes softened or altered when it ceases to be acceptable to more rational thought; thus a helpful beast comes to be supplanted by a fairy godmother.

" Puss in Boots " is another type of the animal benefactor, stories of whose nimble wit and ready resource delight all the world. The mind which in a confused way has identified men with animals, and animals with men, would quite naturally conceive of animals talking, and playing active parts in human affairs. It would be no great effort to the savage imagination to tell the story of a girl who married a porcupine, or of the successful suit of the frog " who would a-wooing go." The *denouement* of the story may or may not be the animal's assuming or re-assuming the human form (as in the German story of the Frog-Prince). That is usually the case in the popular tales that have filtered down to us through generations of story-tellers, and then the transformation into a beast has been the wicked work of some demon, or witchcraft and sorcery have been introduced to explain it. Some of the Tsimsheean Indians of British Columbia believe that they are descended from a frog; and the Dog-rib Indians of Great Slave Lake tell the following story to explain their supposed descent from dogs: A woman was married to a dog, and bore six pups. She was deserted by her tribe, and went out daily procuring food for her family. When she returned she found tracks of children around her lodge, but did not see any one besides her pups. Finally she discovered from a hiding-place that as soon as she left them the dogs threw off their skins (just like the swan-maidens and the werewolves, who will presently be described). She surprised them, took away the skins, and the dogs became children—a number of boys and one girl. These became the ancestors of the Dog-rib Indians. These elements are combined into a story on Vancouver Island, where a tribe of Indians derives its origin from dogs. The legend is found in many other places on the Pacific coast, and there is a somewhat similar one among the Hare Indians of Great Bear Lake. The Eskimos have stories of dog-ancestors; and in Baffinland, the mother of the dogs is their most important deity. But extremely numerous everywhere are the myths in which a human ancestress is said to have given birth to an animal of the totem species. Thus the Snake clan among the Moquis of Arizona are descended from a woman who gave birth to snakes. Similarly, in Western Equatorial Africa, the Bakalai believe that their women once gave birth to the totem animals ; one woman brought forth a calf, others a crocodile, hippopotamus, monkey, boar, and wild pig. In Samoa, the prawn or cray-fish was the totem of one clan, because an infant of the clan had been changed at birth into a number of prawns or cray-fish.

The accusation of bearing animal children is frequently brought against a woman in folk-tales, which so accurately reflect the lines of savage thought, as, in Greek myth, Kronos dines off the foal which he was assured his wife had just borne, when in reality the child was Poseidon. But Pasiphae was the mother of the Minotaur, and Leda's twins were contained in two eggs ; while in the Prose Edda, Gefjon's sons were oxen ; the hag's sons were wolves ; and before the birth of Aed Slane, king of Ireland, his mother brought forth first a lamb, and then a silver trout.

No doubt, many a story is invented to account for the habitual veneration of a particular animal ;

for instance, a Bantu legend explains how the friendly crocodile comes to the aid of a fugitive heir, and is in consequence held sacred ever after.

When it has become a habit to ask the pardon of the animal namesake in the event of unwitting injury, to pray to it for protection, and to make propitiatory offerings to it, it is not surprising that by degrees a particular animal should develop into a deity. Herein we discover the germ of religion and myth ; it remains but to follow its development and cult.

There appear to have been various phases of animal worship in Egypt, and in this place it is impossible to enter deeply into the subject. Maspero points out that the animals were worshipped first, and, later on, the gods who were supposed to be present in the animals. It is thought that the animal-headed deities so often represented in Egyptian art after the twelfth dynasty may have been symbolical, the animal personifying certain qualities which were to be adored ; just as the sacred Scarab is an emblem of the resurrection, wherefore it was always placed in the tomb with the mummy. On the other hand, the beast-gods may have been survivals of totemic badges, and this explanation would account for the local character of their worship—the crocodile, for example, being hated of men in Apollinopolis and put to death, whereas in Arsinoite the sacred creature was served with geese and fish, decked with necklaces and bracelets, and mummified at its death.

Pastoral tribes usually regard the herds as sacred, and this habitual veneration of their cattle may, as Prof. Robertson Smith has pointed out, explain the sanctity of the cow in Iranian and Brahmanical religions, and the worship in Ancient Egypt of the bull-god Apis, the cow-goddess Isis-Hathor, and the ram-god Ammon.

But the savage ancestors of all races have had their animal gods : all the mythologies teem with them. The Algonkins have their Michabo, or Manibozho, a great hare ; Marawa, a spider, is the miracle worker in Milanesian mythology. And even in the case of the more refined Greeks Nature made no leap. They, like all other peoples, must have passed through the stage of savage intellect. We may see survivals of totemism in the various beasts associated in Greek temples with the worship of Zeus, and Apollo, and Demeter, according with their several metamorphoses. For gods would have the power to assume any shape, like Proteus. A bristly boar, and a fell tiger, a scaly dragon, and a lioness with tawny neck, were among the manifold forms which he took.

In Red Indian, in Thlinkeet, and in Australian mythology the gods can become birds ; a tale is told of Apollo, the Sun-god, in the form of a dog ; and we all know how Zeus, " to gain his private ends," took the form of a swan, an eagle, a dove, a serpent, a bull, and an ant, just as the Crow-god in Australian myth turned himself into a little grub on occasion. Metis, too, like other gods and goddesses, had unlimited powers of transformation, and having been persuaded to assume the form of a fly, she was swallowed by Zeus, who had married her, and afterwards feared she might bear a child more powerful than himself.

This device for getting inconvenient persons out of the way is commonly introduced in *märchen*, or folk-stories. It occurs in the Welsh story of Taliesin, where Caridwen, in the shape of a high-crested black hen, swallows Gwion Bach in the form of a grain of wheat. In the same manner, the princess swallows the Jinni in the " Arabian Nights." The idea itself is purely barbaric, and just what would occur to minds at a very low level of culture. Accordingly we meet with it in the tales still told by savages. In a Bushman myth, an important divinity, a Mantis insect, gets swallowed by a supernatural character, who in this manner has made away with a large number of animals in his time. When he is killed these all come trooping out of him alive, like the swallowed victims in the German story of the " Wolf and the Seven Little Kids." The

Kaffirs tell a very similar tale about a voracious swallower, whose victims were disgorged alive. In short, examples of this very myth are found amongst savages all over the world, and every European country has it in some form. The Greek myth of Kronos is on a par with it, and must equally have been invented before the ancestors of the Greeks had emerged from the savage stage of mind. Kronos had been warned to beware of his heirs; consequently he was in the habit of swallowing his children as soon as they were born. But he was deluded with a stone wrapped in swaddling-clothes in the case of his latest born, and he swallowed it unsuspectingly. The babe who thus escaped was Zeus, and when he grew up he compelled his father to disgorge. The stone, being swallowed last, came up first, and then all the children emerged safe and sound.

We may be sure, then, that all the savage and revolting tales about the gods were invented when men were living after the roving fashion of wild beasts. In later times, these traditions, albeit distasteful to the more cultured minds of the Greeks, were preserved because, as Eusebius said, " none dared alter the ancient beliefs of his ancestors," or as Euripides wrote, " In things which touch the gods it is not good to suffer captious reason to intrude." Whenever faith forswears inquiry it stands confessed as the twin-brother of superstition. As Tiresias says in the *Bacchæ*, "We do not show too much wiseness about the gods. Our ancestral traditions, and those which we have kept throughout our life, no argument will overturn; not if any one were to find out wisdom with the highest genius."

It is said that when Pythagoras journeyed to Hades he saw the soul of Hesiod bound to a pillar, and that of Homer hung in a tree, as a punishment for speaking unworthily of the gods. Pindar, who wrote about 480 B.C., felt that it was safer to think nobly of the gods, for so the blame was less, and accordingly preferred to give another explanation of the Pelops affair. According to the legend, Tantalus boiled his son Pelops, and served him to his divine guests. Pindar suggests, "It may be that the bright web of legend, figured in colours of falsehood, beguiles mortals into reports wide of the truth." Euhemerus (316 B.C.), who wrote his "Sacred History" in the time of Alexander the Great, therein treated the stories of the Greek mythology as exaggerated narratives of actual fact. His work was translated into Latin by Ennius. In short, as civilisation advanced, and religious thought was shocked by the impiety and rudeness of many of the divine myths, well-meaning attempts were made to explain them, many and diverse being the theories expounded by the several apologists. In this way new legends were invented to account for the irrational elements in the older myths. The meaning of an original word was supposed to have become corrupted, thus giving rise to absurd and gross misconceptions; or a symbolical interpretation of myths was attempted, just as the modern mythologist thinks that he traces the personification of Sun, Moon, and Dawn, Storm, Wind, and Rain, in the characters that figure in Indian and Greek divine legends. In this way, according to some, the myth of Kronos, for example, simply means that the lord of darkness swallows the power of light— an interpretation not reconcilable, however, with the theory of others that Kronos is the sun; or again, that he is the storm-god who swallows the clouds. " The Mintiras of Malay have introduced the conception of swallowing and disgorging alive into a myth, which explains the movements of sun, moon, and stars."

The safest method of interpreting any myth found amongst civilised people is to accept the irrational element in it without gloss. It will be found to have its parallel in the stories current amongst existing savage races, for a comparison of the myths of different nations reveals their striking similarity; and thus any barbaric conception that tradition has preserved may be traced to its origin in that savage state of mind through which all civilised races have passed.

From the foregoing consideration of savage belief in animal metamorphosis, it will be seen how the germs of myth in the human intellect may be cultivated till they produce the endless series of stories of swan-maidens who doff their bird forms with their feather tunic, like the Hindu Apsaras, or cloud-maidens, and even the Norse Valkyries, who have their shirts of swan plumage. The giant Thiazzi, in his eagle-skin, flaps his wings in pursuit of Loki, clad in the hawk-skin which he has borrowed of Freya. Weyland the Smith and his brothers Egil and Slagfin entrap the three swan-maidens, Lathgund, Allrune, and Swanwhite, when they alight to rest on the sea-strand, and take them as wives. Seven winters they stay with their husbands in peace, but on the eighth they begin to pine, on the ninth they must needs part, and betaking them to their wings, they fly away.

The type of the Swan-coat story is as follows. A man sees a woman bathing, having doffed her charm-dress on the shore. He steals this dress of feathers, and she falls into his power. He marries her ; but after some years she succeeds in recovering the dress, and she flies away. As a rule, he is unable to recover her. The theme occurs in the " Arabian Nights," in the tale of

Hasan, who unlocks the forbidden door and sees ten birds, who are really ten beautiful maidens, doff their feather suits whilst they bathe. The tale conforms to the type, and examples of it are found in Sweden, Russia, Germany, in the Shetland Islands—in short, almost throughout Europe, as well as in Asia and in Africa. In Finland the maidens are geese; elsewhere they are more appropriately described as ducks; or they may be doves, as in Bohemia, Persia, and the Celebes Islands; or pigeons, as amongst the Magyars and in South Smaland. In the guise of a vulture the bird-maiden is found in Guiana, and American Indians tell their version of her widespread story. In the Shetland Isles maidens assume animal shape, and doff seal-skins when they want to bathe. In Croatia she hangs up her wolf-skin before entering the water.

As some of the many European versions of the Swan-coat story are probably familiar to all, a variant may be cited from the Malay Island of Celebes. It has a double interest, accompanying the " Swan " *motif* with the good old nursery theme of " Jack and the Beanstalk." " Seven heavenly nymphs came down from the sky to bathe, and they were seen by Kasimbaha, who thought first that they were white doves, but in the bath he saw that they were women. Then he stole one of the thin robes that gave the nymphs their power of flying, and so he caught Utahagi, the one whose robe he had stolen, and took her for his wife, and she bore him a son. Now, she was called Utahagi from a single white hair she had, which was endowed with magic power, and this hair her husband pulled out. As soon as he had done it, there rose a great storm, and Utahagi went up into heaven. The child cried for its mother, and Kasimbaha was in great grief, and cast about how he should follow Utahagi up into the sky. Then a rat gnawed the thorns off the rattans, and he clambered up by them, with his son upon his back, till he came to heaven. There a little bird showed him the house of Utahagi, and after various adventures he took up his abode among the gods."

There is a Siberian story very similar to this. The lover of folk-tales will doubtless recall in this connection the German story of the " Six Swans," where the little girl's six brothers are turned into swans when the charmed shirts are thrown over them.

Or we have the story of Melusina, the lovely fountain nymph, who married a mortal on condition that she should pass all her Saturdays in strictest seclusion. One day her husband broke his promise, invaded her privacy, and looking through a keyhole, saw her transformed into a mermaid, and disporting herself in the bath. Thereupon she left him, and ever after haunted her husband's castle, like a Banshee, when one of its lords was about to die. Gervase of Tilbury, who wrote about the beginning of the thirteenth century, is the earliest writer to mention the legend, and he tells it of Raymond, lord of a castle near Aix, in Provence. His wife makes him promise never to see her naked. After they have been many years married he tears aside the curtain of her bath, whereupon she instantly changes into a serpent and disappears under the water for ever. The Maoris and the Japanese have variants of this tale, which is very widespread. The well-known story of Undine is similar. It will be remarked that the Melusina type has to do with the observance of a taboo ; hence it has parallels in the immense cycle of stories of " Beauty and the Beast," or " Cupid and Psyche," where it is, however, the husband who has ever and anon to resume his animal form, and the taboo forbids his being looked upon at night when he appears as a man.

In another direction this ingrained belief in transformation would easily develop into the horrible superstition of the werewolf, or *loup-garou*, so common in the Middle Ages, when it was firmly believed that men were in the habit of being transformed into wolves. Werewolf signifies man-wolf, *wehr* meaning " man." *Garou* is a French corruption of wehrwolf, so that the compound *loup-garou* is tautological.

Once upon a time Sigmund and Sinfitela went into a wood, and lit on a house wherein lay two men sleeping, who were under a spell as were-wolves, for their wolf-skins were hanging over them. Every tenth day they were able to come out of their skins. They were kings' sons. Sigmund and Sinfitela put on the skins, and could not put them off again, and fell under the same spell as the others had been under, and howled like wolves ; but they could understand each other's howling. Each of them slew many men. When the day came when they could come out of their skins, they took them and burnt them with fire, that they might do no more harm to any one. As the Swan-maid can lay aside the swan-ring or feather-dress, so can the wolf-skin or wolf-girdle be discarded.

In European legend, however, it is more often the donning of the girdle made of human skin that transforms the human being into a werewolf. According to Slavonic superstition, the Livonian sorcerers bathe yearly in a river, and turn for twelve days to wolves, as did the Neuri for a few days every year in the legend of Herodotus. The were-wolf is rampant, in popular fancy, in modern Greece and in modern Germany, where you must not " talk of the wolf " by name in December, lest the werewolves tear you. They hold no longer place in English folk-lore, though the idea of metamorphosis is transferred from the extinct wolf to some other animals. The familiar episode of the animal being wounded, and the person who bore its shape being found with a similar wound, is met with in the folk-lore of every people (see *ante*, p. 91). In an old Norse book written about 1250 A.D., and giving an account of Ireland, a story is told to the effect that when the holy Patricius was preaching Christianity there, one great race was specially hostile to him, and howled at him like wolves. Patricius implored God to avenge him for the insult, and fitting punishment accordingly fell on them and on their descendants to this day. For " it is said that all men who come from that race are always wolves at a certain time, and run into the woods and have food like wolves. . . . And it is said that some become so every seventh year, and are men during the interval. And some have it so long that they have seven years at once, and are never so afterwards."

A progenitor of the werewolf was at large in classic times. Virgil, in the Bucolics, shows the popular belief ; for in speaking of certain herbs and drugs, the enchantress says (Ecl. viii.), " By the power of these I have seen Mœris oft become a wolf and hide within the woods." Ovid relates how

Lycaon, king of Arcadia, invited Zeus to a banquet, and gave him human flesh to eat. As a punishment for this impious practical joke, Lycaon was transformed into a wolf. From that time, according to Pliny, each year on the festival of Zeus Lykaios (the wolf Zeus) a noble Arcadian was led to the margin of a certain lake. Hanging his clothes on a tree, he plunged into the water and became a wolf. Then for nine years he was doomed to roam the woods ; but if during the whole time he could abstain from human flesh, he might don his clothes once more, and resume his natural form. According to a later legend, those who ate of the human sacrifice offered to Zeus Lykaios were transformed into werewolves, but could resume their original shape if for ten years they abstained from the flesh of men.

These sacrifices to Zeus were, in all probability, developed out of the cannibal feasts of a Wolf tribe. We have many classical examples of religious services in which the worshippers clothe themselves in the skin of the animal whose feast they celebrate. Thus the Hirpi, or " wolves," wore the beast's skin in their wolf-dances ; and in the Attic bear-dance the young girls used to " make up " as little bears, connecting Artemis with the worship of the She-Bear. Similarly, the Mænads wore the dappled fawn-skins in their frenzied worship of Dionysus.

The people of North Germany, according to Tacitus, worshipped the mother of the gods, and wore images of wild boars as the symbol of their belief.

But to return to our werewolf. Let us see what is related of him in South Africa. A certain Hottentot was once travelling with a Bushwoman and her child, when they perceived at a distance a troop of wild horses. The man, being hungry, asked the woman to turn herself into a lioness and catch one of these horses, that they might eat of it ; whereupon the woman set down her child, and taking off a sort of petticoat made of human skin, became instantly transformed into a lioness, which rushed across the plain, struck down a wild horse, and lapped its blood. The man climbed a tree in terror, and conjured his companion to resume her natural shape. Then the lioness came back, and putting on the skirt made of human skin, re-appeared as a woman, and took up her child, and the two friends resumed their journey after making a meal of horse's flesh. Africa is specially rich in stories of man-lions, man-leopards, and man-hyænas.

In Scandinavia there are legends of a man-bear, and in Hindustan of a man-tiger. The werewolf also appears in North America, duly furnished with his wolf-skin sack ; and, indeed, his equivalent in some animal form is believed in everywhere among savages.

But the werewolf of the Middle Ages is a far more terrible and diabolical conception than the barbaric werewolf, which was merely a transformed man. In the savage idea of animal-transformation there was nothing necessarily diabolical ; it was in the course of its final development that the belief acquired its most horrible features, when lycanthropy in its contact with Christianity came to be regarded as a species of witchcraft, the werewolf being supposed to be in league with the devil himself. Hundreds of persons were burned alive on the charge of animal metamorphosis.

It would be out of place to enter here into a discussion of the nature and causes of lycanthropy as a diseased mental state, or of the Berserker insanity characteristic of Scandinavia, in which the frenzied champions are supposed to tread fire, swallow live coals, and bite shields without feeling pain. The fabulous man-wolf (who rightly comes under the notice of the folk-lorist) must be distinguished from the lycanthrope, who imagines himself to be a wolf, and imitates a wolf's actions. Therefore it is unnecessary to cite the terrible instances of persons being seized with homicidal mania, clothing themselves in beasts' skins, and sallying forth by night to devour the unsuspecting wayfarer. It is natural that to the unscientific mind of the Middle Ages these abnormal cases of craving for human flesh should be regarded as the consequences of diabolical metamorphosis. To the enlightened mind of the modern physiologist, however, the explanation is to be found in the obliteration of those qualities which distinguish man from the brute, by an occasional reversion to a primitive ancestral type characterised by bestial instincts, and a mental capacity on a level with that of the lowest savage. A curious instance of relapse into barbarism occurred during the recent (March 1895) native rising on the Niger, when Akassa was attacked and pillaged by the Brassmen. " One of the most prominent figures among the assailants, dressed in the usual waist cloth, was a Brassman who had been educated at King William's College in the Isle of Man, and had a high reputation for piety in British Brass town, where he had been seen in civilised costume a few days before the outbreak. When the Brassmen retired with their prisoners to Nimbo, and proceeded to torture and hack them to pieces, and boil their limbs with rice in large pots, this promising convert was seen by a French missionary to take a leading part in the horrible orgie of cannibalism, with a human foot tied round his wrist."

CHAPTER III

ANIMISM—GHOSTS AND GODS

SOMETHING has already been said in these pages of the theory known as *animism*—that is, the universal attribution of souls to all things, whether animate or inanimate. The savage believes that everything in nature is alike endowed with personal attributes, and, according as his experience teaches, is an object of dread or is harmless. Every death adds a ghost to the number of the spirit-world;

130

these ghosts have power to visit the abode of the living, and their powers are supernatural either for good or evil. Every tree and plant, every stock and stone, every forest and hill, has its indwelling spirit ; the haunted air is crowded with spirits, visible and invisible. Later on these develop into the fairies, sprites, gnomes, and giants of popular fancy, the household spirits, the brownies and pixies, the Irish pookas and leprachauns, who, however, are looked upon as more mischievous and spiteful than really terrible, like the malicious ghost which haunted the imagination of the savage. He is not cheered with the visitations of the hob-goblins and Robin Goodfellows that, in later super-stitious times, would " grind corn for a mess of milk, cut wood, or do any manner of drudgery work—draw water, dress meat, or any such thing." He weaves no pretty fancies about the

> " fairy elves,
> Whose midnight revels by a forest side
> Or fountain, some belated peasant sees,
> Or dreams he sees, while overhead the moon
> Sits arbitress."

Horror of the unseen fills the mind of the savage, just as it quickens the imagination of the civilised child, who therefore fears to be alone in the dark. The following recent occurrence, brought under the writer's notice, well illustrates the attitude of the

131

childish mind towards the supernatural. A mother left her child's bedside with these parting words : " You need not be afraid to be alone in the dark : remember, God is in the room ; He will take care of you." Recalled soon after by muffled screams, she found the little girl with her head under the clothes, in absolute terror. " Oh, mother ! " she implored, " please ask God if He would mind going away : He does frighten me so ! "

This terror of the unseen is an essential element of primitive religion. Baffled here, conquered there, the savage everywhere attributes his ill success to some malignant power, something outside himself. To propitiate this power is his first endeavour, by oblation or satisfaction ; for the motive prompting every sacrifice is either bribe or thanksgiving. That is the obvious explanation of a certain rural sacrifice which was performed in the eighteenth century, on the 1st of May, in many Highland villages. A square trench was cut, a fire lighted on the turf, and a pot of caudle cooked. After spilling some of the caudle on the ground as a libation, each person took up a cake of oatmeal, and turning his face to the fire, broke off a knob and flung it over his shoulder, saying : " This I give to thee ; preserve thou my horses : this to thee ; preserve my sheep." Afterwards they used the same ceremony to the noxious animals : " This I give to thee, O fox ! spare

thou my lambs : this to thee, O hooded crow! this
to thee, O eagle ! "

From the savage's belief in the power of ghosts
grew the rudimentary conception of deity ; and out
of habitual fear grew systematic worship. Man has
his own experience to go by, and nothing else ; hence
he attributes to all things motives like his own.
He can only conceive of a god as a powerful man,
therefore he is influenced by his own predilections
in his dealings with his deity. Fat beasts and the
smell of bullocks and of goats his own soul loveth,
therefore he offers them to his god, in whose sight
also his self-inflicted wounds must be acceptable,
since the wounds which an enemy receives are a
source of satisfaction to the savage himself. Such
crude reasoning as this gives rise to all manner
of ceremonial observances and sacrificial rites, the
modified forms of which are practised amongst the
civilised to this day. Noah must have reasoned in
this way when he offered burnt offerings after the
flood. The sacrifice was accepted, the conciliation
declared : " And the Lord smelled a sweet savour ;
and the Lord said in His heart, I will not again
curse the ground any more for man's sake." And
so did the Argives sacrifice each man to one of the
everlasting gods, Agamemnon slaying a fat bull of
five years to mighty Kronion. Throughout the Iliad
like sacrifices are offered, with sprinkled barley and

libations of gleaming wine, whensoever prayer is made to the gods.

The animistic view of sacrifice is that the soul or essence of the offering is abstracted by the ancestral or other spirit to be appeased, who is hardly of a nature to consume material food or drink. As the negro explained to the traveller who saw him worshipping a tree and offering it food, " The tree is not fetich, the fetich is a spirit and invisible, but he has descended into this tree. Certainly he cannot devour our bodily food, but he enjoys its spiritual part, and leaves behind the bodily, which we see." And the Hindu entreats the ancestral spirits to quaff the sweet essence of the hot dish of rice, as he sets it before the Brahman to eat. So the Chinese, after allowing time for the ancestral souls to consume the impalpable essence of their sumptuous offerings, fall to and eat the material substance themselves. It is the same with other nations. The same conception underlies the Homeric sacrifices. It was the thick clouds from the burning thighs of the slaughtered oxen that, ascending to Olympus, cheered the assembled gods. When once it was conceived that food for the gods was chiefly acceptable in the form of smoke or vapour, it would be but a step from the offering of fumes of burning flesh to the substitution of fragrant woods and resin for a sweet savour;

and to this practice can be traced the origin of the use of incense in the service of the gods. In Revelations, the smoke of the incense went up before God with the prayers of the Saints; and the four-and-twenty elders carried bowls full of incense, " which are the prayers of the Saints."

Polytheism, or the worship of a plurality of gods, seems a natural outcome of the belief in friendly or malicious ghosts, possessing powers of greater or less degree. The religions of all tribes recognise higher spirits or gods above the commonalty of souls, demons, and Nature-spirits, just as the Olympian Zeus, the personal sky, holds sway over the lower gods of earth, air, and sea. Savages have generally the same name for all the powers, whether good or evil, which they recognise as superior to man. The word devil is the same as God; it is a corruption of *deva*, the Sanscrit name for God. The Greek Θεός, the Latin *Zeus*, French *dieu*, and our word deuce, meaning " a little devil," can all be traced to the same root. Similarly, the word demon, now applied exclusively to fiends, originally meant as the Greeks used it, simply a divine or a semi-divine being possessed of supernatural powers. It is by slow degrees that the supernatural beings resolve themselves into opposing hierarchies of good spirits and evil spirits, into gods and devils, thus preparing the imagination for the conception of a supreme god and a supreme devil—in short, for the system of dualism.

A Slavonic word for god is Bôg ; this word, after a marvellous number of modifications, may at length be seen in the name of " bogie," or " bogle," a hideous spectre of evil influence. Set, the devil of later Egyptian mythology, was not originally a god of evil. His worship was as ancient as any ; it was not till the decline of the Empire that he came to be regarded as an evil demon, and his name was effaced from monuments. Horus and Set were the personifications of Light and Darkness, and their combat was the prototype of the subsequent legends of Marduk and Tiamat, Bel and the Dragon, St. George and the Dragon, and many others.

The jinn of Arabian legend are, in many particulars, like the demons of the rabbinical traditions. The jinn are not immortal ; they live in communities, and are ruled over by princes ; they have the power to become invisible, and to assume the form of various animals. There are good and bad jinn ; but a spell can bind them, and they become the slaves of certain talismans.

The Persians have a creation of good and bad spiritual beings, the peris of surpassing beauty, " nymphs of a fair but erring line," who wage perpetual war against the repulsively hideous deevs, with their ugly shapes and goggle eyes, their great fangs and long tails.

Northern races have their white elves, friendly to men, and their dwarfs or dark elves. These dwarfs or trolls live in hills, mounds, and hillocks. They can influence the lives and destinies of mankind, can foretell future events, and can become invisible, or assume an animal form. It is usually their cap that renders them invisible, and if it is seized they are in the power of its possessor.

The spirit-world of the savage is the foundation of the primeval Aryan Nature-worship, upon which are based the religion and philosophy of the ancient civilised world, whether men's thoughts tended towards Pantheism (which is the worship of a plurality of deities, some being subordinate), or towards Monotheism (that is, the worship of one god), which characterises the religion of most civilised people at the present day. (Though, "in a certain sense," as Mr. Lang has said, "probably any race of men may be called monotheistic, just as, in another sense, Christians who revere saints may be called polytheistic.")

Sun and Moon rank high among the Nature-gods, and to this day have obeisance done to them, even amongst ourselves (see *supra*, p. 20). Sun and Moon are regarded by savages as brother and sister, or as husband and wife. Survivals of the ancient

137

rites of sun-worship may be traced in the custom of turning to the East, as well as in the bonfires set ablaze upon the hills on Easter morning, and in the solar rite of the New Fire on Easter Eve, as still observed in the Greek Church. The fire festival at the summer solstice, once celebrated throughout Europe, was observed in France quite recently—the huge straw wheel, which is lighted with a torch and set rolling from the hill-top, being an emblem of the sun, which is called in the Edda " fair wheel." In Christian times these solar rites at midsummer attached themselves to St. John's Eve, just as the yule log and bonfire customs are now associated with Christmastide, though originating in sun-worship. The day adopted by the Church as the anniversary of the birth of Christ was the day of the winter solstice, December 25, which the Romans celebrated in connection with the worship of the Sun-god Mithra, wherefore it is called " Dies Natalis Solis invicti," the Birthday of the Unconquered Sun. The festival of December 25 is of solar and not of Christian origin.

Further interesting evidence of the reality of sun-worship is afforded by the numerous solar shrines. At Abydos a temple was orientated for the sun at the summer solstice. The temple of Amen-Râ at Karnak is directed to sunset at the summer solstice ; the pyramids and the temples at

Gîzeh, Sais, and Tanis were orientated to the sun at the equinoxes. The Sphinx watched for the rising sun at an equinox ; and the Colossi, those two great statues at Thebes, watched for the rising sun at the winter solstice. To pass to Asia, the solar temple at Peking is orientated to the winter solstice ; and, to come near home, Stonehenge, to sunrise at the summer solstice. Stellar shrines are orientated with equal precision. The mention of one example must suffice—the Parthenon, which was directed to the rising of the Pleiades on April 30, B.C. 1530. All these facts are of interest to the student of folk-lore, as affording foundation for the many curious superstitious practices, which are still to be observed among the folk, in connection with sun, moon, and stars.

Fire, too, was worshipped as the manifestation of a personal deity among the Aryan-speaking nations, this worship being probably a development of the rude barbarian's adoration of the actual flame as a fetich. Bare reference must suffice to the ancient ordeal of passing through fire or leaping over flaming brands, which in all probability gave rise to the expression " to haul over the coals."

The Parsis, representatives of the religion of Ancient Persia, are typical fire-worshippers. Hestia, the divine hearth, was the venerable virgin fire-goddess of the Greeks, for whom at banquets first and last, men poured the honey-sweet wine. Like her in name was the Latin Vesta, in whose sanctuary perpetual fire was nourished, the sacredness of this perpetual fire being an article of faith, not alone amongst the ancient Greeks and Romans, but also of the Jews, Chaldeans, Tatars, Chinese, and other Mongolian tribes; Egyptians, Ethiopians, and Japanese; Mexicans, Peruvians, and other tribes of the new world; so that it may fairly be considered universal in ancient times. In the course of time there came to be recognised the two great divisions (as amongst the Persians) of celestial fire and infernal.

The Fire-god, whose worship, a development of sun-worship, was so widespread, took many forms. In the Aryan religion it was Agni, who is entreated by name in the first hymn of the Rig-veda, the oldest and most sacred book of the East. In the Latin word for fire, "ignis," we see the Sanscrit Agni. Tubal-Cain, according to Mosaic account the first artificer in brass and iron, was perhaps as much a fire-god as the Greek Hephaistos, the Latin Vulcan, the Scandinavian Loki, and the Circassian fire-god Tleps, who were all skilled metal-workers. The grim attendants of these subterranean fire-gods, like the hideous Cyclops of the Greeks, are the ugly black dwarfs of fairy mythology, who forge the magic swords and the impenetrable shirts of mail. The great Phœnician God, Moloch, although perhaps not strictly a fire-god, has always been associated with fire, victims being burned within his hollow brazen image. It must suffice just to name in this connection the Persian Asmodeus, who, like the Christian Satan, was placed on the throne of the burning world.

Among the Nature-spirits are the great gods who rule the universe, as our Aryan-speaking ancestors personified Sky and Heaven in their deity Dyu, who could hurl the thunderbolt and pelt rain, and whose name remains in the Greek Zeus, and the Latin Jupiter.

But personification is not necessarily deification. The Egyptians acknowledge the Nile as a god, " but not so Storm, Rain, Wind, Thunder, Lightning, Cloud, Rainbow, or Eclipse, though some of these were personified or represented in mythological form." They recognised divinity only in those cases " where they perceived the presence of a fixed Law, either of permanence or change." The Earth abides, so do the Heavens. Stars in their courses are constant ; but wind and rain observe no such regularity.

Some peoples have special Rain-gods and Thundeı· gods, like the Scandinavian Thor, the thunderer, whose memory we keep in our word Thursday, or *Jovis dies*, *Jeudi*, the day of Jove, who was both the thundering sky and the rainy sky, Jupiter Tonans and Jupiter Pluvius.

North American Indians and South Sea Islanders have their Wind-gods, like Boreas and Zephyros of the Greeks, to whom Achilles sacrificed, praying them to blow, as in Swabia, the Tyrol, and the Upper Palatinate they fling meal in the face of the gale, bidding it cease. Longfellow introduces the native Indian legends of the Four Winds in "Hiawatha." In New Zealand the great deity Maui (who in Tahiti is himself identified with the East Wind) is said to hold the winds in his hands, or, like Æolus, to imprison them in caves, save the West Wind, which is almost always blowing, because he has never been able to catch it. Other mythologies in like manner personify the winds. In Revelations (chap. vii.) four angels stand at the four corners of the earth, holding the four winds.

In barbaric theology the Earth too is worshipped, as the mother of all things—as when the Ojibwa Indian leaves an offering for the great-grandmother Earth, when he is digging up his medicine plants. A good Algonkin would never dig up a medicine without depositing an offering in the earth for the Great Grandmother of all ; and some of the native tribes of India, before eating their food, offer some to the earth. The Khonds of Orissa even offered human sacrifice to their earth-goddess. As Mama-Pacha, or " Mother-Earth," she is worshipped by the Peruvians. She is a divinely honoured personage in the mythology of North American Indians, Caribs, Finns, Lapps, Esths ; and, in our own country, time was when Anglo-Saxons called upon the Earth, " Hail thou Earth, men's mother." The two great parents of the Aryan-speaking race are the Earth-Mother and the Heaven-Father, called in Sanscrit Dyaushpitar, in Greek Ζεὺς πατήρ, in Latin Jupiter. The divine pair still reign in Finn theology as Ukko, the Grandfather (Heaven), and Akka, the Grandmother (Earth). Dēmēter, Terra-Mater, is the later name of the classic earth-goddess Gaia, the " revered divinity " of the Homeric hymn, the mother of gods, and wife of starry Heaven.

> " O universal mother, who dost keep
> From everlasting thy foundations deep,
> Eldest of things, Great Earth, I sing of thee."

It is thought that the English custom of leaving a few ears of corn standing in the field is a trace of earth-worship, just as in various localities particular festival customs may be connected with earth-deities. For example, in many parts of North and South Germany the last sheaf is made up in the form of an animal, or is adorned with the wooden image of an animal. In different districts it is a pig, wolf, he-goat, cock, hare, or cow, and the last sheaf is called accordingly the rye-sow, the straw-cock, the wolf, the cock, the hare, &c. In other places (extending from Scotland and England through the whole of Germany to Slavonic countries) the last sheaf is made into a doll, representing sometimes a man, sometimes a woman. In England it is called the harvest lady, harvest queen, the maiden, kirn dolly, kirn baby, or kern baby (corn baby) ; in Germany, the corn-mother, great-mother, wheat-bride, oats-bride, the old man, the old woman ; in Poland and in Denmark it is variously called. Certain ceremonial rites are performed over this last sheaf, such as drenching it with water, and then there follows a feast.

Then there are the water-deities and the indwelling spirits of the water, the divine sea, and divine springs, rivers, and lakes. The Red Indian makes an offering to the resident spirit of the Mississippi ; Peruvians prayed to their river-deity. From 800,000 to a million pilgrims go annually to a religious festival on the Ganges, the divine river by which the Hindus swear. The annual ceremony of blessing the waters of the Neva is usually performed in the presence of the Czar of all the Russias. Multitudes struggle for some of the newly-blessed water, with which they cross themselves and sprinkle their clothes. The Greek

Skamandros and Spercheios once had temples and priests of their own, though naught but the memory of its once sacred character now clings, like the ghost of Homer, "round Scamander's wasting springs." The Japanese have their Water-god and their Sea-god, to whom they throw cloth, and rice, and bottles of rum, just as the Greek sacrificed a bull to Poseidon, and the Roman to Neptune before a voyage. Xerxes threw a golden goblet and a sword into the Hellespont, which, on a former occasion, he had punished with branding and flogging. Cyrus punished the river Gyndes for drowning a sacred white horse. Achilles fought with Skamandros ; Pheron speared the Nile, and was blind for ten years in consequence. The following interesting case of administering justice to a river is from the *Peking Gazette* of November 1878 : " The Governor-General of the Yellow River requests that a tablet may be put up in honour of the river-god. He states that during the transmission of relief rice to Honan, whenever difficulties were encountered through shallows, wind, or rain, the river-god interposed in the most unmistakable manner, so that the transport of grain went on without hindrance. *Order :* Let the proper office prepare a tablet for the temple of the river-god." One more case from China. Some twenty years ago an edict published in the *Peking Gazette* announced that the river Yung-Ting had filled its channel, and overflowed in several places, a fact that appeared not only surprising but inexcusable, seeing that in the preceding year Li Hung-Chang himself reported that he had caged the dragon! Goats are thrown into the Sutlej to appease it, and prevent its wearing away its banks.

All savages show the same reluctance to save a drowning man, because they fear the water-demon's vengeance if he be cheated of his prey. Similar superstitions as to this have been found among the St. Kilda Islanders, the Danube boatmen, among French and English sailors, as well as among less civilised races.

It is said that the unwillingness of the Chinese to save a man from drowning, or from any peril of life, is due to the belief that the ghost of the last person killed must act as watchman in purgatory until the arrival of a fresh defunct relieves him of the post. Thus, the person who saves a life will assuredly be haunted by the "watching spirit," whom he has defrauded of a successor to release him from servitude. A belief similar to this is met with in many parts of the Scotch Highlands, where the last person buried is thought to act as sentinel over the churchyard, until able to deliver his charge to another. Consequently, if two neighbours die on the same day, the relatives make every effort to be first in closing the grave over their dead, so that the term of watching may be short. In County Cork it is said that the last person buried in any churchyard will have to draw water for all the others there sleeping, until there is another burial.

If a Solomon Islander falls into the river and narrowly escapes the jaws of a shark, his fellow-tribesmen will throw him back as a doomed sacrifice to the god of the river. Tradition says that little children were offered to the sacred river in Esthonia ; the river-god, sometimes seen by mortal eye, being a little man in blue and yellow stockings. The river Tees, the Skerne, and the Ribble have each a sprite, who, in popular belief, demands at times human victims. The river Spey is spoken of as " She," and must have at least one victim yearly.

> " Bloodthirsty Dee
> Each year needs three."

Peg Powler, the sprite of the Tees, is a sort of Lorelei, with green tresses, and an insatiable desire for human life. The foam or froth, which floats in large masses on the river, is called " Peg Powler's suds ; " the finer, less sponge-like froth, " Peg Powler's cream." The sprite of the Ribble is called " Peg O'Nell," and she demands a life every seven years. Unless a bird, a cat, or a dog is drowned in the stream on " Peg's night," some human being is certain to fall a victim there. A story is told to prove the truth of this.

In a Kaffir story, the heroine, who hitherto had never gone out except at night, is sent by her father-in-law to fetch water by daylight. The river draws her in, and she cannot escape from it. Though her father-in-law sacrifices an ox, the river will not accept it instead of the woman. Only at night, when her child is brought down to the river-side, she comes forth to suckle and pacify it. The nurse informs the babe's father of this, and he hides by the river one night, and when his wife comes out he clasps her and tries to draw her away. But the river, whose waters turn into blood, follows her right to the village and takes her back as it subsides, and only the very powerful charms of a medicine woman effect Tangalimlibo's deliverance.

In Germany, millers throw different things into the water on December 6th, St. Nicolas's Day, as an offering to the water-deity. In Northern countries, a certain deity, Neck, is the particular dread of millers. The nixes, those treacherous sprites who lure men to a watery grave, are nymphs of ancient lineage, to whom offerings were systematically made. Christian authorities, by giving a saint's name to springs or wells, have sought to transfer the venera-tion. On Christmas Eve the Bohemians throw a portion of their supper into the well, while repeating an appointed prayer to the water. At the Roman *fontinalia* nosegays were thrown into wells and fountains in honour of their presiding nymphs, as crooked pins are cast into St. Winifred's Well in North Wales, and three stones are offered to the spirit of the stream in Unst (Shetland).

In connection with ancient water-cult, propitiatory sacrifices had to be offered to water-deities before throwing a bridge across their habitat ; and so, in the Middle Ages, the constructor of a bridge was a sort of consecrated character, half priest and half engineer. Such was the Roman pontiff, so called because he made the bridge.

Doubtless some sacrificial rite survives in modified form in the custom, still observed in Cornwall, in parts of Ireland and Scotland, and in Brittany, of leaving small objects, such as pins, buttons, articles of dress, rags, &c., at sacred wells, pools, and springs.

Thus it is seen that many observances, customs, and superstitions of the present day are the outcome of the primitive barbaric belief that everything in nature is animated ; that every place, every object, is the dwelling of a particular spirit. What has already been said (p. 75) must suffice as to the veneration of certain trees, in accordance with this animistic theory. The demons of trees, rivers, fountains, and seas passed into dryads, nymphs, syrens, mermaids, as in the ocean caves dwelt those sister Nereids, children of Nereus, the Old Man of the Sea. " The Rhine has its Lorelei, and all the Northern seas their mermaidens, who sing in irresistibly sweet and plaintive tones, and comb their golden hair." In our own Isles do

" Water-kelpies haunt the foord,"

luring benighted travellers to destruction.

Every hill and mountain in China is the abode of some dragon-spirit ; every house has a niche in it fitted up as a shrine for the particular dragon who protects its destinies. All the mountains in Wales are haunted by female fairies of hideous aspect, just as in classic times the forests and fields, the waves and caves, teemed with satyrs, fauns, fairies, elves, trolls, and dwarfs. In Christian times fairies have come to be regarded as evil spirits, and elves have given place to devils in such connection as devils' dykes, leaps, punch-bowls, &c. So the ancestral spirits in the course of ages have suffered change. They assume the form of Lares, those spirits of the deceased who, according to Roman belief, watch over the living ; or they become guardian angels and patron saints ; whilst in certain morbid forms they are hobgoblins, ghosts, brownies, and bogies. For the brownies,

too, are family spirits, which receive sacrifice in
the Orkneys. In the North the dead who were
worshipped, the ancestral spirits, were called *Anses*.
Elf was another name for the spirits of the dead,
and of divine spirits generally ; though in later Christian times it sinks in Scandinavia to the meaning
of fairy. Our ideas about fairies are derived from
heathen beliefs as to the spirits of the dead. The
same thing has happened in the case of the wight,
which was originally a term for unearthly beings,
or spirits of the dead. Manes are the spirits of
deceased ancestors inhabiting Hades, who are
occasionally brought up again by sorcery. Raising
corpses is a universal feat with witches and wizards,
from the Witch of Endor to the modern spiritualist. Deceased persons reappear as ghosts often
to foretell death to the person they visit. Dread
of ghosts is common to savage and civilised alike.
With a pre-established belief in their existence, the
over-wrought brain would be subject to illusions
supporting that belief. Vampires are the souls of
the dead, who at night feed on the blood of the
living. We can trace their pedigree to the buried
barrow-ghost who could rise, slay, and eat, as in
the Danish tale of Asmund and Aswit. All the
hideous vampire legends grow out of facts concerning primitive cannibals. These demon blood-
suckers have their principal abode in Slavonia and

Hungary, and their name is derived from the Polish word *upior*. Or the vampire may appear in the *rôle* of poltergeist, or knocker, who upsets the furniture and causes disturbances in houses. Similar manifestations assure the modern spiritualist of the visit of some soul of the departed. A Bulgarian sorcerer, armed with a saint's picture, can entrap a vampire into a bottle baited with the filthy food that this gruesome soul loveth, and cork him down.

Besides the Nature-gods that we have been considering, the polytheism of the lower races acknowledges other deities, with the special attributes that savage imagination has seen fit to furnish them withal. Any power transcending his own is regarded by the savage as something supernatural ; therefore the higher culture of the superior stranger entitles him to a place in the savage's spacious pantheon. Europeans received religious homage on their first contact with the red men of the North American continent. Montezuma, supposing Cortés to be an incarnation of Quetzalcoatl, sent human victims to be slaughtered before him. The natives of Africa call the white man a devil ; and the natives of Mozambique draw their devil in the likeness of a white man. The devil can be all one's fancy paints him. He is not always black as the sooty Vulcan, nor with horns and hoofs like Pan and his Satyrs. Like a deity, he can be developed out of a powerful man, or out of a stranger bringing new arts, or out of any person possessed of superior power. All sorts of tales would be woven round this imaginary or real benefactor. Undoubtedly there was a very long fireless period in the earliest stages of man's development, just as there are fireless people at the present day, such as the Dokos in Abyssinia. Australians knew nothing about boiling and roasting food till the advent of Europeans. Then it comes to be related how some wise and superior being tamed fire, taught the use of the bow, and told " the hidden power of herbs and springs." Iron and gold, gems and poisons, music, science and the arts, " such, the alleviations of his state, Prometheus gave to man," according to Greek legend. Similarly, all peoples who have attained to even a low degree of civilisation have their culture-hero, whom they delight to honour, and sometimes deify. Such a benefactor was Wäinämöinen, whose praises are sung in the Kalewala, the epic poem of the Finns. Yehl, the god or hero of the Thlinkeets, could, like all savage gods, assume the form of a bird, and he stole fire as Prometheus did. But the fire dropped from the brand which he carried in his beak upon stocks and stones, and it is still to be obtained by striking flints or rubbing dry sticks together. The Zulus have their Unkulunkulu, " the old, old one," whom they regard both as the first man and as a creator; he, too, imparted to men a knowledge of the arts. Brazilian tribes say that Tamoi, the Grandfather, was the first man; he taught them how to till the soil, and then rose to the sky, where he will receive their souls after death. Many other races besides those mentioned identify the Creator with the First Man, or at least explain a kinship between them. The Hindu Yama was the first man and a solar god, being himself Son of the Sun. He is also Judge of the Dead. In Polynesian mythology, the divine Maui is ancestor of the human race. He, like Yehl, assumed a bird-form, and gave to men the art of procuring fire by friction. The Ahts of Vancouver's Island relate the exploits of a superior being, one Quawteaht, who could assume the form of beasts. The theft of fire is not alleged of him, though he seems to have had it in his possession. It was the cuttle-fish who stole it. Tsui Goab among the Hottentots is the name to conjure with. He died several times and rose again, and has as many burial-places as are claimed for a Christian saint, worship being paid him at these several cairns. In his lifetime he seems to have been a chief and a wizard.

Where ancestor-worship prevails, as for instance in China, the souls of great chiefs and warriors, or any celebrated person, are certain to be raised to divine rank in the course of generations. And this is how it comes to pass that the gods of savage creation are mortal. Like men, the gods of the Hindus were only made immortal by drinking soma. When the young prince Buddha inquired about a corpse he was told that all flesh, gods and men, rich and poor, alike must die. The Scandinavian gods died and were buried ; and Egyptian frescoes represent the burial of Osiris, one of the chief gods of Egypt. The Egyptian gods give to the deceased in heaven " the tree of life, of which they themselves do eat, that he likewise may live." He eats and drinks with the gods the " bread of eternity " and the " beer of everlastingness." In short, the un-cultured mind everywhere conceives of god in the likeness of man ; for even the Nature-gods were anthropomorphic ; and the deeply-rooted idea has prevailed down to recent centuries. Whenever the sense of his own incapacity showed the need of some great artificer, some supernatural miracle-worker, man created gods in his own image ; in the image of man created he him, male and female created he them.

The sacred legends tell how these man-created deities hunted, feasted, rioted, made love, went to war, and retired to bed at sunset. All these things do the Fijian gods of the present day ; nor is this surprising, seeing that the Fijian gods are simply deified mortals, apotheosised men. It seems, therefore, not unreasonable to assume that the Greek gods, in conception essentially parallel with the Fijian, were originally devised in like manner, when the ancestors of the Greeks were in a similar stage of intellectual development to the Fijians.

As the spirit-world is to some extent the reflex of the material world, it might happen in the course of time that one spirit would differ from another in glory, some gods would become subordinate to others, till the idea of one supreme power was reached ; just as, in the evolution of savage society, man warring against his fellow in the pursuit of his own advantage would learn that absolute equality cannot exist, and subordination would mean the recognition of superior power or rank, culminating in a head-man, a chief, or king. When a people lost its independence its gods did not cease to exist, but became the servants of the conqueror's deities.

Monotheism, however, is not necessarily the reflection of kingship in human society, for, as Mr. Lang points out, we find the conception of a supreme god, at least in outline, among races who have not even a chief, while among races with a king (as the Aztecs) there is no specially supreme deity, and no centralised divine government.

To attempt description of the religious systems of the world would be to digress from the plan of this little book. We have not to ascertain why men believe in gods (that being rather the business of the science of religion), but why they tell such strange stories about them, and why, moreover, men all tell the same sort of story, no matter to what race or clime they belong. But, as good and evil spirits find their way into the folk-lore of every people, it is expedient to show that all supernatural beings, however much in the course of evolution they have diverged from the primitive type, under cultivation by this sect or that, yet reveal their ultimate relationship one with another, being all alike cradled in savagery.

Some of the lower races show a rudimentary form of dualism in the opposing attitude of their good and evil spirits. The Devil as the power of Evil plays an important *rôle* in European folk-lore. The Poles, whose proverbial belief it is, like our own, that the devil is not as black as he is painted, say that he carries a man's soul up the chimney, that being his usual way of exit. It is related of an Englishman who died in 1883, and had been for years an inhabitant of Wrexham, that if in his walks a magpie crossed his path, he would make with his stick the sign of a cross upon the ground, and say, " Devil, I defy thee ! "

In the religion of Ancient Persia, which was the most impressive of all systems of dualism, the rival powers of good and evil, of light and darkness, were represented in Ormuzd, Ahura-mazda, the supreme Good, and Ahriman, the supreme Evil. Ormuzd created a fair and beautiful world, but Ahriman came after him, marred and frustrated all the good, and created all the evil that is in it. Like his offspring Satan, he is represented under the form of a serpent. Undoubtedly, in its development, Christian theology has been much influenced by the dualism of the ancient Persians. The Jews possessed no conception of a devil as the author of evil before their captivity in Babylon, and owe it to their close contact with Chaldean and Persian ideas. But this original Satan, the Asmodeus of the Hebrews, the prince of demons, the "adversary," has suffered great degradation during the course of centuries, and in mediæval times we find him in all sorts of grotesque guises, and with very various borrowed attributes. He is the black dog in Dr. Faust's study, or, imitating the classic sylvan deity Pan, he figures as a goat with horns and cloven hoofs. As the prince of the powers of the air, he is attended in his midnight flights by troops of witches mounted on brooms. He is Wayland Smith, the cunning worker in metals; and, like Hephaistos, he is lame from the effects of a fall from heaven. From the Scandinavian Thor, god of thunder, he obtains his red beard and his pitchfork, and his power over thunderbolts ; and probably he gets his name of Old Nick from his appearing as a water-imp or nix. Numerous traditions attest the gullibility of this mediæval devil, who, like the trolls, or " night-folk " of Northern mythology, is frequently foiled by the superior cunning of mortals. For instance, the devil sees a man moulding buttons, asks what they are, and is told that they are eyes. He thinks he will have a new pair himself, and actually consents to being pinioned while they are adjusted. When he is tightly bound to a bench he opens wide his eyes, and receives a blinding stream of melted lead, and starts up in agony, bearing the bench away on his back, only to encounter ridicule. Or, as is related in many a mediæval legend, he offers to help an architect to overcome his many difficulties in constructing a bridge, on condition that he receives in payment the soul of the first being to cross the bridge. The architects in these stories invariably give the promise, but cheat the poor devil by driving cats, dogs, pigs, hares, or fowls across the bridge. In many another way the devil gets cheated of his fee, as when, in " taking the hindmost," he gets only the shadow of the last man in the race, who thus gets off free, but lives shadowless ever after. The Irish on Achill Island at the present day dress all their boys like girls till they are about fourteen years old, in order to deceive the devil, who is always on the look-out for a boy. This precaution reminds one of the Chinese custom of giving a lad a girl's name, so that the gods may be deceived ; for they fear that the gods will deprive them of their boys.

It is interesting to see how very widespread is a particular story often attaching to this gullible devil. Frequently the devil, when displaying his powers, is persuaded to make himself small, and then gets entrapped. Sæmund, the hero of many an Icelandic story, and especially apt at outwitting Old Nick, asked him one day to make good his boast that he could make himself as small as the smallest midge. Sæmund bored a tiny hole in the door-post, invited the devil to walk into it, and then stopped it up with a plug of wood. The devil was not released till he had promised to become Sæmund's servant. But he chafed at his thraldom, and was for ever trying to revenge himself upon Sæmund, who, however, was always one too many for him. Once the devil took the form of a fly, and tried to hide under the film that had gathered on the milk-jug, hoping that Sæmund would swallow him unawares and so lose his life. But Sæmund instead put fly, film, and all into a bladder and laid the package on the altar. There the devil had to bide till after the service, and it is said that he never found himself in a worse case.

In a Danish story the devil gets shut up in a box, and in a Portuguese he takes refuge, after a severe thrashing, in a log of wood. In very many fairy tales diabolic spirits are imprisoned in phials as flies. A ghost that haunted a house in the west of England was served in this way. The man who undertook to lay the ghost, and awaited his midnight visit in a locked room, had a bottle of brandy, with a tumbler and water, and an empty bottle, at hand. When the ghost appeared, the man asked how he got in, and would not believe it was through the keyhole. " At any rate," he said, " if you can get through a keyhole you can get into this bottle, and I won't believe that you can do either." " Here goes, then," said the ghost, as into the bottle he went. Then the man popped in the cork, and took and threw the bottle exactly over the key-stone of the middle arch into the river, and the ghost never was heard of after. The ghost of a child that haunted the " Old Hall," at Hinckley was exorcised by a number of ministers, who, after a short religious ceremony, enticed it into a bottle, which was then securely corked and thrown into the moat.

The Southern negroes of America say that, to secure protection from being hag-ridden, you must hang a bottle half full of water on the bed-post ; get a new cork, stick into it nine new needles, and hang it over the bottle, an inch above its mouth. When the hag has finished her nightly ride on your chest, she will see on departing the cork and the needles, and, her fatal instinct for counting seizing her, she will pause. Then is the moment to cork the bottle, with her semi-fluid corporeal substance inside. You will never be troubled with that hag again. It will be seen that the device of bottling noxious spirits is very common indeed.

In a Russian story, a soldier comes to the rescue of a certain princess, who is visited every night by an evil spirit, which gives her no rest till dawn. The fiend arrives at midnight, and assumes the form of a man. The soldier intercepts him, tricks him in various ways, and finally chastises him till he takes to flight. Every night for a month a different devil is sent to the palace, and receives the same treatment at the hands of the soldier. Then " Grandfather Satan " himself confronts the soldier, and retreats howling. Presently the soldier induces the whole of the fiendish party to enter his knapsack, imprisons them therein by signing it with a cross, and then has it thumped on the anvil to his heart's content. After this he usually carries the knapsack about on his back, with the fiends inside it, till one day some inquisitive women open and let out the unsuspected contents with a crash and a roar. The hero of a Bohemian story likewise " bags " all the demons who had haunted a nobleman's castle, including Satan himself. Then he has them well hammered at a smithy, and only sets them at liberty on their promising never to return.

The Walloons tell a story called " Misery and Poverty," in which again the devil suffers much ignominy. It is very much like the Norse story of " The Mastersmith," and has besides its parallels in France, in Rome, in Holland, and elsewhere. Misery, a blacksmith, and Poverty, his dog, are companions in privation. One day the blacksmith, sorely tempted, sells his soul for a large sum of money to the devil, who will claim his purchase at the end of ten years. In the meantime the blacksmith is enabled to live in the enjoyment of plenty. One day St. Peter and the Lord, passing his way, halt to have their ass shod. Misery sets to work at once, and shoes the ass with a silver shoe. This pleases the travellers, and, as a recompense, they promise to grant any three wishes that the blacksmith may express. After due reflection, Misery asks for a purse that will never let its contents escape, an armchair which will hold its occupant prisoner, and a cherry-tree from which no one, having climbed into it, will be able to descend without his permission. St. Peter, in an urgent aside, has been prompting the blacksmith to ask for Paradise; but Misery would not hear him. The travellers go on their way, and the goodman's three wishes are realised. One evening, the ten years being now accomplished, the devil appears to claim Misery's soul. "You seem tired," says Misery. "Sit down in the armchair whilst I get myself ready." The devil acquiesces, and off goes Misery to make a bar of iron red-hot in the fire. Back he comes, and proposes starting; but the devil tries in vain to get up. Misery then lays into him mercilessly with his red-hot poker, and will not desist till he is promised a ten years' respite. When that period has elapsed, a whole troop of devils come to fetch his soul. It is summer-time and very hot, so Misery invites them to climb into the cherry-tree and refresh themselves. Thereupon, having them in his power, he obtains another ten years' reprieve before letting them go. The ten years pass, and he is invaded by another troop of devils. This time he sets out with them. Having gone a stage together, Misery asks if they are not tired, and offers to carry them for a while if they can get inside his purse. All unsuspicious, in they crawl, and are at his mercy till they promise another ten years. But before these have elapsed the old fellow dies, and so does his dog. They arrive together at the gate of Paradise, St. Peter opens to them, but instantly recognising the man who had so offended him by not taking his hint about Paradise, he shuts the door in his face. Then Misery, still accompanied by his dog, presents himself at the gate of hell. The devil who opens the door happens to be the very one who had such a bad time of it in the armchair. In terrible alarm he slips inside again, bangs the door to, and bolts it. So Misery and Poverty were not received at either place; and that is how it is that they must wander on earth for ever and ever.

In many variants of this story it is Death that is put off in some such manner and cheated of his prey, as when Gambling Hansel, in the German story, like the hearty old lady of eighty in the French version, makes Death climb into the imprisoning fruit-tree, and leaves him up there for seven years; and in the Magyar folk-tale, when the young farmer corks up Death in the spirit flask; or when Bippo Pipetta, in the Italian variant, forces him to enter his magic sack.

In the Norse tale of " The Lad and the Deil," the devil is induced to crawl into a worm-eaten nut, and the smith finds that a precious hard nut to crack, even with his sledge-hammer.

Brother Lustig, in the German story, wishes the nine devils into his magic knapsack, which he then takes to a smithy and lays on the anvil, bidding the smith and his apprentices strike it with all their strength with their great hammers. In this way eight of the devils are done to death, and the ninth only escapes through lying in a fold. Years afterwards, when Brother Lustig presents himself at the door of hell, this very devil peeps out, and recognising the man with the knapsack, and recalling his narrow escape with a black eye from the terrible hammering, he bolts the door again in a fright, and rushing to the devil's lieutenant, begs him, as he values his life, never to let that chap with the knapsack in. Then Brother Lustig applies for admission at the door of heaven; but St. Peter, who had given him the knapsack, and who knows something about him, says he will not have him there. Brother Lustig begs him to take back his knapsack, and he pushes it in through the bars. " Now I wish myself inside the knapsack," says Brother Lustig, and in a second he was in it, and so in heaven, where St. Peter was forced to let him bide.

The devil who is released from the bottle by the woodcutter's son, in another German story in Grimm's collection, is actually fool enough to be persuaded to get inside again before strangling his rescuer, who of course loses no time in thrusting in the cork, and then keeps him prisoner till he has promised a reward for his release.

This last story attaches, in Switzerland, to Paracelsus, of whom it is told that, wandering one day in the forest, he heard his name called by the devil, who was imprisoned in a fir-tree, and promised to liberate him on condition that he procured him a medicine which would cure all the sick, and a tincture that would turn everything to gold. The devil promises, and the doctor proceeds to cut out of the tree a little plug with three crosses marked on it, whereupon the devil crawls out, in the form of a hideous black spider, and, reaching the ground, transforms himself into a tall, thin, squinting, red-eyed man, in a red cloak. He conducts the doctor to a rock, which he strikes open with a hazel-rod. Thence he fetches the promised medicine and tincture. Then they return to the fir-tree, the devil intending to go thence to Innsbrück to fetch the man who had imprisoned him. But Paracelsus craftily compliments him on his power to turn himself into a spider, and the devil politely offers to perform the feat before his eyes. He does so, and crawls again into the little hole, whereupon Paracelsus rams in the plug, cuts three fresh crosses on it, and leaves the devil to his fate. The contents of the bottles turned out to be quite genuine, and by means of them Paracelsus became famous.

Or, as in a Russian tale, it is Woe the Woeful that is so clever at getting into chinks. A merchant invites him to play at hide-and-seek, and induces him to make good his boast by creeping into the axle-box of a wheel. Then he drives in a wedge, and flings the wheel, with Woe in it, into the river. Misfortune, in the fable, gets shut up in a hollow oak-tree, much in the same way as the devil gets wedged in a beech-tree in a German story.

When Donald - Duival M'Kay, the wizard of Sutherlandshire legend, was exploring the Cave of Smoo, he came across a large cask. He bored a hole in it, and out came a little man of an inch and a half long, who, on gradually assuming gigantic stature, said, "Donald, did you ever see so great a wonder ? " "Never, by my troth," replied the wizard ; " but wert thou to shrink again, that would be a bigger wonder still." The giant is simple enough to shrink back into the cask, which Donald loses no time in closing. The fisherman, in the " Arabian Nights," who brings up the copper vessel in his net, and unwittingly liberates the jinni who had been imprisoned therein by the power of Suleymán's magic signet-ring, induces the threatening and ungrateful monster to re-enter the vessel by means of the usual taunting incredulity. The idea is derived from the Muslim legend adapted from the Talmud. Solomon performed his many feats by means of a magic signet-ring. The king of the demons cajoled him out of possession of this ring, and flung it into the sea. Solomon, who was cast by the demon into a foreign land far from his own, eventually, after many wanderings, finds the ring in a fish he is eating, and is enabled by its means to recover his kingdom, and imprison the demon in a copper vessel, which he cast into the Lake of Tiberius.

According to Eastern tradition, Solomon also confined no less than three million demons, with seventy-two of their kings, in a bottle of black glass, which he then threw into a deep well near Babylon. The citizens, however, in the expectation of finding treasure, broke the bottle and set the demons free.

The tract entitled " The Devil upon Two Sticks," printed in 1708, which, like Le Sage's well-known novel " Le Diable Boiteux," is derived from a Spanish romance written in 1641, contains the incident of the devil being delivered from imprisonment in a glass bottle.

The notion of demons being enclosed in vessels prevails also in China, where more than one instance of it occurs. In one legend, the prefect of Shiu-hing, many, many generations ago, dreamed a dream. It was this. Myriads of devils boasted to him that they would overthrow the ruling dynasty. He doubted their power, and obtained their consent to mark each with a red spot on the forehead, so that he might recognise them if, to carry out their threat, the devils should assume an altered form. When he awoke he was troubled at the dream, and determined to consult wise men about it. Outside his yamên he found the ground strewn with small round stones, on every one of which was a red spot. " These are surely the devils I marked last night," thought he, and straightway had the stones collected and secured in earthenware jars, which were then locked in a strong room in his yamên. The door was sealed with the prefect's seal, which was to be renewed by each successive holder of the office. To shorten a long story, it must suffice to add that prefect after prefect for many generations duly re-sealed the door of the devils' prison, till at length, faith in the necessity of this caution being shaken, one unlucky prefect, inappropriately surnamed Luk, neglected to perform the duty, and the door got opened and a jar of devils broken. They caused the city to be submerged below the waters of the river, and it was not until they were recaptured and the door re-sealed that the city again rose above water. After this woeful experience it once more became the care of each succeeding prefect to re-seal the door ; and so time passed on, till in 1854 there arose a prefect surnamed Ma, who utterly despised the devil story, and had the red-spotted stones taken from the strong room and thrown away ! That very year red-turbaned rebels—the devils in human form—captured the city. Here endeth the legend, and, as far as is known, the red-spotted devils are still at large. One thing is certain (" and the rest is lies "), no man surnamed Luk or Ma is allowed to be prefect in Shiu-hing to this day.

In Icelandic folk-lore, the " Sending "—which is a ghost raised by sorcery—" is sometimes induced to assume the form of some small beast or insect, either by taunts or flattery, and to creep into a bottle, or into an empty marrow bone ; and, once there, he is corked up tight for his folly. . . . Woe betide him who, unsuspecting, finds the marrow bone or bottle subsequently, and uncorks it ! The goblin gains ten times his original force by being imprisoned, and ten times his old malignity." In Korea, at the present day, it is the blind who deal with the evil spirits and exorcise devils. A gifted blind man can catch a devil in a bottle and put him in a safe place.

In a story told by gipsies, a dragon gets imprisoned in a jar ; just as, in the Far East, the Buddhist devil *Schimnu* is enticed into a water-jug, the mouth of which is straightway sealed. The time-honoured device is met with everywhere in folk-tales, and recalls how Zeus persuaded his wife Metis to become a fly, that he might swallow her. Loki, the Scandinavian giant-demon, could turn himself into a fly, and get through keyholes (like the ghost) into locked rooms, and could even slip through the eye of a needle.

The Syrian counterpart of Bel, the supreme deity of the Assyrians, was Baal, and, in connection with his credited influence over flies, was known as Baal Zebul. The Hebrews, punning on this name, called him Beel-Zebub (dung-god), and afterwards crowned him " Prince of Devils." But the Septuagint translates Baalzebub, the name of the god of Ekron, by Βάαλ μυῖα, fly-god (2 Kings i. 2). Ahriman in the shape of a fly pervaded all nature.

The devil is outwitted much in the same way in Italy. In a Basque story we find him in a sack, as, in the North, Thor himself did crouch in a glove thumb, wherein from fear and cowardice he was packed away.

Christian story-tellers have transformed the dull demons of olden time into Satan and his attendant fiends, who thus come to figure in these very antique narratives.

An important outcome of Animism is *Fetichism*. In accordance with the general idea that any lifeless object may be the dwelling-place of spirits, that the souls of the dead have power to quit the corpse or return to it, and to become embodied in animal, tree, plant, or lifeless stone, each of these was regarded at an early age as a

172

fetich [1] or charm, to which offerings were made by way of propitiation. A further development of fetichism is manifested in the faith in relics and in the worship of idols. If the soul is present in the corpse, it is present in parts of the corpse ; hence the savage custom of preserving relics of the dead, such as a finger-nail, a tooth, or a tuft of hair, and of paying homage to them, under the belief that the resident spirit will reward and protect the pious worshipper. When we read of a savage making offerings to a shapeless stone, under the belief that the soul of an ancestor has taken up abode therein, it seems inevitable that he should presently begin to shape his fetich, making a rude effigy of a man or an animal, and worshipping it systematically, either as an ancestor, or as a deity. It is but a step from the worship of a dead body to the worship of an object representing that dead body. Into the image of the dead, the spirit of the dead may enter ; so the divine idol comes to be worshipped as the residence of the god himself. Thus the whole apparatus, so complex and elaborate, of idols, temples, priests, and sacrifices may be traced to these crude beginnings in the animism of the lowest savagery.

[1] The Portuguese in West Africa, centuries ago, applied the word *feitiço*, meaning charm or talisman, to the various objects venerated by the negroes.

In India, the image of Vishnu, set up in his temple, is washed and dressed by his attendants, before choice foods are set before him, and an entertainment of music and dancing is given. Saxo gives a wonderful description of the gigantic statue of the divine Suanto-Vitus in Rügen, and of the splendour of his shrine, within which the priest took heed not to breathe, lest the divine presence should be tainted. Once every year, after harvest, beasts were sacrificed before the temple, omens were taken, and a libation poured at the feet of the image, while prayer was made for the increase of the coming crops.

Lucretius says that " the brazen statues which stand near the gates, show their right hands made smaller by the touch of people frequently saluting them and passing by." But, as Mr. Grote points out, speaking of Greek worship, " The primitive memorial erected to a god did not even pretend to be an image, but was often nothing more than a pillar, a board, a shapeless stone, or a post." The rites of stone-worship in India are probably survivals from low civilisation. There Siva is worshipped as a stone, as Artemis, represented by a log, was worshipped in Eubœa ; and from a passage in Isaiah (lvii. 6) we learn that, from the Semitic race, stones received a drink offering and an oblation. Another such fetich is the black stone of the Kaaba.

Pilgrimages are yearly made to Continental shrines

containing relics of a particular saint, just as in ancient times the devout Greek would visit the temple of a particular god, perhaps to be the witness of a human sacrifice at the altar, as a gift to the god of what is dearest to man. In later times we find the substitution of an effigy or dummy, as in China, and as in the rites of Ancient Mexico, the symbolism of human sacrifice being thus retained ; or the victim came to be a beast, a particular animal being associated with each divinity. Thus in course of time a doe instead of a virgin was sacrificed in Laodicæa to Artemis, and elsewhere a bear. Demeter received a pig. Similarly, a goat was substituted for a boy in the sacrifice to Dionysus in Potniæ ; just as, among the early races of South India, goats are sacrificed by the thousand during certain festivals to the deities of the lower cult.

A prominent feature in the practice of very many religions is sacrifice of a mystical or sacramental character. Usually it is a divine animal that is slain, and its body and blood are, either actually or symbolically, partaken of by the worshippers. The animal may be regarded as the incarnation of a god, or it is sacred to a god. Or the victim may be a divine man. But into the subject of " god-eating," as practised, for example, by the Mexicans, and symbolically by the Christian Church, it is impossible to enter. It only concerns us in this place to note that the origin of all observances of this type is to be sought, not among civilised, but rather amongst savage races ; not in an advanced, but in a crude stage of mental development.

It is this recognition of survivals that has given vital interest to the science of folk-lore. For a further example :—In the custom observed amongst ourselves of breaking a bottle of wine over the bows of a ship, may be traced the older practice such as the Wickings used, and such as Captain Cook found in the South Seas, of sprinkling the war-galley with human blood. It is analogous to the custom of consecrating a building by burying alive. Tradition affords many traces of human sacrifice in our own isles (see p. 107). The accounts of Tacitus and other classic authors show that it was frequent among Northern tribes in olden times. There is a Scandinavian tradition about the sacrifice of King Doomwald by his Swedish subjects in time of famine. The reader will be reminded of the theme of Tennyson's poem " The Victim." In the *Heraclidæ* of Euripides, Macaria offers herself as a sacrifice to the daughter of Ceres.

The veneration for the serpent, fed by fear, has survived many other systems of fetich worship ; the form of the serpent being handed down from age to age as the accompaniment of magical power. In every part of the earth inhabited by the serpent, this animal has at one time or other been reverenced by man. Its strange beauty and spectre-like quietude, its miraculous power over the lower animals, its deadly venom, and other qualities and faculties of the serpent, amply account for its being regarded as supernatural. To its habit of attaching itself to human habitations may be traced the notion of its friendliness and guardianship. It was believed to be a reincarnation of a dead man's soul, a messenger from the gods; and whilst still worshipped by Indian tribes, by the Slave Coast negro, by Chinese and Egyptians, and across the Atlantic, the serpent is demonised by Zarathustrians, Jews, Muhammadans, and Christians. The Hebrews, it will be remembered, were open and undisguised snake-worshippers until the reign of King Hezekiah. All sorts of mythologies have women with serpent tails or serpent hair, who have magical power, from Lilith the Hebrew sorceress downwards.

When the ancient Egyptians personified the powers of nature, they gave to evil powers the shapes of noxious animals and reptiles such as snakes and scorpions. " The principal enemy of the natural body was the worm, and from the earliest times it seems that a huge worm or serpent was chosen by the Egyptians as the type of the powers that were hostile to the dead, and also of the foe against whom the Sun-god fought."

The veneration of various other creatures, beasts, birds, as well as plants (see p. 103) is in many instances connected with this fetich theory ; that is to say, the worship is paid to the incarnation in animal or plant form of some divine ancestral soul.

CHAPTER IV

THE OTHER-WORLD

THE very general belief in an invisible world, the abode of invisible spirits, the disembodied souls of all past generations, as held by the lower races, is the natural and almost inevitable outcome of the universal animistic belief which we have been considering. Primitive ideas of another world, the abode of spirits, like all other primitive ideas, pass through stages of development. The abode of the spirits is associated with the place of the burial of the dead ; the locale of the other world, therefore, is in a great measure determined by the mode of burial. The Caribs buried their chiefs on hills ;

the Comanches and the Patagonians also select the highest hill as the burial-ground ; in Western Arabia and in Borneo the practice is the same. Herein is seen sufficient foundation for the belief that the summits of the highest hills, the places most difficult of access, are peopled with spirits ; and the widely prevalent idea that the souls of the dead resort to a high mountain may also be reasonably connected with this particular method of burial. When a European made the ascent of the Sacred White Mountain, or Paik-tu-San, in Korea, the native carriers would not go near the summit, and even as they approached the mountain were careful to propitiate the spirits by placing boiled rice on a fallen tree.

The gods of the ancients resided in high mountains. One of the Indian hill-tribes believes that each mountain peak is the watch-tower of a god. In popular belief, the soul in its wanderings has to climb a steep hill-side, sometimes supposed to be made of iron, sometimes of glass, on the summit of which is the heavenly paradise. This is why the nails of a corpse must never be pared (see p. 53) ; they would be required for that " climb up into heaven " of which the angel speaks to Esdras. Lays and legends tell of the *glass-bergs* and *glass-burgs*, which are the abode of heroes and wise women. Only the good and valiant youth can win the fair princess on the glass-mountain of popular narrative. By a hero Brünhild, in the Norse saga, was delivered from her hall of flames. The transition from a mountain abode to an abode in the sky which the mountain peak, the " heaven-kissing hill," seems to touch, is but an easy step. The Norse *glêrhiminn*, or glass-heaven, a paradise to which old heroes ride, recalls Ezekiel's firmament of " terrible crystal " above the heads of the living creature, and the " sea of glass like unto crystal " in Revelations, before the throne of heaven. The notions of solidity and expansion were both contained in the Hebrew conception of the firmament, which name literally signified something hammered or beaten out. The blue ethereal sky was regarded as a solid crystal sphere to which the stars were fixed, and which was constantly revolving, carrying them with it. This sphere or firmament divided the waters which were under the firmament from the waters which were above the firmament. There were " windows in heaven " through which, when opened, the waters that were above the firmament descended. This was rain. Ilmarinen, in the Finnish epic, forges the firmament of finest steel, and sets in it the moon and stars. The New Zealander thinks there is a hole or crack in the solid firmament, through which the rain can be let down from the reservoir above. The view entertained by the

Greeks and other early nations was essentially the same. The Egyptians believed the sky to be like an iron ceiling, either flat or vaulted, and to correspond in extent and shape with the earth beneath it. The stars were lamps hung from it. This rectangular ceiling stood on a pillar at each of the four corners—the roof-tree of primitive nations.

Or, on the other hand, the practice of cave-burial would engender the conception of a subterranean other-world, not necessarily as the abode of evil spirits, for the barbaric mind does not trouble itself with the destiny, only with the whereabouts, of the soul, and has no idea of a devil or a hell, because the moral nature of the savage has not so developed as to enable him to form theories of retribution. To inquire at what barbaric stage of culture this development takes place, is beyond the province of this little book, and belongs rather to the study of religious history. The idea of bliss is not incompatible with underground abode. Legends tell of many a blissful sojourn in subterranean fairy-halls. In folk-tales, little children who are good fall into wells, and pass through green meadows to the house of friendly Frau Holda. A well-known Chinese legend relates how two friends, wandering among the mountains in search of medicinal herbs, come to a fairy-bridge guarded by two maidens of superhuman loveliness, who invite them to cross into fairyland. The blissful period spent with the fairy-folk seems but as yesterday when it is past ; yet when the friends fulfil their desire to revisit their earthly home, they find that seven generations have lived and died during their absence, and they themselves are centenarians. There are other forms of this Rip Van Winkle story current in China. Wang Chih, a patriarch of the Taoist sect, is said to have been wandering about gathering firewood when he came upon a grotto wherein some aged men were playing chess. He enters, puts down his axe, and watches the game. Presently one old man gives him something resembling a date-stone, after tasting which he is oblivious of hunger and thirst. When one of the players suggests that he has been long enough away from home, Wang Chih proceeds to pick up his axe. The handle has mouldered into dust. Centuries have passed since he left his home, and Wang Chih finds no vestige of his kinsfolk. So, retreating to the hills, he devotes himself to the rites of Taoism, and attains to immortality.

Many a renowned hero has been housed in Hades, where Achilles paced with great strides along the mead of asphodel, where dwell the souls, the phantoms of men outworn. And thither down the dark ways did Hermes lead the gibbering souls of the slain wooers. " Sheol," the ancient Hebrew name for Hades, and the original of our English " hell," was the destination of all the dead, whether good or bad. Sheol literally means " cave " ; cave-burial was the primitive Hebrew practice. As the ghost developed into an everlasting soul, so the cave developed into an underworld, as the abode of all disembodied souls.

In savage belief, the dead rejoin their ancestors. The stationary cave-dwellers, therefore, think they return to an underground region ; while immigrant races must journey back after death to the abodes of their fathers, overland, across rivers, or across the sea, even as their own journeyings forth have been.

So the other-world may be in some distant isle across the seas, or, like hyperborean happiness, may be found in that land of perpetual sunshine beyond the north wind. The Fijian abode of bliss can only be reached in a canoe. The Samoans say of a chief who has died, " he has sailed." It is not at all unusual for savages to place a boat beside a grave ; and many modifications of the practice have been observed. The Chonos of Western Patagonia actually bury their dead in canoes near the sea ; many tribes remote from each other either bury their chief in a boat, or put the corpse adrift in a boat. In short, numbers of peoples bury their dead in boats, and our own Scandinavian ancestors had kindred usages. In Norse narrative, when Balder died, the Âses placed his body on its funeral pyre on board a vessel, set fire to it, and committed it to the sea at high water. When bodies were buried in a boat on land, it must have been so that their ferry was ready, when, on their journey to the underworld, they should reach the water. Everywhere similar observances point to a similar meaning, the general belief amongst savages being that the dead return to their ancestral home.

As the passage of a large river would be the chief obstacle to overcome in any overland migration, it would be natural to conceive the notion, which is found to be so very general, that the crossing of a river is the chief obstacle on the journey which the dead must make to the other-world. One of the North American tribes explains the inability of the soul to pass the river as the reason for its return. Some of the Indian tribes put strings across rivers for the spirits to cross by, that they may be encouraged to return and re-animate the corpse. The Kasi Indians, if they pass a puddle with the funeral *cortège*, will lay down a straw for the dead man's soul to use as a bridge. The popular idea that spirits cannot cross running water may have arisen from the primitive belief as to the river-crossing that the deceased has to encounter. A familiar application of the notion will

185

occur to the reader in the legend of "Tam o' Shanter." It will be remembered that as soon as Tam has reached the "key-stane o' the brig" he is beyond the pursuit of the witches. "A running stream they darena cross."

The Finns, on their way to Minala, their other-world, must voyage across nine seas and a half; the Wickings must cross the Ginnûnga-Gap; and the Red Indian has his Great Water, like the Vaitarani of the Brahmans, the Styx of the Greeks, and the Christian Jordan, across which is the Celestial City.

In Mr. Spencer's opinion, the belief in two or more other-worlds would in course of time arise from the notion of different ranks requiring different other-worlds; the chiefs would have separate ancestral homes. Further, societies consisting of conquerors and conquered, who have separate traditions as to their original home, necessarily have separate other-worlds. These would differentiate into superior and inferior places of abode for the spirits, originating the conception of places for the good and places for the bad, and, by endless modifications here and amplifications there, developing at last into the definite distinction of the separate abode of good and evil spirits—the Paradise or heaven, and the Hell or purgatory.

With man's first belief in a future state came his first idea of Hades, an unseen world, as the abode

of all the dead, good and bad alike. Hades means
" invisible " ; it is quite probable, however, that the
term *Hadi*, meaning Eternity, was the original name
brought from the East, as *Bit-Hadi*, " the house of
Eternity," is found on old Assyrian tablets, and the
name *Hades*, " invisible," was adopted later. The
translators of the New Testament into Coptic rendered the Greek ᾅδης by *amenti*, the name which
the ancient Egyptians gave to the abode of man after
death, and the Copts peopled it with beings whose
prototypes are found on the ancient monuments.

As to the position of Hades, the most general
view is that it is situated below the earth, and the
river of Death must be crossed ere it can be reached.
The Hades of the early Greeks, as systematically
stated by Hesiod, and graphically described by
Homer, was surrounded by the river Styx, across
which Charon ferried the souls in a narrow two-
oared boat. For this he charged a fare ; therefore
the Greeks placed an obolus in the mouth of the
dead (see p. 49).

In the play of Euripides, Alcestis, about to die for
her husband, sees the two-oared boat, and the ferry-
man of the dead holding his hand on the pole, as he
calls to hasten her with vehement words. But the
unburied may he not convey between the dreadful
banks and across the roaring stream, and so when
Æneas, in the Sibyl's company, visited the deep

flood of Cocytus, he saw a forlorn crowd entreating to be taken across ; but the surly boatman thrust them to a distance, and kept them away from the brink, because their bones had not been laid in their place of rest. For the same reason the ghost of Patroclus clamoured for the rites of the dead (see *supra*, p. 59).

Procopius, a historian of the sixth century, speaking of the island of Brittia, by which he means Great Britain, relates a legend which he had often heard from the lips of the inhabitants. They imagine that the souls of the dead are transported to that island, and it is the duty of certain fishers and farmers on the Frankish coast to ferry them over. Those whose turn it is to perform the duty go to bed at dusk. At midnight they hear a knocking at their door, and muffled voices calling. Rising and going to the shore, they see empty boats, which are not their own, and board them and seize the oars. Though they see no one, it is evident when the boat is under way that she is heavily laden, for her gunwales are scarce above water. During the voyage the boatmen hear a voice loudly asking the name and country of each invisible passenger. In an hour they touch land, which their own craft could not reach under a day and a night. Then the boat speedily unloads, and becomes so light that she only dips her keel in the wave.

On the river Treguier, in Bretagne, it is still customary to convey the dead to the churchyard in a boat, over a small arm of the sea called *passage de l'enfer*, instead of taking the shorter way by land. British bards sing of the pool of dread and of dead bones across which souls must sail to reach the underworld ; and a North English song names " the bridge of dread, no brader than a thread," over which the soul must pass. There is a Muhammadan tradition to the effect that " in the middle of hell all souls must walk over a bridge thinner than a hair, sharper than the edge of a sword, and bordered on both sides by thorns and prickly shrubs. The Jews also speak of the hell-bridge narrow as a thread, but only unbelievers have to cross it." The Muhammadans are said also to believe that before the judgment day they must pass over a red-hot iron spanning a bottom-less pit. The good works of each believer will put themselves under his feet.

Much the same meaning appears to lie in the voyage of souls to the underworld, and in their walking the bridge that spans the river. The episode of crossing a river or gulf to reach the land of the dead occurs in North American myth, frequently without any moral sense attached to it. The Hurons say that a dog guards the tree-trunk that bridges the river of death. Some souls are attacked by the dog, and fall. The Choctaws say that only the good can safely walk the long and slippery barkless pine-log, that stretches from hill to hill athwart the deep and dreadful river. The wicked cannot reach the Indian paradise, but fall through the waters to the dark dread land. A very similar legend comes from the Woodlarks, a group of islands off British New Guinea. After death the spirits of the good go to Tum, a small, very fertile island. Dikinikan, a terrible goddess, watches over the beach, and the serpent by her side forms the bridge across to Tum. The favoured pass over safely; but when others attempt the passage the serpent dives, and the deceased fall into the jaws of a shark. Thorkill had to cross water to reach the Teutonic Tartarus. On an earlier voyage he saw a river which could be crossed by a bridge of gold, like the Giallar-brú, the bridge over the river Gioll, that parted earth from the lower world. In the Belgian folk-tale of " The White Wolf," which is a variant of the Cupid and Psyche theme, the heroine has to cross a bridge of slippery ivory in order to regain her lost husband. For this purpose, in one version, she has to be shod with iron. This recalls the hell-shoon and the difficulty of scaling the slippery mountains (see pp. 45, 53).

The ancient Egyptians believed that whilst the dead body was being ferried over the Nile, the soul

in the realms of the underworld was being ferried
over the infernal Nile, to undergo trial in the hall
of the Two Truths, where the good actions of the
deceased are weighed in the balance against the
emblem of Truth, and Osiris pronounces judgment
according to the result, while his son Horus appears
as a mediator. Then the soul may be admitted to
Heaven, returned to earth for a fresh term of life
in the form of some unclean animal, or condemned
to a term of purification in Purgatory.

The psychostasia, or weighing of the conscience,
figured on every Egyptian mummy case, forms the
subject of one of the illustrations embellishing the
funereal papyrus of Ani, which probably dates from
the fourteenth century B.C., and which may be seen
in the British Museum. The centre of the picture is
occupied by the great Balance. The heart of Ani
in the left scale represents his conscience, and is
weighed against a feather, symbolical of the law.
A dog-headed deity sits on the top of the Balance,
while the jackal-headed Anubis examines the indi-
cator. Destiny, as a long-bearded man, stands under
the Balance, with the goddess of Fortune, and
another goddess connected with birth, behind him.
Above these is the soul of the deceased, in the
form of a bird with a human head. Thoth, the
ibis-headed scribe of the gods, notes down the result
of the trial ; while behind him waits the terrible

Amemit the Devourer, with crocodile-head, fore-parts of a lion, and hind-quarters of a hippopotamus. The judgment is pronounced. Righteous and just is Ani ; his case is straight upon the great Balance ; he is without offence and without rebuke. Amemit the Devourer may not prevail over him ; he is to receive cakes, the right of appearance before Osiris, and a permanent allotment in Sechit-hotepu, an abode of bliss, like the Elysian fields.

Any attempt to survey and compare the different religions of the world, with their doctrines of future life, and systems of rewards and punishment, is of course beyond the scope of the present volume. The very striking similarities which they present need not be pointed out. The alphabet of every religion is the same, one key serves to explain them all—namely, the universal animistic belief of the savage. Whether this belief be itself the result of a misunderstanding of normal biological pheno-mena—the hypothesis exhibited in these pages—or whether, according to another conceivable hypo-thesis, it be derived from the savage's acquaintance with rare, abnormal, and not scientifically accepted phenomena, does not affect the issue.

The early conception of Hades was much modi-fied by the constant intercommunication between Greece and Egypt. The Romans in turn absorbed much from the Greeks, and Virgil has given minute details of the nether world called Orcus, which is divided into five regions, the last of which is Elysium, the place of the blest. Without further particularising, it must suffice to say that all the features in the Hell of the Christian fathers, and of the Christian religion generally, may be traced in the Amenti of Egypt, the Sheol and Gehenna of the Jews, and the Orcus of Virgil ; and that the Hells of the Koran and of many other creeds are offshoots from the same originals ; while the Scandinavian Walhalla, with its Purgatory, Niflheim, and its everlasting Tartarus, Nāstrond, are merely variants of the same idea, except that ice and cutting wind, as representing the Norseman's idea of misery, take the place of unquenchable fire in the economy of punishment. The central core, the innermost circle of Dante's Inferno is, not fire, but thick-ribbed ice. The breath of Lucifer freezes ; it does not burn.

It is to the region of eternal cold, only to be reached by water, that Thorkill sails with his men, in the story told by Saxo ; and here the same precautionary abstinence from food must be observed as in the Greek Hades. Persephone tasted of a pomegranate in Hell, wherefore she is for ever doomed to stay there ; but Wäinämöinen, in the Finnish Kalewala, wisely refuses to drink when among the dead.

The same Arctic Hell is described in the old Scottish ballad, " The Ship of the Fiend," in sharp contrast to the abode of bliss—

> " ' Oh what are yon, yon pleasant hills,
>   That the sun shines sweetly on ? '
> ' Oh yon are the hills of Heaven,' he said,
>   Where you will never win.'
>
> ' Oh whatna mountain is yon,' she said,
>   ' Sae dreary wi' frost and snow ? '
> ' Oh yon is the mountain o' Hell,' he cried,
>   ' Where you and I maun go ! ' "

But gladly does the traitor Judas quit the pit of fire once every year, and journey to the healing snows, to cool himself an hour on his iceberg, reaping reward for his sole act of kindness.

The early and childlike conceptions of the lower races as to the locality of the land of souls have had deep-rooted hold on the mind of mankind, even influencing the formation of civilised opinion. Thus savages at the present day—a study of whose beliefs and fancies affords us the best clue to what our own fore-parents thought—locate their underworld in the far-off unknown, the secluded or inaccessible regions of the earth's surface ; or in Hades, across the waters under the earth ; or westward over the sea, where the sun goes down at evening into a fiery abyss. The Mexicans say he goes to lighten the dead. Or the sun and moon themselves may be conceived of as the abode of departed souls. Some savages even place their paradise in the sky, and sometimes it is reached by the " Path of the Dead," which we call the Milky Way. And all the lower races claim to know of their Heaven by direct revelation. " To them the land of Souls is a discovered country, from whose bourne many a traveller returns."

CHAPTER V

MAGIC

WE have seen how the irrational elements in myths may be traced to the mental condition of savages. Now, the belief in demons, magic, sorcery, and witchcraft, which is a prominent characteristic of the savage condition at the present day, is distinctly traceable to Animism,—the investing of all things with life ; it is a remnant of that universal religion of the primeval races of man.

The medicine-man or sorcerer is believed to have intercourse with and power over supernatural beings. Not only can he exorcise evil spirits, but he can also induce them to enter the body of his enemy, causing

196

sickness and death. He thus has power over the living and over the souls of the dead. Death is supposed to be caused by this hostile conjurer, whose powers are practically unlimited, for he can command even the weather, and, as we have already seen, can himself assume, or cause others to assume, the form of any animal. In Ireland it is still believed by many that certain persons can practise witchcraft. " By a spell they will bring a person into an animal or object such as a table, a chair, a bed-post, or such like, and then, by torturing or injuring the animal or object, do the same to the person they want to injure. Or something belonging to a person may be bewitched." A well-to-do man in Connemara, who had always been accustomed to sleep on a head of straw, bought a bedstead, and the morning after sleeping on it found his calf dead. Of course the bedstead was bewitched, and so he chopped it to bits and burned it.

Limited magical power is sometimes ascribed to the layman. For example, in Matabeleland it was the late king himself who did what little rain-doctoring the climate required, and on one occasion ordered the cessation of revolver practice in the European settlers' camp, lest the sound of the guns should frighten the rain away, when he was engaged in his incantations. Saxo tells how the Permlanders, to hinder the voyaging of the Danes, cast spells upon the sky, stirred up the clouds, and drove them into most furious storms. The Samoan rain-makers have a sacred stone which they wet when they want rain, and dry at the fire if they want dry weather. The Lapland wizards sell winds in a knotted cord, to be let out by untying it knot by knot; as it is written of the women in the Isle of Man, who " selle to shipmen wynde, as it were closed under three knotes of threde, so that the more wynde he wold have, the more knotes he must undo." In the Odyssey, Æolus gave the winds to Ulysses tied up in a bag; and in 1814 an old woman at Stromness, in the Orkneys, sold favourable winds to mariners, as saint or witch has claimed to do from time immemorial. Pomponius Mela describes how the priestesses of Sena roused up the seas and the winds by their incantations. Mist, wind, and rain are often produced in folk-tales by magical means. The notion survives in the slang phrase, " raising the wind." When a ship is becalmed, sailors will sometimes whistle for a wind; but in other weather they hate whistling at sea, which act, by the same symbolic magic, raises a whistling gale. By the power of spells, Swanhwid, the daughter of Hadding, overshadowed herself with a cloud of mist, and shrouded her beautiful face in darkness, just as, in Homer, mist was used to cover and hide persons.

Some insight into the principles of savage sorcery

may best be afforded by the citation of a few practical examples. It must be understood that the
special property of any object is supposed to be
present in all its parts, and to be obtained by
obtaining any of those parts. " The powers of a
conquered antagonist are supposed to be gained by
devouring him : the Dacotah cats the heart of a slain
foe, to increase his own courage ; the New Zealander
swallows his dead enemy's eyes, that he may see the
farther ; the Abipone consumes tiger's flesh, thinking
so to gain the tiger's strength and valour." The
Caribs sprinkle a male infant with his father's blood,
to give him his father's courage. Dead relatives
are consumed in pursuance of an allied belief. In
New Zealand, small pebbles are thrust down the
throat of a newly baptized child, to make its heart
callous and incapable of pity. In 1862 some Chinese
in Yunnan ate the heart of a murdered missionary,
and the heart and brains of a celebrated robber who
had been executed, so as to acquire his valour and
cunning. We learn from Strabo that the early
British were cannibals, and used to eat the bodies
of their deceased parents. One of the most interesting inferences concerning the new race recently
discovered by Professor Petrie is that it was their
custom to eat portions of the bodies of deceased
persons. This fact is proved from observation of the
burials. The head was almost always severed from

the shoulders, and the hands often removed ; bones had the ends broken off, and the marrow scooped out ; these and other such facts pointing undoubtedly to ceremonial cannibalism. Yet this remarkably fine and powerful non-Egyptian race, whose existence in Egypt was hitherto unsuspected, and who lived about 3000 B.C., were not ignorant of civilisation. Their pottery, flint - working, bead - making prove them the equals or superiors of the Egyptians. Their drawing and sculpture were very rude, and no writing was known. But some fine wood-carvings were found, and copper needles show that they sewed garments ; and in pottery they excelled, though the potter's wheel was completely unknown.

On the other hand, among the Dayaks, young men will abstain from the flesh of deer, lest it should make them timid ; but all savages will eagerly devour a portion of the carcase of particular animals, in order to acquire courage, strength, fleetness, ferocity, and so forth.

An illustration of this widespread practice is afforded by a passage in a Northern lay upon the favourite subject of the Wolsungs. " Some gave Gothorm wolf's flesh, some sliced serpents . . . before they could persuade him to lay hands on the gentle hero."

Among the Haidahs of the Pacific States, the

inspired medicine-man " springs on the first person he meets, bites out and swallows one or more mouthfuls of the man's living flesh, wherever he can fix his teeth, then rushes to another and another ; " while, among the neighbouring Nootkas, the medicine-man " is satisfied with what his teeth can tear from the corpses in the burial-places."

The horrible European legends of vampires probably grew out of facts like these concerning primitive cannibals ; for the original vampire was the supposed other-self of a ferocious savage still seeking to satisfy his thirst for human blood. The Polynesians speak of departed souls devouring the hearts and entrails of sleepers. Cannibalism " is also found to have a religious significance, on the supposition which has unsuspected survival among advanced races, that eating the body and drinking the blood communicates the spirit of the victim to the consumer."

The same mode of thought as that illustrated above is displayed in the medical prescriptions of past ages ; while the belief in the efficacy of human blood, and portions of the human body as a cure, is prevalent in China at the present day. And we may recall the very numerous instances in folk-tales of the step-mother demanding the heart or the blood of the hated child's pet animal as a cure for her feigned illness. Grimm cites a story from Bornu, which may be briefly told, as apposite in this connection. It is about two faithful friends, a rich man and a poor man. The rich man feigns illness, and, at his instigation, the aged man, who is called in to see him, says that the poor man's son must be killed, for only the sight of his blood can save the rich man's life. The poor man fetches his child, and ungrudgingly gives him to his friend. But a sheep's blood is sprinkled on the floor, and the rich man pretends to be cured by the sight. The boy is kept in concealment. After a time he is restored to his father, and the rich man reveals that his illness was feigned for the sake of proving his friend. A great many instances might be adduced of the sacrifice of one human being as a cure for disease in another. A life for a life is the theme of Longfellow's " Golden Legend." There is recent mention of an alleged sacrifice of a girl near Poona to cure a disease. A fowl, a sheep, and a girl had to be sacrificed. In the course of time animal sacrifice supplanted human sacrifice. In Persia, when any member of a household is very ill, it is the custom to kill a sheep, in order to avert danger from the sick person. Examples of similar practices are recorded as obtaining in the British Isles, where also animals are sacrificed for animal sickness.

The belief that some particular virtue resides in every part of an object or of a person explains the dislike universally shown by savages to having their portraits taken. For they hold that some part of the life must be drawn into the representation of the living thing, and that the possession of a portrait gives fatal power over the person represented. With the portrait a portion of the man's self is carried away, and may fall into the hands of some enemy, who may injure him by conjuring with it. Many believe that it contains the soul of the person portrayed, and refuse to let themselves be drawn or photographed, fearing that as a consequence they would die. This has been the experience of travellers all over the world ; not only amongst the uncivilised. The savage displays the same caution with regard to the cutting of his hair, the parings of his nails, his saliva—anything, in short, that has been a part of himself—to prevent them getting into hostile hands. In Italy, at this day, a man does not like to trust a lock of his hair in any one's hands, lest he be bewitched by its means.

Furthermore, the savage confuses names and things, thinking of the name as an actual part of the person or thing bearing it ; wherefore a knowledge of the name gives power over the person, and puts him in danger of being bewitched. Some people would never dream of revealing the name of a child before its baptism, this ceremony being a safeguard ; for if a witch can get hold of the name, that is all that she wants to cast a spell over the child. From all parts of the world we get instances of this desire to keep a name secret. Sometimes the name of a reigning chief is most rigidly taboo'd, even to the extent of omitting from the language any common word that may resemble that name in sound. Curious freaks are played with a language by this ever-recurring necessity. " No Korean dare utter his king's name. When the king dies he is given a name (a kind of name, an apology for a name) by which his august personality may be distinguished amid the dense masses of history." But his real name, the name he bears in life, is never spoken save by the privileged lips of his favourite wife in the secrecy of the palace harem. The reader may recall, in this connection, the Jews' unwillingness to pronounce the name of Jehovah ; also an occasion when Moses had to content him with the evasion, " I am that I am." It is related that Solomon made heaven and earth to quake by beginning to utter the incommunicable name. Similarly, Herodotus uses great reserve in reference to the name of Osiris. The name of Brahma is a sacred thing in India, and only to be uttered on solemn occasions ; while in China it is a statutable offence to pronounce the real name of Confucius. Such sayings as " Talk of the devil and you will see his horns " must once have borne a serious meaning. Especially notice-

able is the widely prevalent repugnance to name
the dead ; savages will have recourse to any amount
of circumlocution to avoid uttering the dread name,
lest the shade should feel offended. On no account
will a Chinaman tell you the real name of his deceased father. Sometimes a rich Chinese has discovered that his proper name has been the same
as that of one of his ancestors, and has paid a large
sum to government for permission to take a new
name. This superstition prevails amongst distant
and various races all the world over, but nowhere
more notably than in Shetland, " where it is all but
impossible to get a widow, at any distance of time,
to mention the name of her dead husband, though
she will talk about him by the hour."

The ancient Egyptians believed that the name of
a man existed in heaven. " The whole man con-
sisted of a natural body, a spiritual body, a heart,
a double, a soul, a shadow, an intangible ethereal
casing or spirit, a form and a name. All these
were, however, bound together inseparably, and the
welfare of any single one of them concerned the
welfare of all."

We find the same secrecy attaching to names
in Northern saga. Sigfred, in the old play of the
Wolsungs, hides his name from the dragon Fafni,
calling himself " Noble deer." Woden himself
never gives his real name. The dislike to mention-

ing the name of supernatural powers is also very general, and originates from a similar fear of the consequences. The Dayak will not speak of the smallpox by name, but will call it " the chief," or " jungle leaves " ; the Laplander speaks of the bear as " the old man with the fur coat " ; in Annam the tiger is called " grandfather " or " lord," in Bengal " maternal uncle " ; in Siberia also he is not mentioned by name ; the Finns call the bear " beautiful honey-claw." In Canton the name of the porpoise is taboo'd. It is colloquially known as " the black and white terror." The words death and coffin are amongst those rigidly taboo'd in China. Undertakers advertise " boards of old age " and " clothes of old age," death and burial being always spoken of euphemistically if possible. The Jews, being forbidden swine's flesh, avoid the word pig altogether, and call it " the other thing." Similarly, the Furies were styled by the Greeks " Eumenides," or gracious ones ; just as the Irish call fairies Sleagh Maith, or " Good People." Orestes, in the play of Euripides, speaks of seeing three virgins like the night, and Menelaus knows that he is referring to the Furies, but is himself unwilling to name them ; and Electra, speaking of her brother's madness, says she dreads to mention those goddesses, the Eumenides, who persecute him with terror.

Numerous prohibitions exist among savages in different parts of the world with regard to the use of names. A man may not utter his own name ; husband and wife will not utter one another's name ; the son or daughter-in-law will not mention the name of the father or mother-in-law, and *vice versâ.* In a Kaffir folk-tale, the heroine, conforming to Kaffir custom, refers to her husband's relatives as the " people whose names are unmentionable." Among the Algonkin tribes the real names of children which are bestowed upon them by the old woman of the family are kept mysteriously secret, and are hardly ever revealed, even at death, the totem or clan-mark being used on the grave ; they are known by a mere nickname, such as " Little Fox " or " Red Head." If a Lapp child falls ill its name is changed. The same is done in Borneo, so as to deceive the evil spirit that plagues it with disease. Finnish wizards consider it of prime importance to know the birth or origin of a disease, so that they have power over it. Many of their charms begin, " I know thy birth." Then the names of the father and mother are pronounced, and the name of the disease. It is easy to multiply instances of this belief in the name giving power over the person or thing bearing it. We may recall the lines in which the poet shows the motive prompting Asia to inquire of Demogorgon " who made terror, madness, crime, remorse . . . and hell, or the sharp fear of hell ? "

> " Utter his name : a world pining in pain
> Asks but his name : curses shall drag him down."

To know the name of a god or spirit constitutes power of evoking him.

In Egyptian myth, Isis, the wife of Osiris and mother of Horus, " the great goddess "—as she is commonly described—" the divine mother, the mistress of charms or enchantments," meditated how she might make herself mistress of the earth, and plotted to get possession of the sacred name of Rā, which she knew was one to conjure by. So Isis kneaded his spittle with earth and formed a serpent, which she set in the path of Rā to bite him. Then in his anguish he was at length induced to give up his name to Isis, as the price of being delivered from the pain of the snake's venom. This story illustrates the mortality of the gods.

To name an evil spirit brings his power to naught. Once there was a troll whose name was Wind-and-Weather, and King Olaf of Norway hired him to build a church the like of which was nowhere to be seen. The building was to be completed within a certain specified time, and the wages agreed upon were the sun and moon, or St. Olaf himself. Ere long the marvellous structure was completed, all but the roof and spire. In great consternation Olaf wandered over hill and dale; suddenly, inside a mountain, he heard a child cry, and a giant woman hush it with these words : " Hush, hush ! to-morrow comes thy father Wind-and-Weather home, bringing both sun and moon, or saintly Olaf's self." So the saint ran back to the church and bawled out : " Hold on, Wind-and-Weather ; you've set the spire askew ! " Then the giant, with a fearful crash, fell off the roof and burst into a thousand pieces, which were nothing but flint stones.

This primitive philosophy may be traced, too, in a type of *märchen* which is very widely spread, and the *dénouement* of which hinges on the discovery of the name of some being of superhuman powers. It is known as the Rumpelstiltskin type, from the name of the German version, which may be briefly related.

A poor miller boasts to the king of having a daughter who can spin straw into gold. The king sends for her, and giving her a spinning-wheel and reel, locks her in a room in the palace, quite full of straw, telling her that if it is not all spun into gold during the night, she must die. The miller's daughter, quite unable to set about the task, is hopelessly miserable, and begins to weep. Suddenly the door opens and in comes a little man, who inquires the cause of her trouble. " What will you give me," says the manikin, "if I do the spinning for you?" "My necklace," says she. And he takes the necklace, seats himself at the wheel, and whirrs away till all the straw is spun and all the reels are full of gold. The king next morning is delighted, and he craves more gold. So he takes the miller's daughter into a much larger room, full of straw which must be converted to gold before morning. Again she falls a-weeping. In comes the little man. "What will you give me?" asks he. "The ring on my finger," answers the girl. He takes the ring and performs the task. Then the greedy king takes her to a still larger room, and promises to marry her if she spins all the straw therein into gold. This time the girl has nothing left to give the manikin, and so is led to promise her first child if she should become queen. And the king, finding the task accomplished, marries the miller's pretty daughter. A year after she has a beautiful child. Suddenly the manikin enters the room and claims it. The horror-stricken queen offers all the riches of the kingdom if he will but leave her child. No; he prefers to have the child. But he will give her three days' grace, and if during that time she can find out his name she may keep her child. All night the queen is recalling all the names she has ever heard, and a messenger is posting far and wide to learn some other names. When the manikin appears next day, she repeats all the names she knows, but not the right one ; and on the second day she has no better success. On the third day the messenger comes back and says, " I have not heard a single new name ; but as I came to where the fox and hare bid each other good-night, I saw a little house, and a fire burned before it, and round about the fire a ridiculous little man was jumping : he hopped on one leg, and shouted—

> ' To-day I bake, to-morrow brew,
>   The next I'll have the young queen's child.
> Ha ! glad am I that no one knew
>   That Rumpelstiltskin I am styled.' "

How the queen rejoiced ! " Now, Mistress Queen, what is my name ? " said the little man, appearing as usual. At first she suggests Conrad ; " No." " Harry ? " " No." Then, " Perhaps your name is Rumpelstiltskin ? " " The devil has told you," shrieked the little man, and in his anger he plunged his right foot so deep into the earth that in his effort to wrench it out he tore himself in two.

In Ruthenia it is believed that a wizard, if he only knows a man's baptismal name, can transform him by a mere effort of will ; therefore a man should conceal his real name and answer to a fictitious one.

The name-taboo enters into the story (which

has many variants) of the man who marries a fairy or supernatural being, but must never know his wife's name, or she will be forced to leave him. This calls to mind, on the other hand, the Teutonic legend of Lohengrin, the Swan Knight, who forsook his bride because she asked the forbidden questions, and insisted on knowing the name of her champion, and whence he came to her succour. In other tales it is through the accidental discovery of her name that a supernatural being gets into the power of her human lover and is constrained to marry him.

When, in stress of battle, the chivalrous hero of the Middle Ages looked upon his love, thought of her, or named her name, he increased thereby his strength, and was sure of the victory.

> " Above the din her voice is in my ears,
> I see her form glide through the crossing spears.
> Iseult ! "

Similarly, the Roman gambler would invoke a god or his mistress before throwing his huckle-bone dice ; and the Greek, using the kottabos in divination, spoke or thought his mistress's name ere he essayed to toss the wine, without spilling any, out of the cup into the metal basin. So much for " what's in a name."

Beliefs such as those that have been illustrated

furnish the whole equipment of the sorcerer, the "dealer in magic and spells," and explain his systematic practice. His method of procedure is to obtain a part of his victim's body, or a representation of his body, and to do thereto something which he thinks is thereby done to his victim. No wonder, therefore, that the savage is in mortal dread lest his hair, nails, or anything that is his, should fall into the hands of a sorcerer ; and as to giving himself away in the counterfeit presentment of a photograph, it would be literally giving up the ghost.

Not only can the sorcerer create disease by the means described, but he can transfer it from a patient to an enemy by making an image of the latter and practising upon it in a harmful way. For all savages believe in a real connection between an object and its image. Or the evil spirit of a disease may be transferred to an image, which is then destroyed, and so the patient is cured ; as Pliny informs us that a stomach-ache may be transmitted to a puppy or a duck, which will probably die of it. By the same process of reasoning, warts are charmed away at the present day, and the well-worshippers think to rid themselves of their ailments (see p. 12). In the Orkneys, the water in which a sick person has been washed is thrown down at a gateway, that the malady may leave the patient and be transferred to the first passer-by. In the Highlands, a cat is washed in the water and then set free. A Scotch cure for epilepsy is to bury a cock below the patient's bed. This sacrifice reminds one of the dying utterance of Socrates ; for the cock was dedicated to Æsculapius.

Devils are conjured into puppets in Buddhist Thibet and in West Africa, or into a live fowl ; as, in Gadara, they were conjured into swine. According to the usual savage theory, every disease is due to the direct attack of that particular disease-spirit, every disease being thus personified. There is a peculiar custom among the aboriginal tribes of Ranchi in Bengal, known as the Era Sendra, or women's hunt, in which only the women take part. The frenzied performance of these Amazons is supposed to expel the cholera-demon from their villages. Various practices are resorted to by the lower races to keep the disease-demons at bay.

In Ruthenia, cholera is personified as an old woman with a hideous face disfigured by suffering. The modern Greeks personify smallpox in the guise of a supernatural female being, and the Servians call her " goddess." The ancient Greeks knew of a spectral creature called Alphitô (ἀλφιτώ, " a spectre, or bugbear, with which nurses frighten children "—Liddell and Scott). The kindred word Alphos also meant a skin disease.

It is needless to quote familiar passages in the

New Testament which prove the prevalence at that day of the belief that diseases were cured by demoniacal possession. For ages after the doctrine has prevailed. In Elizabethan England, when devil-hunting was common, the priests were the exorcists, and all sorts of prodigies of conjuring were vouched for by the devout eye-witnesses of these exhibitions of the power of the priesthood of Satan. The process of exorcism was a terrible ordeal to the patient. Balls of hair, pieces of iron, knives, nails, lumps of lead, and such like things were brought up by the devil from the mouth of a possessed person by command of the exorcist. The devils expelled from one woman had such names as the following :— Frateretto, Fliberdigibet, Hoberdicat, Cocabatto, Hobberdidance, Lusty Dick, Kellico, Hob, Corner-cap, Puff, Purr, Bonjour, Pourdieu, Motubizanto, and several others. A German woman, distracted with toothache, wished the devil might enter into her teeth, and was possessed by six demons accordingly, who gave their several names. In the year 1788, seven devils, which had thrown a man into fits, were solemnly exorcised by seven clergymen at the Temple Church at Bristol. The ceremony of casting out devils is retained to this day in the rituals of the Greek and Roman churches. The wizards who at this day in the North of Ireland extract elf-bolts (stone arrowheads) from the bodies of bewitched cattle, are, like the Elizabethan exorcist, consistent representatives of their forefathers in primitive antiquity. Compare their practices with savage quackery. The priest among the Dayaks of Borneo pretends to extract stones, splinters, rags, &c., which he declares are spirits, from the afflicted part of his patient. The Fingo witch in South Africa sucks Indian corn, the alleged cause of the pain, from the sufferer's side. The native Australian sorcerer extracts from his own body, by means of passes, a magical essence, and makes it enter his victim's body in the form of a bit of quartz, which causes pain and consumes the flesh. Here, again, is a case for the " sucking cure," of which further examples from many distant regions might easily be cited.

The sorcerer can do this, and more also ; the diseases he can cure he can also inflict, and greatly is his power feared. Even the burning of rubbish that had belonged to any one, such as the refuse of the food that he had eaten, would cause his death. A savage will run his spear into the footprints of an enemy, or put broken glass or poison in them, thinking to lame him thereby. Saxo gives us an instance of this sort of conjuring. The dauntless champion Froger, who was king of a Northern island, and the reputed son of Odin himself, had received from the immortal gods the boon that no man should conquer him, save he who at the time of the conflict could catch up in his hand the dust lying beneath Froger's feet. Frode the Doughty challenged him to a duel, caught up some dust from his footprint, and straightway slew him, gaining by craft what mortal strength could never have effected. On Tuesdays and Fridays Italian witches gather earth from people's footprints, and with this can do great harm.

Briefly, then, the principle of sorcery is, that like affects like. You injure a man by injuring an image of him. A stone roughly resembling any part of the human body will cure a disease of that part. Amongst the civilised it was once supposed that the external character of plants and minerals was an indication of the diseases for which they were remedies. Thus yellow flowers would be given for disorders of the liver, and red for those of the blood ; and the bloodstone was supposed to be hæmostatic. This old medical theory, known as the " Doctrine of Signatures," was nothing more than an elaboration of the savage's notion of sympathetic magic, the principle of like curing like, an instance of which, from Matabeleland, was reported in the *Times* of October 14th, 1893 : " A native, bitten by a white man's watch-dog, claimed compensation for the injury. It was refused, on the ground that the man was trespassing. ' But at least,' said the would-be thief, ' give me a hair of the dog that bit me, to put in my wound, and all will be well.' " In the Edda we read, " Dog's hair heals dog's bite." The same notion obtains in China, where a Hakka woman begged a missionary for a hair from the tail of the dog that had slightly bitten her child.

The custom of making a wax figure of one's enemy, and sticking pins into it, or melting it in the fire, so that the hated person might waste as his image wasted, was common in Europe in the Middle Ages, and still flourishes in India and elsewhere.

> " Why did you melt your waxen man,
>   Sister Helen?
>   To-day is the third since you began."

The answer to this every savage knows.

In Egypt, in the period of the later dynasties, a service was performed daily in the temple of Amen-Ra at Thebes, to deliver the Sun-god from the assault of the great serpent Apef or Apep, and on each occasion it was accompanied by a ceremony in which a waxen figure of Apep was burnt in the fire ; as the wax melted, so the power of Apep was destroyed.

Simætha, in the idyl of Theocritus, plies her magic arts to draw home to her the man she loves. " Delphis troubled me, and I against Delphis am burning this laurel . . . even thus may the flesh of Delphis waste in the burning. . . . Even as I melt

this wax, so speedily may he by love be molten."
By similar magic arts did the enchantress (in the
Bucolics of Virgil) endeavour to draw Daphnis from
the city home. " As this clay hardens, and as this
wax melts, in one and the self-same fire, even so let
Daphnis melt with love for me, to others' love be
hard . . . I, to kindle Daphnis, burn this bay."
The Zulu chews a piece of wood in order to soften
the heart of the woman he wants to wed, or of
the man whose oxen he wants to purchase. The
Devonshire peasant hangs in his chimney a pig's
heart stuck full of thorns, that the heart of his
enemy may be pierced in like manner. Negroes
and savages everywhere practise similar magic to
this. Peruvian sorcerers make rag-dolls, and stick
cactus-thorns into them, in order to cripple people.
In Borneo they make a waxen figure of the enemy
to be bewitched, and gradually melt it ; as Margery
Jordane did with the waxen image of Henry VI.,
Jane Shore with that of the Duke of Gloucester, and
the Countess of Soissons with that of Louis XIV.
Royalty has been much subjected to this ill-treatment. One Agnes Sampson confessed to having
tried to compass the death of King James VI. of
Scotland by hanging up a black toad for nine days
and collecting the juice that fell from it. If she had
been able to obtain a piece of linen that the king
had worn, she could have killed him with this

venom, causing him to suffer as though " lying upon sharpe thornes or endis of needles." Furthermore, it is recorded of Queen Caroline, the unloved and unloving wife of George IV., that " Her Royal Highness made a wax figure as usual, and gave it an amiable pair of large horns ; then took three pins out of her garment, and stuck them through and through, and put the figure to roast and melt at the fire." " What a silly piece of spite," adds the recorder. " The devil teacheth," remarks King James in his " Dæmonology " (Bk. II., ch. v.), " how to make pictures of wax or clay, that by roasting thereof, the persons that they bear the names of may be continually melted or dried away by continual sickness." The death, in the reign of Elizabeth, of Ferdinand, Earl of Derby, was popularly attributed to witchcraft, suspicion being reduced to certainty when " a waxen image with hair like that of the unfortunate earl was found in his chamber ! " The Hindus knead earth with clippings of hair and nails into little figures, and write the name of the enemy upon them, and, after pronouncing magical words, pierce them through. Such a figure, roughly representing a body with head and limbs, made of clay, by a woman in Islay, where belief in its power survives, was recently exhibited before the Folk-lore Society. It is called a Corp Chre. A long incantation is used whilst the operator sticks pins into it. In

Ceylon the sorcerer requires a small waxen or wooden image, or a drawing of the person to be injured by his arts, together with a few hairs from the victim's head, some clippings of his nails, and a fragment of his clothing. Beliefs such as these have been carried very far.

" On All Souls' Eve an old woman went to pray in the now ruined church of St. Martin, at Bonn. Priests were performing the service, and there was a large congregation, but by-and-by the old woman became convinced that she was the only living mortal in the church. She wished to get away, but she could not ; just as Mass was ending, however, her deceased husband whispered to her that now was the time to fly for her life. She ran to the door, but she stopped for one moment at the spot in the aisle where two of her children were buried, just to say, ' Peace be unto them.' The door swung open and closed after her : a bit of her cloak was shut in, so that she had to leave it behind. Soon after she sickened and died ; the neighbours said it must be because a piece of her clothes had remained in the possession of the dead." The Karens of Burmah model an image of a person from the earth of his footprints for malicious purposes ; this is like the ancient practice in Germany of cutting out the turf whereon the person to be destroyed has stood, and hanging it in the chimney, that he may perish as his foot-print dries and shrivels. Horace speaks of the evil wrought by the charms of the Samnites and the enchantments of the Marsi. Hanging and burning in effigy are modified survivals of primitive sorcery. And the hypnotist of the present day, who thinks that a pin scratch on the photo-negative of a hypnotised subject causes pain to, and produces a similar mark upon, the body of the subject, is not in a position to deride the philosophy of the savage, or to despise the practice of the sorcerer.

We see much the same process of thought at work, at the beginning of the present century, in the mind of the New Hampshire woman who so carefully preserved a square inch of her boy's skin which sloughed off from the effects of a burn. When he left his home in after years, his mother would frequently examine this piece of skin, that she might inform herself thereby of his well-being; for she fully expected that the skin would decay in the event of his death. This is a modern instance of the "life-token" (see p. 79), which is met with so frequently in the *märchen* of all lands. In an Argyllshire story, three trees spring up at the birth of the fisherman's three sons, and serve in after years as their life-tokens; for if evil befalls either of the boys, his tree is seen to wither. In a

Breton story, the life-token is a laurel into whose trunk a knife is to be struck daily by the twin-brother left at home. If blood flows, the absent brother is dead. Or again, in the Egyptian story of " The Two Brothers," the jug of beer in Anapu's hand will froth if Bata should die. At this day one may hear it said by our American brethren that if friends, on one's leaving home, stick a piece of live-for-ever in the ground, it will indicate the fortune of the absent one. If he prospers, it flourishes ; if not, it will wither or die. The Magyars say that garnets only show their beautiful red colour while the person wearing them is in health ; for if the wearer ails, the stones turn pale. In British Guiana, when young children are betrothed, trees are planted by the respective parties, in witness of the contract ; and if either tree should happen to wither, the child it belongs to is sure to die. All these cases are on a par with the sympathetic magic of the savage.

A few words must be said upon another feature of sorcery—namely, that based on belief in the power of songs of incantation. This also is illustrated in an interesting manner in numerous *märchen*, where the repetition of some formula, usually rhymed, produces magic effect. The Romans thought that incantations could draw down the moon ; just as all savages believe that they can make the weather. " In Scotland, in the seventeenth century, a tempest was raised by dipping a rag in water, and then beating it on a stone thrice in the name of Satan.

> ' I knok this rag upone this stane,
> To raise the wind in the divellis name,
> It sall not lye till I please again.'

Drying the rag, along with another conjuration, appeased the storm."

> " Rain, rain, go away,
> Come again another day,"

say our children.

When a drought threatens to injure the crops in Croatia, a young girl, generally a gipsy, dresses herself entirely in flowers and grasses, and is then conducted through the village by her companions who sing to the skies for mercy. So also in Greece there are many songs and ceremonies in connection with a desire for rain.

In the Odyssey a " song of healing " was sung over the wounded Odysseus ; and we read of a similar song in the Finnish epic ; while the Indians chant texts from the Veda (one of their sacred books) over the sick. In the Norse saga of Eric the Red, the witch has the song of the warlocks chanted, so as to secure the attendance of " many powerful spirits." Woden hung nine whole nights on the gallows-tree, whose roots no man knoweth, to learn the nine songs of might by means of which spells he brought the magic drink out of Hell. In Brian's saga, the Walkyries weave a Web of War, chanting first a song which foretells Brian's death, then a charm—a song " such as seeresses know how to sing "—which shall save the young king's life.

In Kaffir and Bushman tales, incantations open rocks, like the magic words " Open Sesame " of the " Arabian Nights." Ali Baba's cave has its mythic representative in the cave of Kwang-siu-f'oo in Kiang-si (China). It was accidentally discovered by one Chang, a poor herdsman, who one day overheard some one using the words : " Stone door, open ; Mr. Kwei Ku is coming ; " whereupon the cave opened and the speaker entered. Of course Chang made a point of remembering the magic words for purposes of his own, and it was entirely through an accident that he shut his poor grandmother inside the cave. For, first of all, he explored it alone ; it did not contain treasure, but was a most romantic and extensive grotto. When he told his grandmother, with whom he lived, of this wonderful place, of course the old lady wanted to see it ; so he took her in. Wandering about and admiring the scenery, Chang lost sight of her, and thought she must have left ; so he passed out

225   P

of the door, and ordered it to shut. To his dismay, his grandmother had not returned home. He rushed back to the cave, spake the magic words, but alas! the talisman failed. Just then the genius of the cave appeared on the scene, and Chang made a clean breast of the affair, imploring for his grandmother's release. This, however, could not be. Her disappearance was a matter of fate, the genius said, for the cave demanded a victim. Chang felt that he was not entirely responsible for his grandmother's death, and it was some compensation to know that, in consequence of the particular manner of it, her descendants would ever possess power over demons.

One of the most widespread superstitions of the human race is the belief in the power of the *Evil Eye*. Things may be acted upon magically without any bodily contact. The mere look of an elf can bewitch; so the sick in Ireland are said to be "fairy-struck." The bleared, envious, evil eye of a witch can bewitch a child, dry up the mother's milk, rot an apple, make the cattle sick, or spoil a dress; she can kill snakes with a glance, scare wolves, hatch ostrich eggs, breed leprosy, or spoil a field's crop. This baleful look is what the Germans called *entsehen*; the Italians, *gettare gli squardi*, or the *jettatura*. Hone, in his " Day Book," speaks of " the blink o' an ill e'e." The shepherd Menalcas,

in Virgil's third Eclogue, sings, " Some evil eye be-
witches my tender lambs."

Within this century, a Yorkshire man was accused
of killing a pear-tree by throwing his glances upon
it ; and newspaper cases afford evidence of old
women being accused of " over-looking," and mal-
treated accordingly. Offenbach the composer, who
was of Jewish extraction, was believed by Christians
to have this horrid power, and was often avoided
because of the *jettatura*. Italians believe that various evils result from coming under a glance of a
jettatore, or a person possessed of an evil eye,
and counter-spells of course abound. Within the
present generation, one of the Italian royal family
was said to have the evil eye. At Court, when
the aristocracy came into the presence, they very
carefully protected themselves by holding their hands
behind their backs, with the thumb and middle
finger closed, and the fore and little fingers extended ; for this is one way of protecting oneself
from the evil influence. To do so openly would of
course be insulting. The wearing of coral keeps
one safe from the effects of the *jettatura ;* hence
the little coral charm, shaped like a hand in the
position described, so often seen in Italy. For
the same purpose, corals are worn by children in
Nicaragua, with the addition of an alligator's tooth,
also considered efficacious. It is the common belief

of all the inhabitants of Nicaragua, Indians and Spaniards, unlettered and educated alike, that after a person has been exposed in the sun and agitated, the heat of his body finds vent from his eye, with fatal effect upon young children and infants who may be exposed to its influence. The *ojo caliente*, or " heated eye," as it is called, is so much feared, that children are always sent away, or covered with a cloth, when any person supposed to have it approaches. The deaths of many children are attributed to it. In Africa, Cameron found a mother who carried a baby slung in a goat-skin on her back, wearing an apron made of innumerable thongs of hide, with a charm dangling from each, to preserve the infant from the evil eye and other forms of witchcraft. In Mangalore, one sometimes sees children with an ornament made of two tiger's claws, joined together by silver or gold, suspended round the neck, as a charm against the evil eye ; and farmers, to protect their fields, erect through the middle of them a line of half-burnt bamboos about six feet high. In India, children are supposed to be specially liable to it, and it is a good thing to keep a piece of iron or some cat-gut in a child's bed. A blue string is tied round a colt's neck, and cat-gut round a buffalo's leg, by way of protection. In the north-east of Scotland, a small brooch in the shape of a heart is

worn to turn off the evil eye, and preserve from
the power of fairies. A Turkish nurse objects,
just as a Sutherlandshire woman does, to your
looking at the baby. For Roumanians think that
if you stare at the baby you spoil it with your
eye. To counteract this, the child must be spat
upon. In fact, you must never say that a baby
is pretty, or that any one looks well, without
spitting on the ground. And a notion very similar
to this obtains in Ireland, and is seen in an
English woman's account of what happened to
herself a few decades ago in Limerick. She was
walking to church with her little girls, who were
nicely dressed in new frocks and hats, when a
respectable-looking woman, meeting them, admired
and praised the children, then suddenly spat on
their new hats. It was afterwards explained that
the woman acted thus out of kindness of heart;
for, aware that she possessed the evil eye, she
had spat on the children to prevent their falling
sick. Further space cannot here be given to illustrations of the world-wide belief in the virtue of
saliva as a charm against evil. It must suffice
to recall the Romans' use of it in lustrating an
infant when it receives its name, to say that the
Mandingoes on that occasion spit thrice in the
child's face, and that money is often spat upon
for luck by all sorts and conditions of men. On

two occasions Jesus Christ made use of saliva in the cure of the blind.

In the county of Donegal, a person supposed to have an evil eye is called Suil Bhallor, or Ballor's eye, because of a legend of Ballor, a kind of Cyclops, who had one eye in the middle of his forehead and one in the middle of the back of his skull. A glance from the latter would strike a person dead. He was called Ballor of the Mighty Blows and of the Evil Eye. Crinnawn, his son, is a formidable one-eyed character in an Irish-Gaelic folk-tale, who boasts of being able to kill with the sight of his eye, if he chooses.

Sticking an awl into the footprints of one who has the evil eye is one of the countless ways of averting bad influences. Enough has been said to show that belief in this particular form of witchcraft is practically universal ; for the dread of the evil eye still survives, even in civilised countries. An ancient reference to the idea may perhaps be seen in Matthew xx. 15 : " Is thine eye evil, because I am good ? "

The changing of an infant is sometimes supposed to be effected by the power of the evil eye. It was at one time a common belief that fairies and other imaginary beings carry off young children from their cradles, leaving in their stead a starveling imp of their own, or an animated stump of wood. Chil-

dren so left were called changelings, and were
marked by their peevishness, and their backward-
ness in learning to walk and speak. The superstition is alluded to by Shakespeare, Spenser, and
other poets, and is an essential part of the doctrine
of fairy-lore almost everywhere. Fairies have no
power to change a child that has been christened,
but it must be most carefully watched until that
ceremony has been performed. In Belgium only
people with a " nice face " are allowed to see it,
special precautions being taken against old women
and cats, who may be emissaries of Satan. A little
heart in red or blue silk is hung round the baby's
neck to protect it from sorcery till baptized. An
open Bible near the child is a safeguard in Scotland ;
a single leaf out of it suffices in Germany ; holy
water in Ireland ; a rosary, which a priest has blessed,
in Picardy. To keep a fire burning or a lamp in
the chamber was a means which the Romans practised of preserving the babe against evil spirits.
Iron or steel, in any shape, placed in the cradle,
was equally efficacious. The potency of iron has
already been discussed. The fear of changelings
exists also in China. The Greeks believe that
witches suck the blood of new-born babes ; the
Nereids also lose no opportunity of exchanging one
of their own fractious offspring for a mortal babe.
There are numerous stories about these fairy rob-

beries of children. Martin Luther, besides describing the general behaviour of changelings, gives an account of one which he saw with his own eyes at Dessau. Prescriptions for getting rid of the changeling agree in the most striking manner, the common resort being to make the changeling betray itself. The best way is to brew ale, boil water, or cook food in an egg-shell, in sight of the cradled child. This is certain to make a changeling " sit up " and express wonder as seeing such a laughable sight for the first time in all its born days. Thus the changeling betrays its age, which usually runs into three figures at least ; and when a changeling laughs all is up with it. Hosts of elves, hearing it, bring the right child back, and carry the changeling away.

That there still exists in Ireland a firm belief in fairies and all their works has been lately proved by the deplorable case of Bridget Cleary, who was burnt to death at Clonmel for a changeling. According to the evidence at the trial, this poor young woman had been ill, and her husband consulted the fairy-doctor, who declared that the real Bridget had been stolen away by the fairies, and a changeling left in her place ; that bodily torture would cause this creature to vanish up the chimney, and then the real Bridget would return, riding on a grey horse. Accordingly the tortures were applied.

A red-hot poker was used to force the woman to swallow a horrible decoction made by the herb-doctor, and she was then held over the fire by a number of relatives, the husband firmly believing—or so he alleged in his defence—that this was not his wife, and that he was using the only means to get her back.

CHAPTER VI

MYTHS, FOLK-TALES, ETC.

Origin of myth—Myths of Observation—The Dragon's pedigree—
Famous Dragon-slayers—Nature myths—Greek and savage myths
compared—Creation myths—Myths explaining physical peculiarities in man and animals, and natural phenomena generally—
Beast-fables: their first home—Animal foster-parents—Grateful
beasts—The language of beasts and birds—Some "irrational"
ideas in European and savage *märchen*—The one-eyed cannibal
giant—The common property of all story-tellers—Stories with
a purpose—A distinction between *märchen*, sagas, legends, and
myths—Classification of folk-tales—Drolls—Cumulative stories—
Folk-songs: their antiquity—Popular ballads—Rhymes—Traditional games—Folk-drama—Nursery-rhymes and riddles—Proverbs—The problem of Diffusion—The William Tell legend.

THE foregoing chapters, in attempting a rapid
survey of the beliefs and customs of savage man,
have afforded some insight into the mental condition of our own fore-parents at a period to which
modern history is but a thing of yesterday. The
human intellect, in the earlier stages of the history
of every people, has employed itself in speculations
giving rise to myths, many of which have been
preserved for countless ages. These myths are as
instructive in their way as all the scriptures that
are written for our learning, for they are "an
attempt to find concrete expressions for those ideas

234

and impressions about the relations between man and the physical world that lie at the basis of religion." The serious beliefs of our fore-parents form the staple of our old wives' tales, and linger on in nursery-lore. Time is a great preserver, but no reverencer, as we see when the " hoc est corpus " of the priest elevating the host gets corrupted into the " hocus pocus " of the *prestidigitateur.*

Some myths, which have been classed as Myths of Observation, are the result of roughly putting two and two together ; for instance, " as when a savage builds, upon the discovery of great bones buried in the earth, a story of a combat of the giants and monsters whose remains they are." Siberian tribes, who are constantly unearthing huge bones of extinct animals, think earthquakes are due to the burrowings of mammoths ; scarcely less wild a theory than that contested, in the fourth century B.C., by Pytheas—namely, that the earth was an enormous whale, whose breathings and spoutings caused the tides. Even Kepler, the great astronomer, believed that the world was actually alive, as the Caribs also believe ; for they say, when there is an earthquake, it is their Mother Earth dancing. All countries have their myths in answer to the question, " Why does the earth quake ? " The Greeks said it was the movement of imprisoned cyclops or titans ; while the Norse explain that earthquakes are caused by the agonised struggles of Loki, bound on the sharp stones, and writhing when the snake's venom drops on his face ; for thus was he punished by the gods. Or the dragon Fâfnir shakes the earth as he journeys to the water. To the Indians the earth quakes every time one of the eight elephants supporting the globe is tired of his burden and gives his head a shake. The Japanese say, when the phenomenon occurs, " Another whale has crept away from under our country." In many other countries where earthquakes are felt, the myth of the Earth-bearer is current, the office of supporting the earth being given to various creatures, human or animal. In Polynesia it is Maui who upholds the earth on his prostrate body ; and when he tries to ease his posture, thereby causing the earth to quake, the people shout and beat the ground, to make him lie still. In Celebes it is thought that the world-supporting Hog rubs himself against a tree ; and the Indians of North America say, when the earth quakes, that the world-bearing Tortoise moves. Myths like these are too numerous to cite.

The fossil footprints of birds and beasts of huge size, such as are found in many parts of the world, may have suggested an analogous, though fanciful explanation of all cavities and depressions in rock surfaces ; and so we have the innumerable myths of footprints stamped into rocks by gods or mighty men. The sacred footprint of Ceylon at the top of Adam's Peak is a cavity in the rock, measuring five feet in length and two and a half feet across. Brahmans, Buddhists, and Moslems still climb the mountain to do reverence to it. To the Brahman, it is the footstep of Siva ; to the Buddhist, of Gautama Buddha ; to the Moslem, it is the spot where Adam stood when he was driven from Paradise ; while Christians put in a claim for St. Thomas, or for the Eunuch of Candace, Queen of Ethiopia. And St. Thomas left the impression of his foot in America as well. In Samoa, two hollow places nearly six feet long in a rock are shown as the spot where Tiitii stood when he pushed the heavens up from the earth.

Thus some kernel of truth may be hidden in many a myth, and some are doubtless based on historical tradition. The discoveries of geologists show that the terrifying monsters, the dragons of popular imagination, were not wholly fabulous creations ; their pedigree may be traced to traditional accounts of huge creatures which actually existed in prehistoric times. Typhæus, the monster captured by Zeus, the Python slain by Apollo, Echidna slain by Argos, the Egyptian Apophis, Vitra the serpent of Hindu mythology, the Zoroastrian Ahi, the Prasee Zohak, and, to pass to

Scandinavian myth, the great Midgard serpent, whom Thor will slay at the end of the world— all these may be traced back to gigantic Saurians, such as the Ichthyosaurus, the Plesiosaurus, the Atlantosaurus, those ancient inhabitants of the globe. The dragons of Chinese and Japanese illustration have doubtless as hoary a pedigree. Legends of sea monsters are very numerous and ancient; they are described on Chaldean tablets giving accounts of the Creation; they are repro-duced as " the great whale " in Genesis, and in the huge Leviathan, the swift serpent of Biblical notoriety, who is not to be drawn out with a fish-hook, the typical opponent of Jehovah. There may be a substantial foundation in fact for every such legend as that of Bel and the Dragon, Michael the Archangel and Satan, St. George and the Dragon, the Egyptian Horus and the Croco-dile, and of the combats with the several monsters already named. These are the prototypes of all the dragons of popular tales which heroes slay to free a maid, as Perseus freed Andromeda. Such a story may very well have been founded on fact. For, in accordance with the custom of offering meat and drink to the sacred animals,—as the Poly-nesians offer human flesh to the birds' believed to be their deities incarnate,—so travellers in Africa tell of the alligator which is fed with a white fowl, and of "the shark at Bonny that comes to the river bank every day, to see if a human victim has been provided for his repast."

Ancient Egyptian art has depicted just such a combat as that of Perseus. Horus striking the crocodile is the very prototype of our patron saint, who is represented on our coinage in the act of spearing the dragon. According to the Homeric hymn, there was a spring of pure water guarded by a she-dragon, a great and terrible monster, the nurse of Typhon, who devastated the land ; and the Lord Apollo slew her with his sharp arrows, and left her to rot upon the ground ; whence the place is now called Pytho, and the Lord Apollo, the Pythian. Of course we have a version of the Dragon or Serpent myth from China, the Land of the Dragon Throne, and in its general features it is much the same as our own popular story of St. George ; and the stories of the laird who slew the "worme of Linton ;" of the slayers of the Lambton worm, and the Laidley Worme of Spindlestone Heugh ; and of the plucky Scot named Martin who slew the dragon which had devoured nine maidens.

In the Chinese story the champion is a girl. Nine victims have in turn been yielded to the mighty serpent whose abode is in the mountains east of Fuhkien, and who lusts every year to devour a maiden of the age of twelve or thirteen. Another victim must be found, and the youngest daughter of the magistrate of Tsing Lo insists on offering herself. At the mouth of the serpent's cavern she places several measures of boiled rice mixed with honey, and being supplied with a sword and a dog, the maiden Ki waits till the serpent comes forth to devour the toothsome mess. Then the dog seizes the monster in its teeth, and the maiden hacks from behind, till it withdraws to the mouth of its cave, and dies. Ki recovers the skeletons of the nine previous victims, and leisurely returns home. Hearing of her exploit, the Prince of Sueh makes her his queen.

Imagination shapes fell beasts and gives them title *rôles*, like the monster of Errour in Spenser's " Faerie Queen," and the Apollyon in the " Pilgrim's Progress." Such as these cannot fairly be associated with any actual creatures. Hesiod records the birth of monstrous beings of various forms, such as Thaumas, the great deep ; the harpies winged like birds ; Medusa and the Gorgons with serpent heads ; Echidna, the terrible flesh-devourer, half lovely nymph, half serpent ; Cerberus, the fifty-headed dog of Hell ; the Lernean Hydra, the fearful serpent with a number of heads, whom Hercules slew ; Chimaira, with one head like a lion's, another like a goat's, and a third like a serpent's, slain by

Bellerophon; the Nemæan lion, and the Sphinx, a scaly sea dragon.

The rainbow is a living monster in New Zealand as well as with the Karens of Birma, where it is said to devour men. To the old Greeks the rainbow reaching from heaven to earth was the personal Iris, messenger between gods and men. To the South Sea Islander the rainbow is a heaven-ladder for the use of heroes; to the Scandinavian it is the bridge Bifröst, as in the German folk-tale. It is the bow of Jehovah, of the Hindu Rama, and of the Finnish Tiermes the Thunderer.

The god of thunder in China corresponds to Vajrapani, a well-known Buddhist deity. In North American Indian belief the thunder is caused by a huge bird whose outspread wings darken the heavens. It lives on the mountain tops. An Indian once got a feather from the nest of a thunder-bird, and it measured over 200 feet in length. A serpent-like fish of immense size, with head as sharp as a knife, causes the lightning when he puts out his tongue. The thunder-bird catches this fish for food. The notion of a flapping thunder-bird has occurred to many a savage philosopher, for many a legend is told of it by Caribs, Dacotahs, Brazilians, Hervey Islanders, Basutos, and many other peoples. In Central America the bird Voc is the messenger of Hurakan, the Tempest-god, whose name has supplied us with the word *hurricane*. Some Chinese and Japanese think waterspouts are caused by the ascent and descent of a long-tailed dragon ; and the Moslems still think them caused by gigantic demons. A missionary received the same explanation of the phenomenon from the chief of an African tribe.

" The peasant of the New Forest thinks that the marl he digs is still red with the blood of his ancient foes the Danes ; " as the ancient Greek saw the red blood of Adonis in the summer floods of the river that flowed by Byblos, and " the Maori sees on the red cliffs of Cook's Straits the blood-stains that Kupe made, when, mourning for the death of his daughter, he cut his forehead with pieces of obsidian."

Now we come to what are sometimes classed as Nature-myths, and, in dealing with them, we must bear ever in mind the doctrine of animism, the savage's philosophy of nature. We have seen that man at a low stage of mental development cannot distinguish between things animate and inanimate. Everything is on a level with himself ; vegetables and stones, tools and meat and drink, pots and canoes, animals and trees, all have immortal souls, just like man himself, which pass to the world of spirits. The sun, the moon, and stars are living beings ; ocean, clouds, whirlwind, and tempest are endowed with will, passion, reason. For the savage

can only interpret the actions of nature by considering them on a par with his own actions.   There
was occasion to refer to the Four Winds amongst
the Nature-gods (see p. 142).   They are personified
in many a fairy-tale, and legend deals with them,
as with other natural phenomena, in every savage
mythology.   Only, we, who see naught but a poet's
fancy in the line, " Winds of all the corners kiss
your sails, and make your vessel nimble," must not
omit to trace the savage's philosophy in the Red
Indian fable of the lazy South Wind, Shawondasee,
sighing for the maiden of the prairie with her sunny
hair.   What we call poetry was real life to the
savage.   With the Persians " all the unnumbered
stars were reckoned ghosts of men ; " the Eskimos
think the sun and moon as well as the stars are
spirits of departed men and animals ; while the
South Australians think them living beings who
once inhabited the earth.   In German folk-lore stars
are souls ; when a child dies, God makes a new star.
African Bushmen and North American Indians call
the Milky Way the " Path of Souls."   This tallies
with the Lithuanian myth of the " Path of the
Birds," for the souls of the good take the form of
birds at death.   The Pythagoreans were familiar
with the thought that souls dwell in the Galaxy.
From such poetic ideas as these it is a fall to our
own prosaic name for the celestial road.   In olden

time the great street of the Wætlingas used to run from Dover through London into Wales. Heaven had its Watling Street as well, for this was once the Englishman's name for the Milky Way.

The identification of Sun, Moon, and Stars with persons who once lived, may have arisen from a misinterpretation of names, just as a like misunderstanding contributed to the belief (see p. 96) in descent of men from animals and plants. It is possible that in primitive times the Moon was used, just as now, as a complimentary name for a woman; but, however that may be, it is certain that the Moon supplies names for children. The Karens, for example, use the name " Full Moon." In short, Sun, Moon, and Stars have all been identified with traditional human beings, and all nations have their myths in which the heavenly bodies are endowed with all the attributes and functions of earth-born persons. The Greeks had traditional stories about the stars, which in character precisely correspond with the stories which are current everywhere amongst modern savages. Sometimes they even contain the same incident. Australian natives say that the stars in Orion's belt and scabbard are young men dancing a corroboree. The Eskimos call these same stars the Lost Ones ; for they say that they were once seal-hunters, and they missed their way home.

The Nimtira of the Malayan Peninsula have an elaborate Nature-myth to explain the generation of the stars. Like most rude tribes, these people have the conception of a solid firmament, not unlike the " hammered plate " in the Creation-myth of Genesis. The sky, they say, is a great pot suspended by a cord ; if the cord broke, everything on earth would be crushed. " The Moon is a woman, and the Sun also ; the Stars are the Moon's children, and the Sun had in old times as many. Fearing, however, that mankind could not bear so much brightness and heat, they agreed each to devour her children ; but the Moon, instead of eating up her Stars, hid them from the Sun's sight, who, believing them all devoured, ate up her own ; no sooner had she done it than the Moon brought her family out of their hiding-place. When the Sun saw them, filled with rage, she chased the Moon to kill her ; the chase has lasted ever since, and sometimes the Sun even comes near enough to bite the Moon, and that is an eclipse ; the Sun, as men may still see, devours her Stars at dawn, and the Moon hides hers all day while the Sun is near, and only brings them out at night when her pursuer is far away."

The following Pawnee Star-myth likewise implies a solid overhanging firmament. One hot summer night two girls climbed up on an arbour to sleep in the cool. As they lay talking of the stars above them, one of the girls pointed to a bright particular star as the one she liked best of all. When this girl awoke she found herself in the lodge of a stranger in a strange country, and she cried for her home. The stranger said he was the star that she had chosen, and he had taken her for his wife. Finally she was contented to stay with him. Every night he went on a journey, after combing his hair and painting his face red. Every morning he was back again. After three years the girl had a baby boy. One day she went out to dig turnips. Her husband had cautioned her never to dig deep into the ground, and as a rule she was careful. But this day she dug deep ; she dug right through. Down through this hole she could see the world ; she could see a camp, and a party of men playing the stick game ; they looked very small, like ants. A longing seized her to revisit her home and her people. She went to her husband's lodge and asked him to fetch her a lot of sinews, and for many a night during his absence she worked to make them into a rope. Then she took her child on her back, and carried the rope of sinew to the hole. She drove a strong stake into the ground to secure the end of the rope, and then let it down through the hole. It seemed not quite long enough to reach the earth, but she would risk that. Having enlarged the hole that her body might pass through, she let herself down by the rope, her child on her back. She reached the end of the rope, but the ground was far below her. There was no one to help ; she was sore afraid. Meanwhile her husband, seeking her in vain at the lodge, at last found the hole, and saw her hanging to the rope. He felt very angry, and he dropped a big stone through, which fell on the woman's head and killed her. But, by the power of the Star-man, the child was saved for a striking career, which need not here be recorded.

It is curious that the relic of a mythopœic age should be everlastingly enshrined in our celestial globe. Yet so it is. For the savage habit of giving human or animal names to individual stars, or groups of stars, is kept up by modern astronomers, who " map the starry sky ; " though any resemblance to human or animal forms in the star-groups is only beheld by a vivid imagination.

Australian aborigines say that Yurree and Wanjil, the stars which we, deriving their names from the Greeks, call Castor and Pollux, pursue the Kangaroo (the star we call Capella), and kill him at the beginning of the great heat ; the mirage is the smoke of the fire by which they roast him. In a parallel myth, Orion pursues the Pleiades, who take refuge from him in the sea.

Every one must know the Greek myth about Meropē, the lost Pleiad. The seven Pleiades were seven maidens, daughters of the giant Atlas. Six of them were loved by the gods, but the seventh had only a mortal lover, and she, poor Meropē, when they were all changed into stars, hid her light for shame.

Now, the aborigines of Australia have likewise a myth to account for the disappearance of one of these seven stars, who, according to them, were a queen and her six attendants. The Crow made love to the queen, who refused him. But the Crow knew that the queen and her maidens were wont to hunt for edible grubs in the bark of trees. So he changed himself into a grub, and hid in the bark of a tree. The six maidens failed to pick him out with their wooden hooks. But he allowed the queen to succeed with her pretty bone hook, and, once he was drawn out, he turned into a giant and carried her off. Since then there have only been six stars in the group.

In Bushman lore, the stars and sun and moon are mortals, or even animals, that have been translated to the skies. Myths to this effect abound everywhere. It may be remembered, for example, how the Egyptian priests told Plutarch that the soul of Isis was translated into the Dog-star.

The Indians of Central Brazil believe the sun to be a ball made of a feather of the red Arra. It is stuck in a pot, the lid of which is lifted in the

morning and closed at night. The moon is a ball
made of the yellow tail-feathers of a weaver-bird.
The night sky is covered with animals and every
conceivable object. The Milky Way is a hollow tree ;
there is a bird-net in it, and an ant-bear embracing
a hunter. A starless space in the Southern sky is a
hole through which a tapir once fell. The question
is, how did these things get up there. Well, they
say that once on a time the whole affair was upside
down ; the sky was below, the earth above, and
mankind lived in heaven. But this heaven was no
paradise ; on the contrary, it was a most unhealthy
place, and people died rapidly. So a mighty magician, to put an end to the state of affairs, overturned
the whole system. The unhealthy heaven was sent
up, while man remained below to inhabit the more
promising earth.

In Australian legend the Moon was a native cat,
who fell in love with some one else's wife, and was
driven away, to wander ever since. A tribe of the
Himalaya say that the Moon falls in love every
month with his mother, who throws ashes in his
face, causing the dark spots that we see. The in-
constant Moon in Slavonic legend is the King of
Night, and his spouse is the Sun. He was severed
in twain, as we see him in the sky, for faithlessly
loving the Morning Star. Among the Mbocobis of
South America also, the Moon is a man, and the Sun

is his wife. The Algonkin Indians, on the other hand, say that the Moon is a woman, and eclipses are caused when she holds her son in her arms, so preventing one's seeing the light of her countenance. The Sun is her husband, and when he is eclipsed or obscured, it is because he is holding their son in front of him. Another Algonkin legend describes Sun and Moon as brother and sister. The Peruvian's Sun and Moon, Ynti and Quilla, are brother and sister, and father and mother of the Incas; just as the Egyptian Osiris and Isis were at once brother and sister, and husband and wife. This was a justification for the sister marriages in Peru and Egypt. The celebrated queen Hatasu, daughter of Thotmes I., was married to her younger brother Thotmes II.; the Inca heir-apparent, by marrying a sister, continued the pure heaven-born race.

Sun and Moon are thus personified in every savage mythology, and many are the stories told concerning them.

The Moon was a man, according to an old Mexican text. A god threw a rabbit in his face, and disfigured him for life. There seems no end to the myths of different races accounting for the spots on the Moon. To the Indians and Mongolians they look like a hare. This is the legend told by the people of Ceylon : " While Buddha, the great god, sojourned upon earth as a hermit, he one day lost his way in a wood. He had wandered long, when a hare accosted him : ' Cannot I help thee ? Strike into the path on thy right ; I will guide thee out of the wilderness.' Buddha replied, ' Thank thee, but I am poor and hungry, and unable to repay thy kindness.' ' If thou art hungry,' said the hare, ' light a fire, and kill, roast, and eat me.' Buddha made a fire, and the hare immediately jumped in. Then did Buddha manifest his divine power ; he snatched the beast out of the flames, and set him in the Moon, where he may be seen to this day." The Eskimos say that the Moon is a girl, whose cruel brother, the Sun, disfigured her face ; she is always fleeing from him. An old Norse fable tells us that Mâni, the Moon, translated from the earth two children, called Hiuki and Bil, who, like our Jack and Jill, had gone to fetch a pail of water. They can now be seen in the Moon carrying the pail on a pole between them. Teutonic legend sets a man in the Moon " bering a bush of thornis on his bake," as Chaucer describes him. According to the Christian revised version of the story which prevails in Germany and elsewhere, this was a punishment for theft, trespass, or cutting firewood on a Sunday; the precedent for punishment of such offence being found in the case of the man in the Book of Numbers, who was stoned to death by the congregation of Israel, for gathering sticks on the Sabbath.

Shakespeare alludes more than once to the Man in the Moon ; for example, in " Midsummer Night's Dream " : " One must come in with a bush of thorns and a lanthorn, and say he comes to present the person of Moonshine." The natives of the Solomon Islands tell the following legend of the Man in the Moon. " The actors are, it seems, the usual three." There was once a girl named Leonivulu, whose father's name was Tuasakai. She wanted to marry a good-looking young man called Silitamburara, and her father made no objection. But a cripple named Gengoukouka madly loved the girl, and meeting her walking by the shore one evening after dark, he personated her accepted lover, and prevailed on her to accompany him to his house. Here she discovered the deception, and escaping next day, complained to her father. Tuasakai was wroth, and pursued Gengoukouka with intent to kill ; but the lame youth managed to get for safety to the Moon, where he has lived ever since, spending his time in making white shell armlets out of the large clam shells.

Eclipses are explained by a variety of myths. A native race of South America " thought the Moon was hunted across the sky by huge dogs, who caught and tore her till her light was reddened and quenched by the blood flowing from her wounds." The Indians howled and drove off the dogs, and the

Moon recovered of the bite. Other races likewise shout, and shoot their arrows into the sky, to drive the devouring beast from Sun or Moon. Civilised nations have their myths of the Eclipse-monster. The Chinese make official announcement of his coming, and encounter him with gongs and bells and regularly appointed prayers. Tacitus relates how the Moon suddenly languished in a clear sky, and the Roman soldiers, whose intended mutiny against Tiberius was thus frustrated by the gods, strove in vain, by clang of brass and trumpet blast, to drive away the darkness. In the seventeenth century it was recorded that the Irish and Welsh ran about, during eclipses, beating kettles and pans, thinking to assist the heavenly bodies.

Then there are the myths of sunrise and sunset ; stories of the Day being swallowed up by Night, and liberated again at dawn ; fancies which seem like mere poetic imagery. With the Egyptians the Sun is the child of Earth and Heaven, Seb and Nut. Day and Night are brothers, children of the Sky. Just as the worship of Nature-gods passes into, or is combined with, the worship of apotheosised men, so Nature-myth develops into heroic legend. Perseus slays the monster and frees Andromeda, as the Sun slays the devouring Darkness.

Maui, the hero of New Zealand myth, and the youngest of five brothers of the same name, took fire in his hands, and, because it burnt him, sprang with it into the sea. This set a volcano burning. When he sank in the water, the sun for the first time set, and darkness covered the earth. When he found that all was night, Maui pursued the sun, and brought him back in the morning. Thus the sun is born from the ocean ; his light is extinguished at sunset, and returns at dawn. According to the Egyptian myth, which the Greek myth of Uranos resembles, " Nut, the sky-goddess, was wife of Seb, the earth-god, from whose embrace she was separated by Shu, the god of the air. When this separation was effected, earth, air, and sky came into being."

Further motive for myth-making is supplied by the desire to account for the parentage of a tribe ; examples of such have already been cited (see pp. 112, 113) ; or to account for the names of places.

The most stupendous of all the insoluble problems has been lightly disposed of in the Creation-myths of every savage race. This is the Huron account of the making of the world : In the beginning there was nothing but water, peopled by various aquatic animals and birds. A divine woman fell down through a rift in the sky. It is thought that her husband—perhaps by accident—gave her a push. Two loons were flying over the water, saw her falling, and saved her from drowning by placing themselves beneath her, while they loudly called for aid. All the creatures of the sea heard and drew nigh. The tortoise, a mighty animal, consented to relieve the loons of their precious burden. It was unanimously agreed that this woman must have earth to live on, and the beaver, the musk-rat, the diver, and others dived to the bottom of the sea, and endeavoured, but without success, to bring some up. Some remained so long below, that when they rose they were dead. The tortoise searched their mouths, but found no trace of earth. At last the toad went down, and came back, after a long time, terribly exhausted, and nearly dead. But the tortoise found in its mouth some earth, which he gave to the woman. She placed it carefully round the edge of the tortoise's shell, and this was the beginning of the dry land, which grew and grew, on every side, till it formed a great country. The tortoise sustained it all, and has done so ever since The woman who fell from heaven bore on earth two sons of opposite dispositions, one good, the other evil. The latter, in rebellious obstinacy, by breaking through his mother's side, killed her. From her buried body sprang the various vegetable productions which made the new earth fitting habitation for man. The twins could not agree together, therefore separated. The good brother created the innocent and useful animals, while the bad brother made all the fierce and monstrous creatures. In African legend the earth was first peopled by beings who fell through the sky. The notion is widespread, and is familiar in Polynesian myths, which account for the appearing of the first settlers. When white men first appeared in Samoa, it was thought that they had broken through the heavens; and to this day white men are called Papalangi, or " Heaven-Bursters."

But, to return to Creation-myths. By much the same means was the earth formed according to Algonkin legend. At first there was nothing but water, over which floated a raft of wood carrying animals of all species, and with them the Great Hare himself, chief of all. He, longing to disembark, tried to induce some animals to dive and bring up some earth from the bottom. The beaver tried hard to excuse himself, and when finally he did plunge down, it was only to return nearly dead, with not a trace of mud on his paws. The otter had no better success. Then the musk-rat volunteered, and after twenty-four hours under water rose to the surface dead, but with a grain of sand between its claws. With this the Great Hare created the earth, which is borne upon a raft. As to the sea and the firmament, the Algonkins explain that they have existed from all time.

Many savage tribes have a tradition of the Deluge

which involves re-making the dry land by means of
the diving device. Thus, the Californian Indians
say that when the whole earth was covered with
water, there were no living creatures save an eagle
and a crow. They held converse, standing on a
stump that projected above the surface of the
watery expanse. Between them they managed to
create a duck to enliven the solitude. One day
the duck dived to the bottom, and came up with
earth on its bill. The eagle and the crow thought
the matter worth looking into. The mud looked
promising, though they had never seen anything
like it. So they agreed to keep the duck constantly employed diving for mud, which they divided
between them, making two heaps, one on either
side of the stump. After an unavoidable absence
the eagle returned, to find that the crow had not
been dividing fairly, having kept much the larger
portion himself. The eagle's heap, so the Indians
say, was what is known as the coast range of
mountains, while the crow's was the Sierra Nevada
range. But the eagle in his anger reversed the
position of the two heaps, and so the mountains
remain even to this day; while all men honour
the eagle and despise the crow.

Another legend from North America says that
the coyote and the eagle created our earth. The
coyote scratched it up with his paws out of nothing-

ness ; only, the eagle complained that there were no mountains for him to perch on, and so he fell to work and scratched up ridges. When he flew over them his feathers dropped down, took root, and became trees ; and the pin feathers, bushes and plants. In the creation of animals and man the coyote and the fox participated, the first being an evil spirit, the other good. The coyote wanted to make men mortal : " Let them die," he said. The fox said, " Let them come back." But nobody ever did come back, for the coyote's advice prevailed. Last of all, the coyote brought fire into the world, for the Indians were freezing. He stole it from a place in the far west, from the two old hags who guarded it ; and this is how he contrived to get it safely home. He got together a great company of animals, from the lion down to the frog, and stationed them in a line all the way to the far-distant land where the fire was, the weakest animal nearest home, and the strongest near the fire. Watching his opportunity, the coyote seized a brand in his teeth and well-nigh flew over the ground, the hags giving chase. He reached the lion, who ran with the brand to the next animal, and so on down to the frog. Whilst the ground-squirrel was carrying it, he ran at such a pace that his tail got afire, and he curled it over his back, and so burned the black spot behind his shoulders which he bears to this day. He chucked the fire into the frog's open mouth, and the frog gulped it down. He gave a great jump, but the hags seized him by the tail (he was a tadpole at the time) and tweaked it off. Frogs have been tailless ever since. He swam under water as long as he could hold his breath, then he came up and spat the fire into a log of drift-wood, where it has ever remained. When the Indians rub two pieces of wood together the fire comes forth.

In another legend of the North American Indians, the lizard, in his attempt to steal fire, accidentally set light to the dry grass, and so set all the country ablaze, and did a lot of mischief.

First of all things existed the moon ; next came the coyote, says the legend of another tribe. Between them they created all things. This is how the coyote made man. Having finished the world and the inferior creatures, he called a council of them to deliberate on the creation of man. The lion was the first to speak. He would like to see man covered with hair, and with terrible fangs, strong talons, and a mighty voice like his own. " Ridiculous to have a voice like yours," said the bear ; " why, you scare away the very prey you want to capture. No ; man should have prodigious strength, but he should move silently, and withal swiftly." The buck said that in his opinion man would look foolish without a magnificent pair of antlers on his head, to fight with ; and he agreed with the bear that it would be absurd to make him roar. Good ears and eyes would be more useful to him than a mighty throat. The mountain sheep protested against the antlers, which would only be caught in the thicket. If man is to have horns, let them be rolled up like a stone on each side of his head ; then he could butt hard. " Stuff and nonsense," said the coyote, whose turn it was to speak. " Every one of you wants to make man after his own image." They might just as well take one of their own cubs and call it man. The coyote conceded that each of the speakers had certain good points. Man would have to be like himself, of course, in having four legs, five fingers, &c. The lion's voice would do well enough, for man need not roar all the time ; the bear's feet were not a bad shape to copy ; the grizzly was happy, too, in having no tail, for, in his (the coyote's) own experience, that organ was only a harbour for fleas. The buck's eyes and ears would do. Then there was the fish, which was naked ; he certainly favoured a man without hair. His claws should be long, like the eagle's. But when it comes to the question of wit, they must all acknowledge that it would be necessary to make man, in this respect also, like the coyote himself—cunning and crafty. The beaver said he had never heard such twaddle in his life. No tail, indeed! Why, man should have a broad, flat tail, so that he could haul mud on it. The owl said that all the animals seemed to have lost their senses. How on earth could a man get on without wings. "Wings!" sneered the mole. "Man would be certain to bump his head against the sky. Besides, if he has wings and eyes both, he will go flying too near the sun, and have his eyes burnt out. Now, without eyes, he could burrow in the cool, soft earth, and be happy." "A man must have eyes," squeaked the little mouse, "or how can he see what he is eating?" The council broke up quarrelling, some of the members behaving quite spitefully. Then each animal took a lump of earth and began moulding a man after his own idea, but the coyote made the one he had been describing. It was so late before they began, that night fell upon them, and they lay down to sleep, leaving the models unfinished. But the cunning coyote stayed awake, and finished his man and gave it life, and spoiled all the other models. Thus it was that man was made by the coyote.

The Caribs, in their account of the Creation, say that the Great Spirit sat on a mora-tree, and picking off pieces of the bark, threw them into the stream,

and they became different animals. Then the Great
Spirit made a large mould, and out of this fresh, clean
clay the white man stepped. After it got a little
dirty the Indian was formed, and, the Spirit being
called away on business for a long period, the mould
became black and unclean, and out of it walked the
negro. All the Indian tribes of Guiana rank themselves far higher than the negro race, and the Caribs
consider themselves the first of the tribes.

One European Creation-myth must complete the
series. This version, probably of Tatar origin,
embodies the belief of the Mordvins, a race occupy-
ing Russian territory. It is unlike the versions
hitherto related in containing the dualistic idea of
an evil spirit trying to frustrate the designs of the
good spirit. Formerly, when there was no land,
Cham Pas, the supreme god, was drifting about on
a stone in the open sea, reflecting how to create a
visible world. He spat in the sea and drifted on.
Presently, on looking back, he perceived that his
spittle had turned into a great hill, drifting in his
wake. He struck it with his sceptre to destroy it,
when out leapt Shaitan, the Devil. Cham Pas was
glad to have a companion with whom to take counsel
in the creation of the world. " Go to the bottom
and fetch sand," he said ; " only, take care that you
mention my name." Shaitan dived, but, in his pride,
would not mention God's name—only his own ;

accordingly, a flame rose at the bottom of the sea and scorched him, and he could not get a single grain. Cham Pas sent him down again, saying the flame would not touch him did he mention God's name. But this time also he got burnt, because he would not pronounce the name of Cham Pas. With renewed warning, God sent him down a third time. Shaitan mentioned the name of Cham Pas and took a mouthful of sand, part of which, however, he retained by stealth in his cheek, thinking that he too would make a world. Cham Pas scattered the sand upon the sea, and it grew till it became dry land. At the same rate grew the sand in Shaitan's cheek, making him howl with pain as his head swelled. He was obliged to confess what he had done. Cham Pas struck him on the head, and bade him spit out the sand. This he did with such violence that the unconsolidated earth quaked, thus originating deep places, ravines, and valleys. Shaitan's sand formed the hills, peaks, and mountains. And Cham Pas cursed Shaitan and sent him to the bottom of the sea, to the place of the dead, to the fire that burned him, there to suffer punishment for ever and ever.

An inexhaustible theme for the myth-maker is the fanciful explanation of physical peculiarities in man and beast, as well as of natural phenomena generally. It has served for every clime and every age, as the following examples, ancient and modern, will show.

When St. Peter took the piece of money for Cæsar's tax out of the fish's mouth, he left the impress of his finger and thumb on the fish. The Scotch say that this accounts for the black marks on the haddock.

Ina, the heroine of a South Sea myth, used to bathe in a pool, and got on friendly terms with an eel. " At last the fish took his courage in both fins and made his declaration. He was Tuna, the chief of all eels. ' Be mine,' he cried, and Ina was his. For some mystical reason he was obliged to leave her, but (like the White Cat in the fairy-tale) requested her to cut off his eel's head and bury it. Regretfully but firmly did Ina comply with his request, and from the buried eel's head sprang two cocoa-trees, one from each half of the brain of Tuna. As a proof of this, be it remarked that when the nut is husked we always find on it ' the two eyes and mouth of the lover of Ina.' "

Chinese legend accounts in a similar way for the two eyes of the cocoa-nut. The Prince Liu Yeh quarrelled with Prince Yueh, and sent a man to assassinate him. His head, which the assassin suspended on a tree, was metamorphosed into a cocoa-nut, with two eyes on the shell. Thus the

fruit acquired the name of Yueh-wang-t'ou, or
" Prince Yueh's head."

The inquirer may learn from the Icelandic Her-
verar Saga why eagles have short tails. King
Heidrik boasted of his power to solve all riddles.
So Odin himself, disguised as a blind man, visited
him, and asked him hard questions. The king
answered them all, his replies, like the questions,
being given in verse. He bade the blind man
ask another. Then the god asked what Odin
whispered into the ear of Baldur before he was
burned on his funeral pyre. And Heidrik thereupon drew his sword and struck at his questioner,
saying, " None can answer that but yourself."
Odin had just time to transform himself into an
eagle, but the sword smote off his tail ; wherefore
eagles ever since have had short tails.

Where the turkey-buzzard struts, the following
story is told to account for its total baldness. When
the animals were leaving the ark, Noah administered
to each some fitting advice before landing them on
a wicked world. And to the turkey-buzzard he
said, " My children, if you see a man stoop down,
look out for yourselves, lest he be picking up a stone
to heave at you." The turkey-buzzard thanked
him for the hint, then added, " Suppose the man
has a stone ready in his pocket, what then ? "
Noah was taken aback ; the shrewdness of the

remark bereft him of rejoinder ; and he decreed that the turkey-buzzard must henceforth be born bald, in token of its great sagacity.

In West Highland folk-lore, the same dialogue takes place between the hoodie and the shrewd young one she is catechising ; and in Ireland, between the old and the young crow. But Noah was not by to commemorate these cute young birds.

The crow, by the way, was originally white. Hesiod has told us why the crow is black. Apollo was in love with Coronis, but she was unfaithful to him. The crow was the bearer of this distressing news, and Apollo in his anger cursed it, that it should ever after be black.

Scripture also teacheth why the partridge flies low. It was because Dædalus was turned into a partridge, and he had seen his son Icarus perish through a lofty flight. This made him cautious.

It is not recorded how Little Bo-Peep's sheep came to lose their tails ; but take almost any animal that has a short tail, and folk-lore will tell the reason why. Now, why has the bear a stumpy tail ?

A fox jumped into a waggon which was laden with fish, and, as it went along, threw a number out into the road, and then slipped off himself and fell to feasting. A bear came along and asked him concerning his remarkable catch of fish, and the fox volunteered to show the bear how he could do likewise. So they went together that night on to the ice, and the fox told the bear to put his tail down through a hole, that the fish might bite. " Sit very still," said the fox. The bear presently shifted a little, and his tail was slightly pulled, for it was freezing to the ice. " Don't be in a hurry," said the fox ; " you are strong, and can get a good haul." So the bear waited ; and the next time he moved, his tail was pulled a little harder. " Not yet," said the fox ; " more will take hold." When morning was come, the fox ran towards a house on the bank and set the dogs barking. This so alarmed the bear that he pulled with all his might, and left his tail frozen hard to the ice. Bears have had short tails ever since.

This is a Russian and an Onondaga story. A Norse story is like it, but without the waggon in-cident. A French story and a Scotch story account in the same way for the stumpy tail of a wolf. Brer Rabbit, according to " Uncle Remus," lost his long bushy tail through this same practical joke, perpetrated by Brer Fox. In Bornu, a hyæna puts his tail into the hole, that the weasel may fasten the meat to it ; but the weasel fastens a stick to it instead, and the hyæna pulls till his tail breaks. The common origin of this story of the Tail-Fisher is unmistakable. The hyrax, according to a Zulu fable, went without a tail, because, on the day when tails were given out, he sent for his instead of troubling to apply personally. And a Russian story tells how the hare lost her tail. It was thus :—

The fox and the hare were sent in quest of a magic fluid. Their way lay between grinding hills (like the Symplegades). The fox went and returned in safety ; but the hare, on her way back, was not in time quite to clear the meeting cliffs, and her tail was jammed between them. Since that time hares have had no tails to speak of. The Californian Indians, who claim descent from the prairie wolf, explain the loss of their tails by saying that the acquired habit of sitting upright has utterly destroyed that beautiful member.

The following Serbian myth accounts for the hollow in the sole of man's foot. The Devil stole the sun and stuck it on a lance, which he left planted in the ground whilst he went bathing with an Archangel. The Archangel dived and brought up some sand. The Devil spat on the ground, and a magpie arose from his spittle, to mount guard while the Devil also dived. He was no sooner under than the Archangel made the sign of the cross, and the water was frozen over ; then off he flew to heaven with the impaled sun. The magpie screamed. The Devil could not get out till he had sunk again in search of a stone to break the ice. He managed to overtake the Archangel just as he had got one foot in heaven, and he caught hold of the other foot and tore off a large piece of flesh. The Archangel complained to God, who decreed, in order to pacify him, that every man should henceforth have a hollow on the sole of his foot.

A Hottentot myth gives the origin of the hare's cleft lip. The moon sent the hare to men to deliver this message : " Like as I die and rise to life again, so you also shall die and rise to life again." But the hare said instead : " Like as I die and do not rise again, so you shall also die and not rise to life again," and then returned and told the moon what he had done. The moon struck at him with a hatchet, meaning to split his skull ; but the blow fell short, and the hare escaped with his life, though the hatchet slit his lip, as it has remained ever since. But the hare clawed at the moon's face, and made the scars which we still see.

The reader may learn from " Uncle Remus " why the negro is black, the opossum has no hair on its tail, the guinea-fowl is speckled, and why chickens are always scratching.

The Prose Edda gives the traditional reason why the sea is salt. There was once a golden time of peace and plenty, when every one had whatsoever he wanted. For the Giant Frodi had a mill which ground out peace and plenty, and withal such an abundance of gold, that golden armlets lay untouched from year's end to year's end on the king's highway. In Frodi's house were two maidens, a giant's daughters, whom he had bought as slaves, and he kept them grinding at that mill until they lost all patience and ground no longer peace and plenty, but fire and war. Then came a mighty sea-rover by night and slew Frodi and all his men, and carried off the maids and the quern. When they had got well out to sea he bade them grind salt, and they ground with a vengeance. The ship was full and sank, the maids of the mill and all. So the quern was lost for ever, and the sea remains salt to this day.

The mysterious " sampo " in the Finnish Kalewala is a mill, " for corn one day, for salt the next, for money the next." Eventually it gets lost in the sea, and, no doubt, accounts for the saltness. The reader is doubtless, too, reminded of the quern in the Norse story, which ground everything, from a Christmas dinner and a whole larderful of dainties to the herrings and broth which nearly submerged an entire parish. Next it ground gold, and, finally, the salt, which sunk it and the ship to the bottom of the sea, where it grinds away still.

Certain of the myths related above are obviously

the result of the exercise of a rudimentary literary faculty ; they are, that is to say, conscious fictions. The most important class of these take the widely-spread and primitive form of fables about beasts, kinship with whom is everywhere recognised by early man. How, indeed, can he arrive at thinking himself a creature quite different from an animal, when he sees that the latter has the same habits and ways as himself.

> " He sat among the woods, he heard
> The sylvan merriment ; he saw
> The pranks of butterfly and bird,
> The humours of the ape, the daw.
>
> And in the lion or the frog—
> In all the life of moor and fen,
> In ass and peacock, stork and log,
> He read similitudes of men."

Thus savage myths tell of the ancestors of mankind living with animals as near relations ; and we see survival of this sense of affinity in the unwillingness of certain tribes to kill particular animals, and in the exemplary kindness shown towards them which is a striking trait in the Oriental. No Korean, for instance, ever kills a snake ; however poor and hungry he may be, he will share his evening meal with the reptiles that crawl round his dwelling.

There was no moral lesson intended in the original Beast-Fable, nor has it entered into those which are told at the present day by Australians,

Kamchadales, Polynesians, North American Indians, Basques, and Transylvanian Gipsies. To the irrational mind of the savage, as has been amply demonstrated in these pages, the beast with human attributes seems natural enough ; it is no fictitious creature invented to preach morals. And it is amongst savages, who ascribe to the lower animals the power of speech, and a nature resembling their own, that beast-stories had their first home. Later on, with progressive culture and a growing moral sense, these develop into the didactic apologue, and reach the class of fables proper, which are due to conscious literary art. It is unnecessary in this place to trace the literary pedigree of what are known as Æsopic fables,—the greater number of the genuine fables of mediæval times being associated with the name of Æsop, whom it is usual to place in the sixth century B.C. Suffice it to say that the ultimate source of many of the fables that have come down to us, whether the Greek of Babrius, or the Latin of Phædrus, was the *Jatakas*, or Buddhist Birth Stories, and other Indian tales which have found their way westward. The ancient Persian Fables of Bidpai were translations of old Indian originals, represented in the *Pantschatantra*, the *Hitopadesa*, and the Arabic *Kalilah wa Dimnah*, which the pure fable of mediæval times followed so closely.

Good examples of stories in which animals play human parts, and which have for their theme the triumph of cunning over mere strength, are those stories of the negroes in the Southern States of America, which " Uncle Remus " tells to the little boy. Stories similar to these are still told by the natives of many parts of Africa ; indeed, the beast-fable is found all over the world. True Æsopic humour informs the stories of Zulus and Hottentots. In Bushman lore the hare, as among American negroes the rabbit, plays much the same clever part as the fox in our European examples. " Even in the advanced civilisation of Ancient Egypt the beast-fable held an important place. ' The Lion and the Mouse ' is found in a papyrus dating from 1200--1166 B.C., the days of Rameses III." Four excellent examples of beast-fables, resembling more particularly the African, have been found in the cuneiform inscriptions of Babylonia, among the fragmentary records of Assur-bani-pal's library. There is no doubt, therefore, as to the venerable and hoary antiquity of even the written fable. Its composition depends mainly " upon a sympathetic and humorous observation of certain animals, whose adventures conform to their supposed character and their known habits."

> " And lo ! the Beasts no more were dumb,
> But answered out of brakes and trees."

A single illustration must suffice. This fable, told in China, is of Indian origin.

" A tiger having seized a monkey, was about to devour him ; but the monkey, bethinking himself of some means of escape, suggested that he was too small to make a good meal for a tiger, and offered to conduct his captor to a neighbouring hill where a far more noble prey might be captured. This was a stag, who, rightly assuming that the tiger had come for a most unfriendly purpose, concluded that his only chance was to put a bold face upon the matter, and accordingly addressed the monkey as follows : ' How is this ? You promised me ten tiger skins, and you have only brought one ; you still owe me nine.' The tiger, hearing this, became alarmed, and instantly decamped, vowing that he never thought the monkey could be so treacherous."

Like the beast-fable, the folk-tale also cannot be profitably examined without such insight, as the foregoing chapters have afforded, into the beliefs and customs of our fore-parents. These savage beliefs are distantly echoed in the irrational elements of many European tales, and establish their claim to a very remote antiquity. In all our folk-tales the relations between heroes and animals are usually kind and helpful. Every one can recall legends of children being suckled by animals, or fed

by birds. The wood-pecker, the bird of Mars, pur-
veyed for his children Romulus and Remus (as
the ravens fed Elijah) when the wolf's milk did
not suffice them. A she-wolf nourished the infant
Dietrich, whence his name Wolfdietrich ; a hind
offered her milk to Sigurd, in the Northern saga.
In Greek legend, Atalanta was suckled by a bear ;
the Ainos of Japan say that their first ancestor
was suckled by a bear, and that is why they are so
hairy. Semiramis was exposed when an infant by
her mother the fish-goddess, and miraculously preserved by doves. To be thus protected and reared
by bird or beast is the widely-prevalent fate of the
hero race, according to universal legend and countless folk-tales. And not alone to babes and suck-
lings in distress do the " helpful animals " appear.
Whenever a hero is in danger, swans, ravens,
wolves, stags, bears, and lions join him to render
aid. That is how animal-figures in the scutcheons
and helmet-insignia of heroes are in many cases to
be accounted for, while others may be referred to
the hero's power of transforming himself.

Then, again, there is the " Grateful Beast,"
who is cast for a most important *rôle* among the
dramatis personæ of the folk-tale. Nothing is more
common than for a hero to do some kindness to a suffering animal, who afterwards shows his gratitude by
signal service to his benefactor at a critical moment.

Beasts in household tales converse, and so do birds, but in an unknown tongue. Only the specially favoured can understand them. Frequently a knowledge of birds' language comes of eating a white snake, as in the German story. That famous king had the wisdom of serpents; nothing was hidden from him. And no wonder. Every day after dinner he ate in solitude of a secret dish, which none but himself might uncover. Curiosity one day overcame the king's servant; he lifted the cover, and saw a white snake on the dish. In a moment he had tasted it, and as the morsel touched his tongue he heard the sparrows chattering together, and knew what they were saying; for eating the snake had taught him the language of animals. According to a Scotch saga, the middle piece of a white snake, roasted by the fire, gives a knowledge of supernatural things to any one who shall put his finger into the fat which drops from it. Siegfried in the Volsunga-Saga, like Sigurd in the Western Wolsung-Lay, understands the birds' talk when he has tasted the heart of the dragon Fafni. In the saga of Seeburg, the serving-man tastes a piece off a silver-white snake, and immediately knows what the fowls, ducks, geese, doves, and sparrows in the yard are saying of the speedy downfall of the castle. Pliny records the same result from eating serpent's flesh. In Iceland one sufficiently safe way of acquiring a knowledge of the language of birds is recorded : " Take the tongue of a hawk, and put it in honey for two days and three nights ; place it then under your own tongue, and you will understand the language of birds. It must not, however, be carried elsewhere than under the tongue, for the hawk is a poisonous bird." In other cases the knowledge is acquired by means of a herb, which one need only put in the mouth to understand what the cocks crow and the dogs bark. Or, accidental stepping on the golden herb (possibly the mistletoe) causes one to fall asleep, and understand the speech of dogs, wolves, and birds. Or if, on Midsummer Eve, when the fern bursts into wondrous bloom, you can catch this bloom, you will be able to make yourself invisible, as well as to understand animals' language. Arabian and Persian traditions represent Solomon as acquainted with the language of beasts and birds. Helenus the seer, whom Æneas consulted, understood the language of birds and the omens drawn from their prophetic flight. All the talking birds of the folk-tales are the direct consequence of savage belief, but for which we should probably never have heard the saying, " A little bird told me."

Other of the leading " irrational " or unnatural ideas in European as well as in savage household tales may be briefly cited. In each case they are derived from the beliefs and ideas of savages; for when they occur in civilised tales, they must be regarded as a survival from a past of savagery, or as having been borrowed in recent times from tales of the uncivilised. A girl marries a frog, afterwards transformed into a man (the story is told by Zulus, Russians, Magyars, Scots, Germans); or she marries a man who is afterwards transformed by sorcery or witchcraft into an animal (a *motif* that is employed universally); she is accused of bearing puppies (a very common incident in European tales; compare the myths in which a human ancestress is said to have given birth to an animal of the totem species, *ante*, p. 112); she receives counsel from a talking bird or animal (animals are akin to men); finally, her traducers fail to compass her death, for when thrown into the lake she is transformed into a turtle; when the turtle is eaten, the carapace turns into a plant; the peel (which is the life thereof) into a bird; the bird into a tree; and so on, the girl's soul for ever escaping (compare the savage belief in a separable soul, and see the stories given in illustration, *ante*, pp. 83, 84). Cinderella (of whose world-famed, truly popular story nearly four hundred separate versions are on record) holds converse with her dead mother at the grave; or, according to other accounts, she talks with the animal into whose shape her mother's soul passed at death. (Savages believe, as we have seen, in the possibility of communion with the dead, also that the human soul quits the dead body and passes into animal shapes.) All sorts of inanimate objects in folk-tales obey incantations. Drops of blood speak, as in the Finnish Kalewala, in the Norse story of the Mastermaid, in the German story of Sweetheart Roland, and in the Biblical story of the murder of Abel ("The voice of thy brother's blood crieth unto Me from the ground"). Drops of spittle speak in stories told in Russia, in Zululand, in the Scotch Highlands, and among the Basques, as in the German story where the witch is ready to kill and cook Hänsel because he is fat; but Grethel sets him free, and with him takes to her heels, after spitting in front of the hearth. " Will the water soon be ready ? " cries the witch. " I am just fetching it," answers the spittle, and so on, whilst the children are getting away.

That witch was a cannibal; many such figure in European as well as in savage *märchen*. The man-eating ogre smells human flesh (" Fee, fi, fo, fum ") wheresoever he stalks—that is to say, all over Europe, from Iceland to Portugal, from Norway to Italy, from Russia to Greece; he scents the blood of Hottentots, Zulus, Canadian Indians, Asiatics, South Americans, and Polynesians, even as the Eumenides in the Greek tragedy smelt out Orestes, and Hidimbas, the râkshasa in the Mahâbhârata (the Indian Epic), smelt man's flesh from afar. If this ogre (whose Italian name *uorco* is derived from Orcus, the ancient god of the lower world) is one-eyed, like the Lapland giant Stalo, the Gaelic Crinnawn, the Tatar Depêghöz, and Sindbad's man-eating giant, he is usually blinded with a red-hot poker, as Odysseus blinded the Cyclops Polyphemus.

Rhyming charms and mystic formulæ are employed in *märchen* to create mist or darkness or dazzling light, as the savage medicine-man uses incantations when he makes the weather. So, magic words and magic wand open the treasure-filled rocks, call spirits from the vasty deep, cause food and raiment, chariot and horsemen, to appear, and, in short, effect all sorts of conjuring. Nothing is impossible :

" The dead return to life,
Rivers are dried, winds stayed."

And so, fertile fancy, wielding the wizard's wand, gives us all the transformations and enchantment of delightful fairyland. "All impediments in fancy's course are motives of more fancy," and with all the marvellous " properties " ready for use, the wishing-box, -lamp, -bell, tarn-cap and fairy-purse, the seven-league boots, the magic swords, all other talismans, how easy it is to spin yarns.

It would be impossible in this place to catalogue even a tithe of the several incidents that are met with in folk-tales. Some of the most familiar have been given. They are the common property of all story-tellers. The same incidents differently combined compose the infinitely various stories, whose elemental likeness yet links them in an endless chain that girdles the globe, making kin of all mankind. *Ut ansa trahit ansam, ita fabula fabulam ;* as a chain's link draws a link, so does a story a story. They are countless : some invented solely for the gratification of the imagination ; others, again, seeming to have arisen from a few ideas of right and wrong, of duty or expediency. They are designed perhaps to serve as awful warnings, like the Biblical story of the bears that ate the rude little boys for making game of old age.

> " For wisdom dealt with mortal powers
> Where truth in closest words shall fail,
> When truth embodied in a tale
> Shall enter in at lowly doors."

We often meet with *märchen* exhibiting the reward of virtue and kindness, the punishment of greed or avarice ; the disaster following disobedience, as in the case of opening a forbidden door (witness the " Blue Beard " set of stories), or of infringing a marriage-taboo. See, for example, what calamity befell poor Psyche because she dared to disregard the prohibition, and lit a lamp and looked upon her sleeping bridegroom. This is the old-world, immortal story which everybody knows. For, take away the names of Cupid, Psyche, and of Aphrodite, the jealous mother-in-law, and what is left is nothing more nor less than a traditional popular tale.

> " The wise reeds talked in the river
> When this tale came to be born,"

and the social institutions of the savage imposed all sorts of restrictions, such as the following : Husband and wife may not meet by daylight ; the name of the husband is strictly taboo'd ; husbands may not see their wives unveiled for three years after marriage, and so on ; for these are the usages of savages at the present day. " Beauty and the Beast " is one of the innumerable stories which treat of the advancement of the beautiful youngest daughter, and the revengeful jealousy of the elder sisters. " Cinderella " is another example. Similarly, it is invariably the elder sons who are jealous of a fortunate junior. The natural explanation of this common incident in folk-tales is, that in polygamous countries the youngest child is the heir. A survival may be seen in the old custom of *Jüngsten Recht*, as it is called, or Borough English, which is of very wide diffusion.

Nursery-tales, or *märchen*, deal with the adventures of imaginary heroes and heroines, and are highly coloured with the supernatural. Among these may be cited " Jack and the Beanstalk." " Jack the Giant-Killer," "Cinderella," "Blue Beard," and "The Sleeping Beauty," as popular favourites. When the self-same traditional stories profess to deal with real occurrences, the adventures being attributed to supposed ancestral heroes, they are called *Sagas*, or heroic epics. By being tacked on to the gods, they enter the realm of Mythology. This term is sometimes applied to the collected myths of a nation, but belongs more especially to the myths or legends of cosmogony, of gods, and of heroes. The mythical stories connected with historical personages, or particular places, are usually called Legends. Folk-tales, *Volks-märchen*, or *Contes populaires* have been handed down by oral tradition from remote antiquity. At various times they have been lifted into literature, as, for instance, when we recognise them in the Odyssey and Rig-veda, in the "Thousand and One Nights," or, again, under more or less disguise of elaboration, by Boccaccio (1348), Straparola (1500), Basile (1637), and by Perrault (1697), or in old French fabliaux.

The Brothers Grimm, at the beginning of this century, were the first to collect the stories, for scientific purposes, from the lips of people living in Hesse and Hanau ; since their time, thousands of stories have been printed from all quarters of the globe.

Attempts have been made to classify all known

283

folk-tales under certain prominent types, so that each story in a new collection may be at once referred to the group to which it belongs. This is possible with a large number of stories, but others cannot be so simply identified. Seventy such types, forming a representative list, are given in the Folk-lore Society's " Handbook."

In a separate class must be placed the Drolls, or Comic Tales, of which the German " Clever Elsie " is a well-known example. The Danish " Not a Pin to Choose between Them " is another. In this story a man sets out in quest of three greater fools than his own wife, and easily finds them. Similar noodles supply the light comedy in stories told in India and all over Europe. The ludicrous adventures of " The M'Andrew Family," most delightful noodles, are recorded in Mr. Jacobs' " More Celtic Tales."

" Cumulative " stories are piled up by the repetition of all preceding steps upon the addition of each new one, as in " The House that Jack Built," and " The Old Woman and her Pig."

Popular folk-songs, or *Volkslieder*, play an important part in the scheme of folk-lore. Their study really began with Scott's " Minstrelsy of the Scottish Border " (1802–3).

The folk-song is probably older than the folk-tale. Stories told in rhyme are much more easily remembered, and all things worth remembering were rhythmically arranged and sung. Thus we find laws and ceremonial formulæ preserved in verse, as well as traditional narratives. It will be remembered that in many folk-tales the magic words which are to effect some miracle, and all invocations, are repeated in verse, or jiggling rhyme. The whole of the famous story of " Cat- skin " is preserved in more than one version of an English folk-song. But folk-songs or ballads, as a rule, differ from folk-tales, inasmuch as they lay claim to credibility. The characters in folk-tales whose adventures, disasters, and successes excite our interest, eventually attain their desires, and live happy ever after. The story of the popular ballad, on the contrary, has usually a tragic or a melan- choly ending. The lovers are united only in death (see pp. 73–4, *supra*). Songs tell of the dead mother coming back to comfort her sorrowing children, and of the dead lover who rises from the grave to console his beloved, as in the Swedish ballad of " Little Christina." She hears a light tapping on her chamber door ; she lets her dead betrothed come in, and she washes his feet with pure wine. The cock crows, and the dead must depart. The young girl follows her lover to the graveyard, and sits on his tomb. But he bids her go back to her dwelling- place. " Every time a tear falls from thine eyes," he says, " my shroud is full of blood ; every time thy heart is gay, my shroud is full of rose leaves." Love and Death are favourite themes of popular poetry ; others are afforded by Nature, War, and the Chase. Winter dies and Spring revives ; the time of the singing of birds is come ; the nightingale sings to the rose, the brooks murmur in cadence, and the pines are stirred to music by the wind in their tops ; lovely it is to rest at noontide and at evening. Popular poetry has a special interest in thus reflecting the emotions and sentiments of the folk. Their highest aspirations are sure to have been committed to their traditionary songs.

The skalds or bards chanted the praises of the popular heroes or headmen, till it became a custom for every fighting chief to have his own particular bard or bards. They went unarmed into the fight, and encouraged the combatants with their songs, as military music heartens the warrior of to-day. As the profession of bard declined, that of the ballad-monger took its place. These wandering minstrels sang for pay to any audience they could find, being welcome alike to courtly dame and lowly taverner, in the days when books were few, and newspapers were not at all. In the East, story-teller and ballad-monger are just where they were centuries ago. Like the immortal Homer, most of the wandering minstrels who carried the popular songs from village to village were blind men.

Italy is, *par excellence*, the land of song, the Italians being the most poetical people of Europe. The popular British ballad of Lord Ronald, otherwise Rowlande, which has been met with in Germany and Sweden, is still sung in Tuscany, Venetia, and Lombardy. Everywhere the poisoned food is the same—" roasted eel," or " eels boil'd in broo'." It is thought that the Italian version, sung 250 years ago in Verona, was most likely the original.

But besides the ballad, the love-song, the harvest-song, and the slogan, all popular rhymes connected with places (see p. 147), with superstitions, or with the weather come under the head of folk-poetry, as well as all lullabies and nursery-songs, and rhymes for children's amusements generally. Much attention has been paid to children's rhymes and formulas of play, which have been found to be handed down from immemorial antiquity, and to reflect the life, and even the religion, of long-past times. The games and rhymes of English children of to-day, and of their American cousins, are identical with those of Germany, France, Italy, and Sweden. It must be borne in mind that these are *traditional* games, handed down from generation to generation ; it is only of late years that descriptions of the games, and their rules, have been published. In the singing games, of which the tragic story of Jenny Jones is a remarkable specimen, we seem to get an insight into the nature of the earliest acted tragedy which developed into primitive drama. The mumming-plays, which may still be witnessed in certain of our own country districts, are folk-tales in' dramatic verse. The nursery-rhymes and riddles of the most distant and varied nations present the same striking identity. In China, as well as all over Europe, children repeat the well-known invocation beginning—

" Snail, snail, put out your horn."

Civilised and savage alike delight in asking riddles ; obviously they belong to a higher grade of savagery ; the original kind are old-fashioned problems, with a real answer, not like the modern verbal conundrum. Savages propound such as the following Zulu riddle : " Guess some men who are many and form a row ; they dance the wedding-dance, adorned in white hip-dresses." The answer to this is, " The teeth." The Basutos ask, " What throws itself from the mountain-top without being broken ? " Answer, " A waterfall." Of such is the famous enigma of the Sphinx, and Samson's well-known riddle, with its matter-of-fact answer.

The folk-lorist has another wide field for exploration in the department of old rhymes and old proverbs, which have preserved for our enlightenment much of the wisdom of the folk. History, as well as philosophy, may frequently underlie " wise saws ; " as, when one hears that " 'Tis time to yoke when the cart comes to the capples," in an English county, we know that the Celts here, at all events, have lived beyond the Teutonic Conquest, for *capples* is a corruption of a Celtic word for horses. Every country, whether civilised or savage, has its store of proverbs, and many collections have been made. Five thousand proverbs have been collected, orally, in Ulster ; and other abundant harvests attest the need of some scientific classification. The Servians say, as we do, that the Devil is not so black as he is painted. Saxo, the Dane, quotes many a proverb which finds an echo with us :—A friend is known at need ; any port in a storm ; the bird is infamous that fouls its own nest ; if there be a will for the deed, a way will open.; and, it takes cunning to catch a fox. " Set a thief to catch a thief " is ever our advice : " A thief myself, I know a thief's foot-prints," says an epigram of Callimachus.

The proverbial philosophy of uncivilised races may also bear comparison with our own. In West Africa they say, " He fled from the sword and hid in the scabbard," which is as forcible as our own " Out of the frying-pan into the fire." Sometimes a popular saying has its origin in a fable or story, as when we liken to the old man with his donkey the person who is anxious to please all and satisfies none. A favourite Chinese fable affords an example of this. Pigs in Korea are generally black; but a white one having once made its appearance, the king thought it worth offering to the Chinese Emperor, and accordingly sent ambassadors to present it. When they reached Peking, however, so many white pigs were to be seen, that the ambassadors thought it would be ridiculous to carry out their mission. Hence, " to offer a white pig to the Emperor " is equivalent to our " carrying coals to Newcastle," or the Greeks' " owls to Athens." The Chinaman, by the way, buys " a cat in a bag," not " a pig in a poke."

In conclusion, something further must be said as to the problem which has been repeatedly presented to the reader by the citation of myths and stories throughout these pages, and that is, the startling similarity in the substance of these stories, even when we compare those told by Hottentots, Maoris, Annamese, Samoans, Red Indians, or Eskimos with stories told in any European country. It has been found that certain incidents, plots, and characteristics occur everywhere—" as the ill-treatment of the youngest son or daughter, who is eventually successful, and is often the heir ; the substitution of a false bride for the true ; the abduction of a bride by a youthful hero, and the pursuit by her giant (or supernatural) father, who is outwitted by cunning ; a supernatural husband or wife, who is for some cause obliged to abandon a human mate ; forbidden chambers, and the disasters that follow from their being opened ; descents into the world of gloom, and the danger of eating there ; husband and wife forbidden to see each other or name each other's names ; the souls of the dead entering animal forms ; and the interchange of kindly offices, as if on equal terms, between men and beasts." Then again, it is not only the savage tales that contain the unnatural and irrational elements ; these, as has been shown, are commonly met with in European tales.

That the irrational elements in myths and tales have their origin in the uncivilised imagination is a conclusion that can scarcely be controverted. What rational being, for example, could conceive of an attachment (unless " *à la* Plato ") for a bashful young potato ? whereas a girl, in a Wallachian tale, actually marries a pumpkin ; and elsewhere, so a story goes, a girl is the mother of a gourd. Who would dream of an iron stove for a husband (as in the German story), except people on the same mental plane as the Hurons, who habitually married their girls, with a formal ceremony, to their fishing nets ? When, therefore, incidents such as these are related in civilised countries, we may either suppose that they have been handed down from the savage past in which they were conceived, or that they have been borrowed in recent times from the uncivilised.

A comparison of the myths and tales of different peoples throws this light upon their structure. They are survivals of a primitive stage of culture through which all races pass, and in which they much resemble each other, both in the crude workings of their minds and in the rude work of their hands. The same problems presented themselves to the aboriginal races in all parts of the world, and we see in myths their attempted solution. What was the origin of the world? How explain the sun's behaviour? Why does rain fall? These are the eternal questions—some, like Tertullian's, still unanswered. *Unde homo et quomodo, et unde Deus?* (Whence is man and how, and whence is God?) How was I born? said the Greek epigrammatist, whence am I? Why did I come? to go again. And so we have our Creation-myths, and those accounting for all natural phenomena; and with myths have many minds been appeased.

Another class of myth are mere fanciful inventions of the indulged imagination, like the romances of civilised times. The extraordinary and striking similarities of fancy displayed on this side of the globe and on that, call for some explanation. Has one nation borrowed its tales from another ? Did all tales start from one centre and spread to all the corners ? Have they been handed down from the common ancestors of the separate peoples ? Have identical ideas sprung up independently ? These are the problems which beset the student of folk-lore. No one theory, standing by itself, affords adequate explanation, but each may fit some particular case.

Where there is a common language there is a common stock of legends. We find similar tales in Greece and Norway, because both peoples have preserved them as their common heritage. But when Eskimos and Zulus tell similar stories, this explanation does not hold. In this case the stories have either been independently invented, or they have been carried from one part of the world to another. Aryan and non-Aryan legends may contain common mythical elements, and yet not be of common origin. In fact, nearly every myth which is found in different forms amongst different Aryan-speaking peoples can be paralleled by similar tales from the remotest quarters of the globe. For instance, our " Jack and the Beanstalk " myth is found among Zulus and American Indians, the central idea of all its variants being alike, by virtue of the like nature of the minds that conceived them. Again, because Australians have a star-myth resembling the Greek myth of the Pleiades, it is not necessary to conclude that they borrowed it from a European, or that they are a detached branch of the Indo-European race, who spread from one centre, bearing their tales with them. The ancestors of the Greeks and the Australians, wishing to explain certain phenomena, may both have hit upon the same idea, men's minds working alike under like conditions.

On the other hand, we meet with widely-scattered stories which are unmistakably of common origin. Such as the Tail-fisher stories given above (see pp. 266–7) ; their only difference is in the local colouring, the plot serving equally in Europe, Asia, Africa, and America.

" A wanderer is man from his birth,"

and the migrations of people in prehistoric times may well have secured the transmission of myth. Furthermore, the importation of myths is a natural consequence of traffic in slaves, and of the practice of obtaining wives from alien tribes, and of taking captives in war. Also, as a probable channel of communication, that ubiquitous, wandering, and specially gifted Oriental race, the Gipsies, must not be forgotten.

Undoubtedly the appearance of certain stories in Europe, Egypt, and South Africa tends to prove a historical connection, near or remote, between those regions. And it is possible to trace certain stories to their original home, just as one may trace the invention of the hammock to South America and the West Indies, whence it has spread over the world, carrying with it its Haitian name, *hamac*. But there is not necessarily a historical connection between distant countries in which similar customs are found to prevail, or in which, as has been said, similar myths are told. The likeness in the inventive faculty of remote peoples is traced in their chipped stone implements, in their pottery, and in their use of fire, and may equally be exhibited in their myths. To seek for a common origin of barbaric conceptions is as vain as to seek for a common origin of all barbaric culture, or for a single primitive language. Every savage group, as we know, has its own dialect, and coins its own expressions. No language becomes durable until it is the means of communication between numerous tribes aggregated into one people ; not till then can it disseminate story-germs.

The well-known exploit of William Tell, the wonderful marksman, may be cited as an instance of a myth which, in its general features, was known to our Aryan-speaking ancestors before they left their original cradle—wherever that may have been. Probably there was no such person as William Tell. At any rate, his existence is no less hypothetical than that of Mrs. 'Arris herself ; and whatever the patriotic Swiss may delight to tell, as to his shooting the apple from his son's head in 1296, his story has no historical value whatever. Saxo tells the same story of a Danish hero named Palnatoki, one of King Harold's body-guard, as occurring in the year 950. The story appears also in England, in the Ballad of William of Cloudeslee ; it appears in Norway, in Finland, and in Russia ; in Persia it is told by a poet born in 1119 ; and there is reason for supposing that it was known in India. Of one of their own marksmen, Samoyeds, Turks, and Mongolians have precisely the same tale to tell ; and probably the explanation lies in the fact that these have borrowed it in recent times from the Aryan-speaking nations, who have inherited their fireside legends, as well as their languages and their customs, from a common ancestral stock. An examination of the Welsh story of the faithful Gellert and its variants leads to the same conclusion as to its Aryan origin.

Those who would contend that the popular tales were carried to Europe from India within historical times, and diffused chiefly through literary channels, such as translations of Eastern story-books and the like, should be disconcerted by the discovery that popular tales resembling those of India and Europe are found on papyri of Ancient Egypt, dating 1400 years before our era.

SELECTED LIST OF BOOKS

BARING-GOULD. *Strange Survivals.* 1892.

BUSK. *The Folk-songs of Italy.* 1887.

CLODD. *Myths and Dreams.* 1885.

THISELTON DYER. *The Folk-lore of Plants.* 1889.

ELTON. *Origins of English History.* 1882.

FISKE. *Myths and Myth-makers.* 1873.

Folk-lore Society's Publications.

FRAZER. *The Golden Bough.* 1890.

GRIMM. *Teutonic Mythology.* 4 vols. 1880–1888.

HALL. *Pedigree of the Devil.* 1883.

Journals of the American Folk-lore Society.

LANG : *Custom and Myth.* 1884.
   Myth Ritual and Religion. 1887.
   Cock Lane and Common Sense. 1894.

MARTINENGO-CESARESCO. *Essays in the Study of Folk-songs.* 1886.

POWELL and VIGFUSSON. *Corpus Poeticum Boreale.* 1883.

SPENCER. *Principles of Sociology.* 1877.

TYLOR : *Early History of Mankind.* 1865.
   Primitive Culture. 3rd edition. 1891.

INDEX

INDEX

INDEX

INDEX

137 *ff*; rain-gods, thunder-gods, 141; wind-, 142; earth-, 142; not immortal, 155
Good and evil spirits, and dualistic deities, 135, 136
Gorgons, 240
Goths, ancestor-worship by, 63
Granny's divination, 24
Grateful beast, 275
Graves, objects placed in, for use of the dead, 48
Great Britain as isle of souls, 188
Great Hare, the, 115, 256
Greece: sneeze salutation, 7; chiromancy, 28; armpitting, 57; the σκιά, 68; butterfly-soul, 71; sacred animals, 115; barbaric element in myths, 117; werewolf, 124; new fire, 138; fire-god, 140; legend of gift of fire, 153; anthropomorphic gods, 156; conception of firˌaˌment, 182; voyage to other-world, 186, 187; Hades, 192; personification of disease, 214; rain-charm, 224; changelings, 231; earthquake-myth, 235; star-myths, 244, 247, 293; Uranos-myth, 254
Greek epigram, on telling bees, 24; on soul's egress, 42
Grimm, 70, 166, 201, 283
Gudrun, 28
Guiding beasts, 104
Gunthram, King, legend of, 42

HADES, 183, 184, 186, 187, 192, 193, 194
Hag-ridden, 161
Haidahs, 200
Hair of dog, 12, 218; human hair, precautions respecting, 203, 213
Hamadryad, 79
Hamlet, ghost in, 60
Hammock, 295
Hand numerals, 38; marks as prophylactics, 107
Hara-kari, 51
Harald, shade of, propitiated, 48
Hare, Easter, 32; an object of disgust, 81; magical character of, 81; witch in form of, 81;

as witch's associate, 91; eating-taboo in Britain, 101; as totem, 102; sacred to Eostre, 102; hare crossing path unlucky, 109; name for last sheaf, 144; in the moon, 250, cleft lip of, 269
Harpies, 240
Haruspication. *See* Divination
Harvest, 32, 143; harvest lady or queen, name for last sheaf, 144
Hat, raising the, 6
Haunted house, 59, 161
Hearth-cult, 64, 139
Heathen apologists, 118
Heaven, personified, 141; and Earth, universal father and mother, 143
Heaven-bursters, 256
Hebrides, low culture in, 5
Hecuba, play of, 61
He-goat, name for last sheaf, 144
Hela, 45
Helenus, 110, 277
Hell, shoes, 45, 190; hell-bridge, 189; Arctic, 194; Woden visits, 225. *See* Hades
Helpful animal, 111
Hephaistos, 140, 158
Herb-doctor, 233
Hercules, 240
Hermes, 29, 183
Hermotimus, 43
Herodotus on ancestor-worship, 62; the Neuri, 124; Osiris, 204
Heroic epics, 283
Herondas, 41
Hesiod on days, 21; punished for impiety, 118; on Hades, 187; on monsters, 240; on crow's blackness, 266
Hestia, 139
Hiawatha, Four Winds in, 142
Hill, soul must climb. *See* Mountain
Hindmost, devil take, 159
Hindu, telling the bees, 24; hell-shoe, 46; suttee, 51; suicide for revenge, 61; religion, trees in, 80; respect for cattle, 100; animistic sacrifice, 134; im-mortality, secret of, 155; corp chre, 220; rainbow, 241

309

INDEX

311

INDEX

fice, 51, 52; laying barrow-ghost, 58; blood-mingling, 99; idolatry, 174; voyage to Hades, 193; on weather-making, 197; witchcraft, 216; proverbs, 289; William Tell legend in, 296

Scamander, 145

Scandinavia: widow-sacrifice, 52; swanmaiden, 121; man-bear, 127; Berserker rage, 128; mortal gods, 155; human sacrifice, 176; burial in boats, 184; Walhalla, 193

Scarab, 114

Schiller, 42

Scold-bridles, 32

Scotland: superstition, 9; hooping-cough cure, 12; empty cradle, 19; Easter egg, 31; banshee, 64; witch as hare, and variants, 91, 92, 93; totemism, 98; descent claimed from seal, 101; swanmaiden, 121; "watching spirit," 146; sacred wells, 149; folk-legend, 168; selling wind, 198; name-taboo, 205; disease-transference, 213; cure for epilepsy, 214; corp chre, 220; life-token, 222; incantations, 224; Evil Eye, 228; changeling, 231

Scott, Sir Walter. See Hell-shoe, Silver bullet, and Folk-songs

Sea, burial at, 58

Sea-god, 145

Sea-monster, shot with silver bullet, 94; descent claimed from, 98; legends of, 238

Seal, Irish regard for, 100, 101; descent claimed from, in Scotland, 101; sealmaiden, 121

Seb and Nut, 253, 254

Second-self, belief in, established, 40. See Ghost, Soul, Spirit

Seer, powers of the, 26

Self-possession, 6

Semitic totemism, 97; fetichism, 174

Separable soul, 36 ff; in Egyptian, 80; and other folk-tales, 83 ff, 278

Serpent, as fetich, 176; worship, 177; devil as, 158; flesh, virtue of, 276

Servia, 214, 289

Set, 136

Seven, the number, 23

Shadow, the soul in the, 67, 68

Shadowless man, 159

Shakespeare, on odd numbers, 22; transmigration, 70; changeling, 231

Shaman, 64

Shark, human victims for, 239

Sheaf, the last, 143

Shelley, 42, 207

Sheol, 184, 193

Shoes, hell-, 45

Shoe-throwing at weddings, 18

Shoulder-blade in divination, 28

Shropshire, superstition in, 9

Siam: Crown Prince of, 49; prayers to the dead, 49; soul's exit, 65

Siberia, folk-tale from, 84, 122; earthquakes, 235

Sicily, wheat cast on bride in, 18

Sieve and shears, 28

Sigfred hides his name, 205

Sigmund as werewolf, 124

Sigurd, 276

Silver bullet, 94

"Singing Bone," folk-tale of the, 77

Singing games, 288

Siva, 174

Six Swans, story of, 122

Skalds, 286

Skamandros, 145

Skerne, river, 147

Skin, animal's, use of, 126

Skulls bored for ghost's egress, 66

Sky personified, 135, 141

Slaves, sacrifice of, 51

Slavonic, widow - sacrifice, 52; feast of the dead, 55; werewolf superstition, 124; word Bôg, 136; vampire, 151; Nature-myth, 249

Sleep, experience during, 40; connected with death, 44

Sleeper, objection to waking, 41

Sling and stone, 33

Slogan, 287

Slovac legend, 76

Smallness of the ghost, 59, 60

Smallpox personified, 214

317

INDEX

INDEX

WADDERS, rice at wedding used by, 18 ; totemism, 103
Wahuma, divination of the, 25
Wäinämöinen. *See* Kalewala
Walkyries. *See* Valkyries
Walling-up. *See* Burying alive
Walloons, charm carried by, 11 ; folk-tale, 163
Wart-charms, 12, 213
Warwickshire, Easter hare in, 32
Water, blessed on Easter Sunday, to protect cattle, 8 ; deities, spirits, 144 *ff*; human sacrifice to, 146 *ff*; worship, 149 ; dead must cross, 184 *ff*; spirits cannot cross, 185
Water-kelpies, 150
Water-lilies, danger in plucking, 103
Waterloo, poppies on field of, 72
Waterspouts, myth of, 242
Watling Street or Milky way, 244
Wax-figure, melting, 218 *ff*
Wayland Smith, 158. *See* Weyland
Weapon-salve, 12
Weapons in tombs, 44, 50, 57
Weasel, soul as, 44, 72
Weather-, lore, 20, 110 ; making, 197, 224 ; prophecies, 24, 110
Wedding, throwing rice, hops, wheat, shoes, &c., at, 17-18
Weighing the soul, 191
Wells, sacred, 12, 149, 213 ; offerings at, 13, 149
Well-worship, 149, 213
Welsh, variant of Midas story, 78 ; belief in animal ancestry, 98 ; story of Gellert, 296
Werewolves, 112, 123 *ff*; of the Middle Ages, 128
Weyland the Smith, 120. *See* Wayland
Wheat cast on bride, 18 ; wheat-bride, name given to last sheaf, 144
Whinny-moore, the, 45
Whirlpool, spirit of, 74
White Mountain, sacred, 180
Wicking, burials, 44 ; sacrifice, 176 ; voyage to other-world, 186
Widow-sacrifice, 51

Wight, 151
Wiltshire, tooth-ache charm in, 11
"Wind-and-Weather" story, 208
Wind, personified, 142 ; *see* "Four Winds ; " buying and selling, 198 ; raising the, 198
Wind-god, 142
Witch of Endor, 26, 151
Witches hinder butter-making, 7, 93 ; steal children, 8 ; bespell cattle, 8 ; cannot cross iron, 15 ; transform themselves and others, 88, 90 ; rule weather, 89 ; witch as hare, 91 ; fox, 92 ; butterfly, 93 ; cat and horse, 94 ; magpie, 94 ; raise the dead, 151 ; ride brooms, 158
Witchcraft, iron against, 8, 15, 16, 231 ; lycanthropy as a species of, 128 ; in Ireland, 197, 215 ; with name, 203 *ff*
Withershins, evil spells wrought, 20
Wives, capture of, 33, 34, 294
Wizards. *See* Sorcerers
Woden, sworn brotherhood of, 99 ; his raven and wolf, 104 ; hides his name, 205 ; on gallows tree, 224
Wolf, and Seven Kids, 116 ; name for last sheaf, 144
Wolsungs, 200, 205, 276
Wolves, descent claimed from, 98, 110
Woman gives birth to animals, 112, 113, 278
Wood-mare, name for echo, 70
World pervaded by spirits, 74
Worship, sun and moon, 20 ; ancestor-, 62, 63 ; ghost-, 62 ; tree-, 80, 81, 149 ; totem-, 96 *ff*, 103 ; animal-, 104, 114 ; plant-, 103 ; Nature-, 137 ; fire-, 139 ; earth-, 142 *ff*; water-, 148 *ff*; fetich-, 173, 178 ; serpent-, 177
Written charms, 14

XERXES, 145

YAMA, 154
Yawning, as case of "possession," 64
Yehl, 153, 154

321   X

APPENDIX

BIBLIOGRAPHY OF FOLK-LORE

[NOTE.—This list is compiled for the use of English readers, the selection being therefore restricted as much as possible to English works. Foreign books are given only when they are unquestionably the best on the subject, or because none exist in the English language, and no attempt is made to provide a guide to the mass of foreign literature on Folk-lore.]

As this work is, in the main, an exposition and interpretation of the facts of Folk-lore according to the principles of the Anthropological School, the reader is referred, for what is still the fullest and most authoritative statement of the facts of early belief and practice, to

Dr. Tylor's *Primitive Culture*, 2 vols., 1903, in which the more or less entirely backward races are drawn upon for instances and examples.

The specific relation of rite or institution to story is dealt with by

Mr. Andrew Lang in *Custom and Myth*, 1884, whilst the same author's *Myth, Ritual, and Religion*, 2 vols., 1899, is concerned more definitely with the particular aspects of early psychology, connoted by the title.

Mr. Edward Clodd's *Myths and Dreams*, 1885, discusses the psychological basis of certain features of Folk-lore.

Special and important aspects of the early culture underlying modern European Folk-lore are dealt with in their world-wide significance by

APPENDIX

Mr. J. G. Frazer, *Totemism,* Edinburgh, 1887.

Mr. Crawley, *Sexual Taboos (Anthropological Journal,* vol. xxiv.), *Food Taboos (Folk-lore,* June 1875), the gist of these papers is partly reproduced in the same author's *The Mystic Rose,* 1902.

Mr. E. Sidney Hartland, *The Legend of Perseus,* 3 vols. 1894–96. (The theory of Life: its origin and manifestations.)

Special application of the hypotheses urged in the preceding works

(*a*) to Semitic Religion,

will be found in **Prof. Robertson Smith's** *Lectures on the Religion of the Semites,* Edinburgh, 1889.

(*b*) to the early stage of European culture,

in **Mannhardt's** *Wald- und Feld-Kulte,* 2 vols., Berlin, 1875–77, describing and expounding the ritual of early agriculture which has survived to the present day.

Mr. Frazer, in *The Golden Bough,* 3 vols., 1900, has applied Mannhardt's method and theory to setting forth and explaining the facts connected with belief in an external soul, with all its implications.

Dr. Jevons' *Introduction to the Science of Religion,* 1897, applies the same method and principles to an account of the probable origin and development of the religious sentiment.

The foregoing works are based equally upon the survivals in European Folk-lore and the culture of non-European backward, or early races.

For European Folk-lore specifically :

In **Prof. K. Pearson's** *The Chances of Death, and other Studies in Evolution,* 2 vols., 1897, it is contended that Aryan culture can be traced back beyond the patriarchal stage studied by Hearn and Fustel de Coulanges to a matriarchal stage.

MacLennan's *Works* (see *infra,* p. 347) should be consulted in this connection.

Mr. G. Laurence Gomme's *Ethnology in Folk-lore,* 1892, essays to determine and discriminate the racial elements in European Folk-lore.

For a collection of general ethnological facts the student is referred to :

A. Featherman's *Social History of the Races of Mankind,* 7 vols., 1881–91.

The religious basis of European Folk-lore may be studied historically and geographically in :

GREEK RELIGION.

Farnell, *The Cults of the Greek States,* vols. i., ii., 1896–97.

Jane Harrison, *Prolegomena to the Study of Greek Religion,* 1903.

ROMAN RELIGION.

Granger, *The Worship of the Romans,.* 1896.

Jevons, *Plutarch's Romane Questions,* with Dissertations on Italian Cults, &c., 1892.

L. Preller, *Römische Mythologie,* 2 vols., 1881–83.

SCANDINAVIAN RELIGION.

Corpus Poeticum Boreale, by **Vigfusson and Powell,** 2 vols., Oxford, 1883 (giving the old poetical sources of mythology).

Saxo Grammaticus, translated by **Oliver Elton,** 1894 (the mediæval, learned account of the Northern mythology).

Anderson, *Norse Mythology : the Religion of our Forefathers,* Chicago, 1875.

V. Rydberg, *Teutonic Mythology,* 1889.

CELTIC RELIGION.

Prof. Rhŷs, *Hibbert Lectures,* 1886.

Kuno Meyer, *The Voyage of Bran.* With Essays upon the " Irish Vision of the Happy Otherworld," and the " Celtic Doctrine of Re-birth," by **Alfred Nutt,** 2 vols., 1895–97.

SANSCRIT RELIGION.

H. H. Wilson, *Works,* 1862 (comprising *Essays on the Religion of the Hindus,* 2 vols.).

Monier Williams, *Religious Thought and Life in India,* an account of the Religions of the Indian Peoples, 1883.

H. Oldenberg, *Vedische Religion,* 1895.

A. A. Macdonell's articles on Vedic Religion, in *Grundriss der Arischen Philologie,* 1897.

The social and economic basis of European and Asiatic Aryan Folk-lore may be studied in

Hearn, *The Aryan Household, its Structure and its Development,* 1879.

Fustel de Coulanges, *La Cité Antique.*

G. L. Gomme, *Folk-lore Relics of Early Village Life,* 1883.

The Village Community, 1890.

For the Folk-lore of the British Isles :

(*a*) Folk-lore of the English-speaking districts :

Brand, *Popular Antiquities of England, Scotland, and Ireland,* by Sir Henry Ellis, 3 vols. This still remains the best repertory of English Folk-lore. It has been very largely supplemented by the

Publications of the Folk-lore Society, 1878–1903, and by the items of Folk-lore contributed to *Notes and Queries,* and reprinted as

Choice Notes and Queries, 1859.

William Hone, *Everyday Book, Year Book, and Table Book,* 4 vols., reprinted 1881–82. (A Collection of English Mythology, Folk-lore, Popular Antiquities, Customs, &c.)

J. O. Halliwell, *Popular Rhymes and Nursery Tales,* 1849.

Child, *English and Scottish Popular Ballads,* 10 vols., Boston, 1882–95.

Chambers, *Popular Rhymes of Scotland,* 1870.

Joseph Jacobs, *English Fairy Tales,* 1890 ; *More English Fairy Tales,* 1894. 2 vols., with notes and parallels.

Addy, *Household Tales and other Traditional Remains.* Collected in the counties of York, Lincoln, Derby, and Nottingham, 1895.

Wm. Henderson, *Notes on the Folk-lore of the Northern Counties of England and the Borders,* 1879 (F.-L. Soc.).

Charlotte Burne, *Shropshire Folk-lore,* 3 parts, 1883–85.

W. Gregor, *Notes on the Folk-lore of the North-East of Scotland,* 1881 (F.-L. Soc.).

(*b*) Folk-lore of earlier Celtic-speaking districts in which English has been introduced within the last few centuries :

Hunt, *Popular Romances of the West of England ; or, The Drolls, Traditions, and Superstitions of Old Cornwall,* 1881.

W. Bottrell, *Traditional and Hearthside Stories of West Cornwall,* 1870, 1885.

Mrs. Bray, *The Borders of the Tamar and the Tavy,* 2 vols., 1879.

A. W. Moore, *The Folk-lore of the Isle of Man,* 1891.

(*c*) Folk-lore of Celtic-speaking districts :

Silva Gadelica, A Collection of Tales (Early Mediæval) in Irish. Translated by **Standish H. O'Grady,** 2 vols., 1892.

Joseph Jacobs, *Celtic Fairy Tales,* 2 vols., 1892–94, with notes and parallels.

J. F. Campbell, *Popular Tales of the West Highlands,* 4 vols., Edinburgh, 1860–62.

Waifs and Strays of Celtic Tradition ; vol. ii. *Folk and Hero Tales from Argyllshire,* Gaelic and English, by MacInnes, with Notes by Alfred Nutt, 1890 ; vol. iii. *Folk and Hero Tales,* by McDougall, 1891 ; vol. iv. *The Fians,* by J. G. Campbell, 1891.

T. Crofton Croker, *Fairy Legends and Traditions of the South of Ireland,* 3 vols., 1826.

P. Kennedy, *Fireside Stories of Ireland,* 1895.

J. Curtin, *Hero Tales of Ireland,* 1894. *Myths and Folk-lore of Ireland,* 1890. *Tales of the Irish Fairies,* 1895.

D. Hyde, *Beside the Fire : Irish-Gaelic Folk-tales,* 1890.

W. Larminie, *West Irish Folk-tales and Romances,* 1893.

Mabinogion, translated from the Welsh by Lady Charlotte Guest, with Notes by Alfred Nutt, London, 1902.

E. Owen, *Welsh Folk-lore,* 1896.

Prof. Rhŷs, *Welsh Fairy Tales in Y Cymmrodor,* 1881 *sqq.* (For Breton Tales, see **Luzel** and **Sébillot,** under "French Folk-lore.")

TEUTONIC FOLK-LORE.

Jacob Grimm, *Teutonic Mythology,* 4 vols., 1880–88.

Benj. Thorpe, *Northern Mythology,* 3 vols., 1851–52.

Grimm, *Household Tales,* translated from the German by Margaret Hunt, 2 vols., 1884.

B. Thorpe, *Yuletide Stories . . . .* from the Swedish, Danish, and German, 1853.

Keightley, *The Fairy Family,* ballads and metrical tales, illustrating the fairy mythology of Europe, 1857.

SCANDINAVIAN FOLK-LORE.

G. W. Dasent, *Popular Tales from the Norse,* Edinburgh, 1888. *Tales from the Fjeld,* 1896.

W. A. Craigie, *Scandinavian Folk-lore,* 1896.

Baring-Gould, *Iceland, its Scenes and Sagas,* 1863.

Powell and Magnusson, *Icelandic Legends,* collected by Jón Arnason, 2 vols., 1864–66.

NEO-LATIN FOLK-LORE.

FRENCH.

Perrault, *Contes du Temps Passé,* with Introduction by A. Lang, Oxford, 1888.

E. H. Carnoy, *Contes Français,* Paris, 1885.

J. F. Bladé, *Contes Populaires recueillis en Agenais,* Paris, 1874. *Contes Populaires de la Gascogne,* 3 vols., Paris, 1886.

Em. Cosquin, *Contes Populaires de Lorraine,* 2 vols., Paris, 1887.

F. M. Luzel, *Contes Populaires de la Basse Bretagne,* 3 vols., Paris, 1887.

Léon Pineau, *Les Contes Populaires du Poitou,* Paris, 1891. *Le Folk-lore du Poitou,* Paris, 1892.

Paul Sébillot, *Coûtumes Populaires de la Haute-Bretagne,* Paris, 1886. *Contes Populaires de la Haute-Bretagne,* Paris, 1880. *Littérature Orale de la Haute-Bretagne,* Paris, 1881.

BELGIAN.

E. Monseur, *Le Folk-lore Wallon,* Bruxelles [1892].

Bulletin de Folk-lore [Wallon], 1891, &c.

ITALIAN.

Basile's *Pentamerone,* translated by J. E. Taylor, 1848.

T. F. Crane, *Italian Popular Tales,* 1885.

R. H. Busk, *The Folk-lore of Rome,* collected by word of mouth from the people, 1874.

The Italian reader is referred to

Straparola, *Le tredici piacevoli notti* (1st ed. 1550).

Giuseppe Pitré, *Biblioteca delle Tradizioni popolari Siciliame,* 20 vols., Palermo, 1871–96. *Novelle Popolari Toscane,* Firenze, 1885.

SPANISH.

(Very little Folk-lore represented in English.)

R. H. Busk, *Patrañas, or Spanish Stories,* 1870.

Mrs. Middlemore, *Round a Posada Fire,* 1881. *Spanish Legendary Tales,* 1885.

Marin, *Biblioteca de las Tradiciones Populares Españolas,* 11 vols., Sevilla, Madrid, 1883–86.

Caballero, *Cuentos, Oraciones, Adivinas y Refranes Populares é Infantiles,* Madrid, 1878.

Maspons y Labrós, *Lo Rondallayre,* Barcelona, 1871. *Cuentos Populars Catalans,* Barcelona, 1885.

Milá y Fontanals, *Observaciones sobre la Poesia Popular.*

PORTUGUESE.

Pedroso, *Portuguese Folk-tales,* 1882 (F.-L. Soc.).

Theophilo Braga, *Contos tradicionaes do Povo Portuguez,* 2 vols., Porto, N.D.

F. Adolpho Coelho, *Contos Populares Portuguezes,* Lisbon, 1879.

NEO-GREEK FOLK-LORE.

Lucy Garnett, *The Women of Turkey and their Folk-lore,* 2 vols., 1890–91. *Greek Folk Poesy,* 2 vols., 1896.

E. M. Geldart, *Folk-lore of Modern Greece,* 1884.

Rennell Rodd, *The Customs and Lore of Modern Greece,* 1892.

Abbott, *Macedonian Folk-lore,* 1902.

E. Legrand, *Contes Populaires Grecs,* Paris, 1881.

J. G. von Hahn, *Griechische und Albanesische Märchen,* 2 vols., Leipzig, 1864.

SLAVONIC FOLK-LORE.

W. R. S. Ralston, *Russian Folk-tales,* 1873.
The Songs of the Russian People, as illustrative of Slavonic Mythology and Russian Social Life, 1872.

W. Denton, *Serbian Folk-lore,* 1874.

Roumanian Fairy Tales and Legends, 1881.

A. H. Wratislaw, *Sixty Folk-tales,* from exclusively Slavonic Sources, 1889.

I. F. Hapgood, *Epic Songs of Russia,* New York, 1886.

J. Curtin, *Myths and Folk-tales of the Russians, Western Slavs and Magyars,* 1890.

NON-ARYAN EUROPEAN FOLK-LORE.

W. Webster, *Basque Legends,* 1877.

Castren, *Vorlesungen über die Finnische Mythologie,* Petersburg, 1853.

J. M. Crawford, *Kalewala,* 2 vols., New York, 1889.

W. F. Kirby, *The Hero of Esthonia, and Other Studies in the Romantic Literature of that Country,* 2 vols., 1895.

J. Abercromby, "Legends of the Mordvins" (*Folk-lore Journal,* vol. vii.).

J. **Abercromby,** *The Pre- and Proto-historic Finns,* 2 vols., 1898.

Ch. Billson, *The Popular Poetry of the Finns,* 1900.

Jones and Kropf, *The Folk-tales of the Magyars,* 1889 (F.-L. Soc.).

FOLK-LORE OF INDIA.

E. T. Dalton, *Descriptive Ethnology of Bengal,* Calcutta, 1872.

H. H. Risley, *The Tribes and Castes of Bengal,* 2 vols., Calcutta, 1891.

Sir H. M. Elliot, *Memoirs on the History, Folk-lore, and Distribution of the Races of the North-Western Provinces of India,* 2 vols., 1869.

W. Crooke, *An Introduction to the Popular Religion and Folk-lore of Northern India,* 1897.

Sacred Books of the East, edited by **Max Müller,** 40 vols., Oxford, 1879–1900 [still proceeding].

The Jataka ; or, Stories of the Buddha's Former Births, translated from the Pāli by various hands, under the editorship of **Prof. Cowell,** Cambridge, 1895, &c.

The Fables of Bidpai, edited by **J. Jacobs,** 1888.

Barlaam and Josaphat, English Lives of Buddha, edited by **Joseph Jacobs,** 1896.

Th. Benfey, *Pantchatantra* (German), 2 vols., Leipzig, 1856.

Kathá-Sarit-Ságara, or Ocean of the Streams of Story, translated from the original Sanskrit by C. H. Tawney, M.A., 2 vols., Calcutta, 1880–84.

J. Jacobs, *Indian Fairy Tales,* 1902. (Notes and Parallels.)

M. Frere, *Old Deccan Days;* or Hindoo Fairy Legends current in Southern India, 1870.

Lal Behari Day, *Folk-tales of Bengal,* 1883.

A. Campbell, *Santal Folk-tales,* Pokhuria, 1891.

J. H. Knowles, *Folk-tales of Kashmir,* 1888.

Natêsa Sâstri, *Folk-lore in Southern India,* 3 parts, Bombay, 1884, 1886, 1888.

Steel and Temple, *Wideawake Stories* (from the Punjab and Kashmir), Bombay, 1884.

M. Stokes, *Indian Fairy Tales,* 1880.

C. Swynnerton, *Indian Nights' Entertainments;* or Folk-tales from the Upper Indus, 1892.

Rájá Rasálu. The Adventures of the Panjáb Hero, Rájá Rasálu, and other Folk-tales of the Panjáb, Calcutta, 1884.

R. C. Temple, *Legends of the Punjâb,* 2 vols., Bombay, N.D.

North-Indian Notes and Queries: A monthly periodical, edited by **Wm. Crooke, B.A.,** 5 vols., Allahabad, 1891–1900 [still proceeding].

Marjory Wardrop, *Georgian Folk-tales,* 1894.

R. H. Busk, *Sagas from the Far East; or Kalmouk and Mongolian Traditionary Tales,* 1873.

W. R. S. Ralston, *Tibetan Tales derived from Indian Sources* (from the German of von Schiefner), 1882.

EGYPTIAN AND MEDIÆVAL ORIENTAL FOLK-LORE.

Flinders Petrie, *Egyptian Tales,* 1896.

G. Maspéro, *Contes Populaires de l'Egypte Ancien,* Paris, 1882.

De Rochemonteix, *Quelques Contes Nubiens,* Paris, 1888.

Sir Richard Burton, *The Thousand and One Nights,* 12 vols., 1894; also **Lady Burton's** edition, 5 vols., 1887–88.

Lane, *The Arabian Nights,* 3 vols., 1882.

PERSIAN FOLK-LORE.

W. A. Clouston, *Persian Tales from Various Sources,* 1892.

CHINESE FOLK-LORE.

De Groot, *The Religious System of China, its Ancient Forms, Evolution,* [&c.], 2 vols., Leyden, 1892–94.

J. H. Gray, *China : A History of the Laws, Manners and Customs of the People,* 2 vols., 1878.

J. Doolittle, *Social Life of the Chinese, with some Account of their Religions, Customs, Opinions,* 2 vols., 1886.

N. B. Dennys, *The Folk-lore of China and its Affinities with that of the Aryan and Semitic Races,* 1876.

Herbert A. Giles, *Strange Stories from a Chinese Studio,* 2 vols., 1880.

H. N. Allen, *Korean Tales, a Collection of Stories from the Korean Folk-lore,* 1889.

JAPANESE FOLK-LORE.

Sir Ed. J. Reed, *Japan : its History, Traditions, and Religions,* 2 vols., 1880.

A. B. Mitford, *Tales of Old Japan,* 2 vols., 1871.

AINO.

E. J. Batchelor, *The Ainu and their Folk-lore,* 1901.

Basil Hall Chamberlain, *Aino Folk-tales,* 1888 (privately printed, F.-L. Soc.). *Language, Mythology, &c., of Japan,* Tokio, 1887.

AUSTRALIAN FOLK-LORE.

Edward Curr, *The Australian Race, its Origin, Languages, Customs,&c.,*4 vols.,Melbourne,1886–87.

James Dawson, *Australian Aborigines : the Languages and Customs of several Tribes of Aborigines in the Western District of Victoria, Australia,* Melbourne, 1881.

Fison and Howitt, *Kamilaroi and Kurnai : Group Marriage and Relationship, and Marriage by Elopement. Drawn chiefly from the Usage of Australian Aborigines,* Melbourne, 1880.

Brough Smith, *The Aborigines of Victoria,* 2 vols.

Lumholtz, *Among Cannibals ;* an account of Four Years' Camp Life with the Aborigines of Queensland, 1889.

H. Ling Roth, *The Aborigines of Tasmania,* 1890.

Mrs. K. L. Parker, *Australian Legendary Tales,* 1896. *More Australian Legendary Tales,* 1898.

Matthew, *Eagle-Hawk and Crow,* 1899.

POLYNESIAN FOLK-LORE.

R. H. Codrington, *The Melanesians : Studies in their Anthropology and Folk-lore,* Oxford, 1891.

Wm. Ellis, *Polynesian Researches, during a residence of nearly eight years in the Society and Sandwich Islands,* 4 vols., 1831.

H. B. Guppy, *The Solomon Islands and their Natives,* 1887.

Geo. Turner, *Samoa a Hundred Years ago and long before.* Together with Notes on the Cults and Customs of twenty-three other islands in the Pacific, 1884.

W. W. Gill, *Myths and Songs from the South Pacific,* 1876.

H. H. Romilly, *From my Verandah in New Guinea,* Scenes and Traditions, with an Introduction on New Guinea Folk-lore by A. Lang, 1889.

MAORI FOLK-LORE.

Sir George Grey, *Polynesian Mythology and Ancient Traditional History of the New Zealand Race as furnished by their Priests and Chiefs,* 1855.

White, *Ancient History of the Maori,* 2 vols., 1887–88.

E. Shortland, *Maori Religion and Mythology,* illustrated by Translations of Traditions, Karakia, &c., 1882.

R. Taylor, *New Zealand and its Inhabitants,* illustrating the Origin, Manners, Customs, Mythology, Religion, Rites, Songs, Proverbs, Fables and Language of the Maori and Polynesian Races in general, 1870.

K. McCosh Clark, *Maori Tales and Legends,* 1896.

NORTH AMERICAN FOLK-LORE.

J. G. Müller, *Geschichte der Amerikanischen Urreligionen,* Basle, 1867.

R. M. Dorman, *The Origin of Primitive Superstitions, and their Development into the Worship of Spirits, and the Doctrine of Spiritual Agency among the Aborigines of America.* Philadelphia, 1881.

H. H. Bancroft, *The Native Races of the Pacific States of North America,* 5 vols., 1875–76.

Geo. Catlin, *Illustrations of the Manners, Customs and Condition of the North American Indians,* 2 vols., 1876.

Journal of American Folk-lore, 1888–1903.

Annual Reports of the Bureau of Ethnology, 23 vols., 1879–1900.

D. G. Brinton, *American Hero-Myths:* a Study in the Native Religions in the Western Continent, Philadelphia, 1882.

The Myths of the New World. A Treatise on the Symbolism and Mythology of the Red Race of America, 1896.

H. R. Schoolcraft, *The Myth of Hiawatha and other Oral Legends,* Philadelphia, 1856.

C. G. Leland, *The Algonquin Legends of New England,* 1884.

Washington Matthews, *Navaho Legends,* 1897 (Am. F.-L. Soc.).

G. B. Grinnell, *Blackfoot Lodge Tales.* The Story of a Prairie People, 1893. *Pawnee Hero-stories and Folk-tales,* with notes, 1893.

Charles F. Lummis, *The Man who Married the Moon, and other Pueblo-Indian Folk-stories,* New York, 1894.

S. T. Rand, *Legends of the Micmacs,* New York, 1894.

Emile Petitot, *Traditions Indiennes du Canada Nord Ouest,* Paris, 1888.

ESKIMO FOLK-LORE.

H. Rink, *Tales and Traditions of the Eskimo* (from the Danish), Edinburgh, 1875.

SOUTH AMERICAN FOLK-LORE.

Im Thurn, *Among the Indians of Guiana:* being Sketches, chiefly Anthropologic, from the Interior of British Guiana, 1883.

J. H. Bernau, *Missionary Labours in British Guiana ;* with remarks on the Manners, Customs and Superstitious Rites of the Aborigines, 1847.

Von den Steinen, *Unter den Naturvölkern Central-Brasiliens,* Berlin, 1894.

Garcilasso, *First Part of the Royal Commentaries of the Yncas.* Translated by Clements R. Markham, 2 vols., 1869–71 (Hakluyt Soc.).

Narratives of the Rites and Laws of the Yncas. Translated from the original Spanish MSS., 1873 (Hakluyt Soc.).

De Acosta, *The Natural and Moral History of the Indies,* 2 vols., 1880 (Hakluyt Soc.).

Sylvio Roméro, *Contos Populares do Brazil,* Lisbon, 1885.

AFRICAN FOLK-LORE.

Revoil, *Contes Berbères,* Paris, 1882.

J. Rivière, *Contes de la Kabylie,* Paris, 1882.

Hanoteau, *Poésies Populaires de la Kabylie de Jurjura,* Paris, 1867.

Bérenger Feraud, *Contes de la Sénégambie,* Paris, 1885.

A. B. Ellis, *The Ewe-speaking Peoples of the Slave Coast of West Africa.* Their Religion, Manners, Customs, Laws, Language, &c., 1890. *The Tshi-speaking Peoples of the Gold Coast of West Africa.* Their Religion, Manners, Customs, Laws, Language, &c., 1887. *The Yoruba-speaking Peoples of the Slave Coast of West Africa.* Their Religion, Manners, Customs, Laws, Language, &c., 1894.

Mary Kingsley, *Travels in West Africa,* 1897.

H. Chatelain, *Folk-tales of Angola,* Boston, 1894.

W. H. J. Bleek, *Report concerning Bushman Researches,* with a short account of Bushman Folk-lore, Cape Town, 1875.

Reynard the Fox in South Africa ; or, Hottentot Fables, Cape Town, 1864.

Bishop Callaway, *Nursery Tales, Traditions, and Histories of the Zulus,* Natal, 1866–68. *Religious System of the Amazulu,* 1884 (F.-L. Soc.).

Theo Hahn, *Tsuni-Goam, the Supreme Being of the Khoi-Khoi* [Hottentots], 1881.

G. McC. Theal, *Kaffir Folk-lore,* 1886.

D. Macdonald, *Africana ; or, the Heart of Heathen Africa,* 2 vols., 1882.

Sir Harry Johnston, *British Central Africa,* 1897.

E. Steere, *Swahili Tales as told by Natives of Zanzibar,* 1870.

J. Sibree, *The Great African Island.* Chapters on Madagascar, 1880.

"Malagasy Folk-lore and Popular Superstitions," published in *Folk-lore Record,* ii., iv., 1879, 1881.

" Oratory, Songs, Legends, and Tales of the Malagasy," published in *Folk-lore Journal*, i., 1883.

" Malagasy Folk-tales," published in *Folk-lore Journal*, ii., 1884.

L. Dahle, *Malagasy Folk-lore*, 1877.

C. Baissac, *Le Folk-lore de l'île Maurice*, Paris, 1888.

NEGRO-AMERICAN FOLK-LORE.

J. C. Harris, *Uncle Remus : Legends of the Old Plantations. Uncle Remus and His Friends*, 1893.

Mary A. Owen, *Old Rabbit, the Voodoo and other Stories*, 1893.

Chas. C. Jones, *Negro Myths from the Georgia Coast* (chiefly animal stories), Boston, 1888.

Alcée Fortier, *Louisiana Folk-tales* (Am. F.-L. Soc.).

Charles L. Edwards, *Bahama Songs and Stories*, Boston and New York, 1895 (Am. F.-L. Soc.).

For the storiological side of Folk-lore, in so far as not dealt with in any of the above-mentioned works, the student is referred to :

E. Sidney Hartland, *The Science of Fairy Tales*, 1891, Mythology and Folk-tales, 1901.

Joseph Jacobs, *The Fables of Æsop*, with a History of the Æsopic Fables, 2 vols., 1889.

W. A. Clouston, *Popular Tales and Fictions*, 2 vols., 1887.

Marian Roalfe Cox, *Cinderella.* Three hundred and forty-five variants of Cinderella, Catskin, and Cap O'Rushes, &c., 1893 (F.-L. Soc.).

The foregoing works are concerned chiefly with stories and customs. For the special study of Folk-poetry and music the following works are recommended :—

BRITISH.

Child, *op. cit.*, under " Englisli Folk-lore."

Chambers, *op. cit.*, under " English Folk-lore."

Halliwell, *op. cit.*, under " English Folk-lore."

J. Ritson, *Ancient Ballads and Songs,* 1877.

Sir Walter Scott, *Minstrelsy of the Scottish Border,* 4 vols., 1902.

Baring-Gould and Sheppard, *Songs and Ballads of the West,* 1890–91.

G. F. Northall, *English Folk-rhymes,* 1892.

T. Crofton Croker, *Popular Songs of Ireland,* 1886.

GERMAN.

H. S. White, *Deutsche Volkslieder* (a Selection in German, with English Introduction and Notes), 1893.

L. Erk, *Deutscher Liederhort,* 1893 [in progress].

DANISH.

R. C. Prior, *Ancient Danish Ballads,* 3 vols., 1860.

FRENCH.

J. Tiersot, *Histoire de la Chanson Populaire en France,* Paris, 1889.

E. Rolland, *Recueil de Chansons Populaires,* 6 vols., Paris, 1883–88.

343

APPENDIX

ITALIAN.

R. H. Busk, *The Folk-songs of Italy,* 1887.

Martinengo Cesaresco, *Essays in the Study of Folk-songs,* 1886.

A. d'Ancona, *La Poesia Populare Italiana,* Livorno, 1878.

SPANISH.

J. G. Lockhart, *Ancient Spanish Ballads,* 1870.

J. W. Crombie, *The Folk-poetry of Spain* (in *Poets and Peoples of Foreign Lands*).

Milá y Fontanals, *op. cit.,* under "Spanish Folk-lore."

F. R. Marin, *Cantos Populares Españoles,* 5 vols., Seville, 1882–83.

PORTUGUESE.

Cte de Puymaigre, *Choix de Vieux Chants Portugais,* Paris, 1881.

GREEK.

Lucy Garnett, *op. cit.,* under "Neo-Greek Folk-lore."

E. Legrand, *Chansons Populaires de la Grèce,* Paris, 1885.

Flor. Macpherson, *Poetry of Modern Greece,* 1884.

SLAVONIC.

Aug. Dozon, *L'Epopée Serbe: Chants Populaires Hero-iques traduits,* Paris, 1888.

W. R. S. Ralston, *op. cit.,* under "Slavonic Folk-lore."

I. F. Hapgood, *op. cit.*, under "Slavonic Folk-lore."

Légendes Slaves : Recueil de Chants Nationaux et Populaires (from Bohemia, Moravia, the Carpathians, the Danube, &c.), Paris, 1890.

INDIAN.

Toru Dutt, *Ancient Ballads and Legends of Hindustan*, 1882.

C. E. Gover, *Folk-songs of Southern India*, 1872.

JAPANESE.

Niponese Rhymes and Japanese Jingles, 1892.

POLYNESIAN.

Gill, *op. cit.*, under " Polynesian Folk-lore."

GAMES.

H. C. Bolton, *Counting-out Rhymes of Children*, 1888.

W. W. Newell, *Games and Songs of American Children*, New York, 1883.

Alice B. Gomme, *English Singing Games*, 2 vols., 1894.

Traditional Games of England, Scotland, and Ireland, 2 vols., 1894–97.

MAGIC, WITCHCRAFT, AND SORCERY.

J. Ennemoser, *History of Magic*, 2 vols. (Bohn), 1854.

Thos. Wright, *Magic and Sorcery*, 2 vols., 1851.

Sir Walter Scott, *Demonology and Witchcraft*, 1830.

F. Lenormant, *Chaldean Magic; its Origin and Development,* 1877.

R. C. Thompson, *The Devils and Evil Spirits of Babylonia,* 1903.

Charles Godfrey Leland, *Etruscan-Roman Remains in Popular Tradition,* 1892.

Gypsy Sorcery and Fortune Telling, 1891.

Aradia, or the gospel of the Witches of Italy, 1899.

V. Rydberg, *Magic of the Middle Ages,* New York, 1879.

H. J. Bell, *Obeah: Witchcraft in the West Indies,* 1893.

F. T. Elworthy, *The Evil Eye: an Account of this Ancient and Widespread Superstition,* 1895.

R. C. Maclagan, *Evil Eye in the Western Highlands,* 1902.

DEMONOLOGY.

Moncure D. Conway, *Demonology and Devil-lore,* 2 vols., 1878.

SPECIAL ASPECTS OF FOLK-LORE.

Birds.

C. Swainson, *The Folk-lore and Provincial Names of British Birds,* 1886 (F.-L. Soc.).

Animals.

A. de Gubernatis, *Zoological Mythology; or, Legends of Animals,* 2 vols., 1872.

Rolland, *Faune Populaire de la France,* 6 vols., 1882.

PLANTS.

Thiselton-Dyer, *The Folk-lore of Plants,* 1889.

H. Friend, *Flowers and Flower-lore,* 1889.

A. de Gubernatis, *Mythologie des Plantes,* 2 vols., Paris, 1878–82.

Rolland, *Flore Populaire de la France,* 4 vols. [in progress].

MEDICINE.

W. G. Black, *Folk-medicine,* 1883 (F.-L. Soc.).

M. Bartels, *Die Medicin der Naturvölker,* Leipzig, 1893.

CHILDREN.

H. Ploss, *Das Kind in Brauch und Sitte der Völker,* 2 vols., Leipzig, 1884.

WOMEN.

H. Ploss, *Das Weib in der Natur- und Völkerkunde,* 2 vols., Leipzig, 1891.

MARRIAGE.

MacLennan, *Studies in Ancient History,* comprising a Reprint of Primitive Marriage : an Inquiry into the Origin of the Form of Capture in Marriage Ceremonies, 1886.

The Second Series, comprising an Inquiry into the Origin of Exogamy, 2 vols., 1896.

Robertson Smith, *Kinship and Marriage in Early Arabia,* Cambridge, 1885.

Westermarck, *The History of Human Marriage,* 1891.

APPENDIX

E. Crawley, *The Mystic Rose,* 1902.

Schröder, *Die Hochzeitsbräuche der Esten,* &c., Berlin, 1888.

E. J. Wood, *The Wedding Day in all Countries and Ages,* 2 vols., 1869.

SEA.

F. S. Bassett, *Legends and Superstitions of the Sea and of Sailors,* 1886.

P. Sébillot, *Légendes, Croyances et Superstitions de la Mer,* 2 vols., Paris, 1887.

THE END